Lecture Notes in Computer Sc

Commenced Publication in 1973
Founding and Former Series Editors:
Gerhard Goos, Juris Hartmanis, and Jan van Leeuwen

Sven Overhage   Clemens A. Szyperski
Ralf Reussner   Judith A. Stafford (Eds.)

Software Architectures, Components, and Applications

Third International Conference
on Quality of Software Architectures, QoSA 2007
Medford, MA, USA, July 11-13, 2007
Revised Selected Papers

 Springer

Volume Editors

Sven Overhage
Augsburg University
Business Informatics and Systems Engineering
Universitätsstraße 16, 86159 Augsburg, Germany
E-mail: sven.overhage@wiwi.uni-augsburg.de

Clemens A. Szyperski
Microsoft Research
One Microsoft Way, Redmond, WA 98052, USA
E-mail: clemens.szyperski@microsoft.com

Ralf Reussner
University of Karlsruhe (TH)
Am Fasanengarten 5, 76131 Karlsruhe, Germany
E-mail: reussner@ipd.uka.de

Judith A. Stafford
Tufts University
Computer Science, 161 College Avenue, Medford, MA 02155, USA
E-mail: jas@cs.tufts.edu

Library of Congress Control Number: Applied for

CR Subject Classification (1998): D.2.4, F.3, D.4, C.4, K.4.4, C.2

LNCS Sublibrary: SL 2 – Programming and Software Engineering

ISSN   0302-9743
ISBN-10   3-540-77617-6 Springer Berlin Heidelberg New York
ISBN-13   978-3-540-77617-8 Springer Berlin Heidelberg New York

Springer is a part of Springer Science+Business Media

springer.com

© Springer-Verlag Berlin Heidelberg 2007
Printed in Germany

Typesetting: Camera-ready by author, data conversion by Scientific Publishing Services, Chennai, India
Printed on acid-free paper   SPIN: 12213993   06/3180   5 4 3 2 1 0

Preface

At the beginning of the 21st century, both software engineering and business application development are facing a variety of challenges. On the one hand, there is significant pressure to streamline the development process and reduce the costs to create, deploy, and maintain software applications. On the other hand, software applications have to fulfill constantly growing demands, in particular as they are being recognized as integral parts of an organization's competitive advantage and as their significant impact on the corporate (e-) business strategy becomes obvious.

Nowadays, software applications have to satisfy rapidly evolving functional and extra-functional requirements. Similarly, the importance of software in technical applications is also constantly growing, as more and more software contributes to the value of various products and technical processes. In both domains, the enterprise and the technical product, software becomes more and more critical, as its failures can have dramatic impact on enterprises, users, and the environment. Cross-cutting these demands, managing the application complexity, flexibly adapting applications to changes in the business environment, and reducing the development time are of primary concern in today's development projects.

In order to better comply with these challenges, designing software architectures of good quality becomes a critical success factor. A software application is organized by its architecture that partitions it into elements and defines relationships among them. For this, we usually use multiple views, each with a different organizing principle. In addition, a software architecture supports reasoning about properties that are emergent and cannot be ascribed to particular elements. These properties are described using a language of quality attributes. Often, quality attributes, such as the system's performance or reliability, have a pervasive impact, are difficult to reverse, and preclude or constrain other properties. For these reasons, they have to be taken into account already during the design phase.

The conference on the Quality of Software Architectures (QoSA) is concerned with all of these topics. It brings together researchers and practicioners from a variety of disciplines to promote a better understanding of how to develop software architectures of good quality. This year's conference combined presentations of carefully reviewed papers, industrial experiences, keynotes, and discussion sessions that delved into topics of interest. In particular, it addressed:

- Architecture design principles and design decisions based on architectural knowledge
- Defining, measuring, and evaluating architecture quality
- Managing architecture quality, tracing architectural decisions upstream to requirements and downstream to implementation

- Preserving architecture quality throughout the lifetime of a software system
- Reasoning about emergent architecture properties such as performance and reliability

According to QoSA's tradition, the themes addressed in the call for papers were broad. The papers selected for QoSA 2007 present recent research and experiences on the topics listed above. From 42 submitted papers, 13 were selected as papers for this conference proceedings volume (for an acceptance rate of 31%). Each paper received at least three reviews and was discussed in depth during special mini-panel sessions at the conference. The selected papers are complemented by a written version of Murray Woodside's keynote on "Resource Architecture and Continuous Performance Engineering."

The conference, held in Medford, MA, featured an additional "Industrial Day" event with inspiring presentations from invited speakers, a variety of tutorials, and a panel discussion. As in 2006, this year's QoSA was organized in conjunction with the International ACM SIGSOFT Symposium on Component-Based Software Engineering (CBSE 2007). Together with the Workshop on the Role of Software Architecture for Testing and Analysis (ROSATEA 2007), they formed the week-long conference and workshop series as Federated Events on Component-Based Software Engineering and Software Architecture (COMP-ARCH 2007).

We thank the members of the Program Committee and the additional reviewers for their thoughtful and timely reviews that helped us in selecting the best papers. We are indebted to Judith Stafford and George Heineman for their invaluable work that made the COMPARCH vision come true. For their support and their work as QoSA Steering Committee, we thank Steffen Becker, Christine Hofmeister, and Ralf Reussner. We thank the generous sponsors of QoSA 2007: Tufts University and University of Karlsruhe (TH). Finally, we are grateful for the support of our COMPARCH sponsors Siemens, Addison-Wesley, and The MIT Press. Without the commitment of all the above people and sponsors, this conference would not have been possible.

August 2007   Sven Overhage
                                                          Clemens Szyperski

Organization

Organization Chair

Judith A. Stafford, Tufts University, USA

Program Chairs

Sven Overhage, University of Augsburg, Germany
Clemens Szyperski, Microsoft, Redmond, USA

Steering Committee

Ralf Reussner, University of Karlsruhe, Germany
Judith A. Stafford, Tufts University, USA
Christine Hofmeister, Lehigh University, USA
Steffen Becker, University of Karlsruhe, Germany

Program Committee

Antonia Albani, Delft University of Technology, The Netherlands
Colin Atkinson, University of Mannheim, Germany
Len Bass, Software Engineering Institute, Pittsburgh, PA, USA
Don Batory, University of Texas at Austin, USA
Jan Bosch, Intuit, Mountain View, USA
Alexander Brändle, Microsoft Research, UK
Michel Chaudron, Technische Universiteit Eindhoven, The Netherlands
Ivica Crnkovic, Mälardalen University, Sweden
Ian Gorton, Pacific North West National Laboratory, USA
Hassan Gomaa, George Mason University, USA
Volker Gruhn, University of Leipzig, Germany
Wilhelm Hasselbring, University of Oldenburg / OFFIS, Germany
Jean-Marc Jezequel, University of Rennes / INRIA, France
Philippe Kruchten, University of British Columbia, Canada
Patricia Lago, Vrije Universiteit, The Netherlands
Nicole Levy, University of Versailles, France
Tomi Mannisto, Helsinki University of Technology, Finland
Nenad Medvidovic, University of Southern California, Los Angeles, USA
Raffaela Mirandola, Politecnico di Milano, Italy
Robert Nord, Software Engineering Institute, Pittsburgh, USA
Frantisek Plasil, Charles University, Czech Republic

Iman Poernomo, King's College, UK
Sasikumar Punnekkat, Mälardalen University, Sweden
Andreas Rausch, University of Kaiserslautern, Germany
Matthias Riebisch, Technical University of Ilmenau, Germany
Bernhard Rumpe, University of Technology Braunschweig, Germany
Christian Salzmann, BMW, Germany
Jean-Guy Schneider, Swinburne University, Australia
Johannes Siedersleben, T-Systems, Germany
Michael Stal, Siemens, Germany
Hans van Vliet, Vrije Universiteit, The Netherlands
Kurt Wallnau, Software Engineering Institute, Pittsburgh, USA
Wolfgang Weck, Independent Software Architect, Switzerland

Cooperating and Supporting Partners

Tufts University, Medford, MA, USA
University of Karlsruhe (TH), Germany
Siemens AG
Addision-Wesley
The MIT Press

Table of Contents

Architecture Evolution

Architecting Process and Architectural Knowledge

Resource Architecture and Continuous Performance Engineering

Murray Woodside

Dept. of Systems and Computer Engineering
Carleton University, Ottawa, Canada

Abstract. The concept of resource architecture has been introduced to describe the association of operations with resources, and interactions between these operations. This paper explains resource architecture with examples, and how it can be used in performance engineering throughout the life of a project.

1 Introduction

Performance engineering of software is a problem that is not under control at the time of writing. It has serious effects in many projects, it cannot be predicted when serious problems will emerge (or not), and every decision in software development and deployment potentially affects it. The current status of the field, and some of its possible future evolutions, are discussed in [16]. That paper argues the importance of an integrated life-cycle methodology that combines prediction from models of architecture with measurement-based diagnosis and testing of products, called here "Continuous Performance Engineering". This paper describes how "Resource Architecture", a concept introduced in [14], can be the basis of Continuous Performance Engineering.

Insight and evaluation both require a system perspective, which comes from architecture, combined with sources of data, which can come from expertise (for prediction) and from measurement. Within the continuous process we can identify three viewpoints on this combined information, shown in Figure 1.

- Architecture comes first and gives a framework,
- Design/deployment/configuration adds essential detail, resources (such as processors), parameters of the configuration (such as buffer and thread pool sizes), and workloads, and
- Runtime provides opportunities to measure actual behaviour and performance.

The second viewpoint is useful for predictive analysis, illustrated in Figure 2. The distinction is made between the Amodel (a software model, e.g. expressed in UML) and Pmodel (a performance model, possibly expressed in a queueing language).

The third viewpoint provides empirical verification. We argue here that architecture (in the form of Resource Architecture) underpins it, as well as the second, and integrates them.

S. Overhage et al. (Eds.): QoSA 2007, LNCS 4880, pp. 1–14, 2007.

Software Architecture   Completed Design, Deployed and Configured (Plan)   Runtime Behaviour and Performance

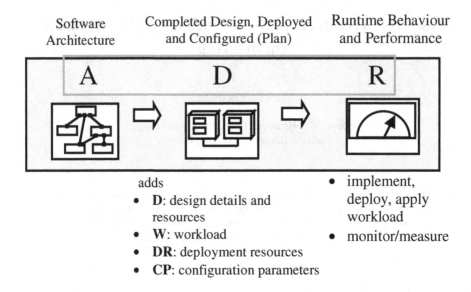

adds
- **D**: design details and resources
- **W**: workload
- **DR**: deployment resources
- **CP**: configuration parameters

- implement, deploy, apply workload
- monitor/measure

Fig. 1. Viewpoints in Continuous Performance Engineering

No attempt will be made here to provide a comprehensive background survey, instead the reader is referred to [16].

"Completion" { *workload W, Deployment Resources DR*
Configuration Parameters CP

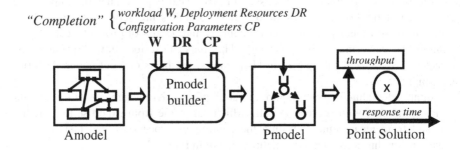

Fig. 2. Constructing a Performance Model (Pmodel) for Evaluation

2   Underlying Factors: Resources and Behaviour

Performance is determined by how behaviour uses resources. This includes physical resources like processors and logical resources like process thread pools, buffer pools and connections. We assume here that "architecture" includes a specification of behaviour, possibly defined by UML (see for instance [17]) interaction or activity models.

2.1 Representing Behaviour and Resources Together

To show the interaction of behaviour and resources we shall use a scenario representation that describes Steps, Resources, and special steps that acquire and release resources. Resources include processors and logical resources. A Step has an associated processor, and the detailed acquisition and release of the processor during the Step are not shown explicitly (since they are usually under the control of the operating system and not the architect). Architecture is represented by "Modules", such that each Step is associated with one module and each module is associated with one processor. Interactions between modules are not included as such, but as behaviour transitions from one module to another. The modules have a dual role, partly to tie the Steps into the architecture, and partly to represent the Task resources managed by the operating system, which are associated with models which are also OS tasks or processes.

Figure 3 shows four examples of scenarios, using a simplified version of the "Core Scenario Model" 0[9, 10] which was developed for this purpose. Figure 3(a) shows an application (AppModule) which executes two Steps S1, S2. The module is a Resource, that is it is a schedulable OS task with a thread pool with one or many threads. Before the task can begin, the task resource must be acquired, and this is associated with input of a request for execution. In Figure 3(b) the application makes a blocking request to Server, so the Server task resource must also be acquired.

In Figure 3(c) the same service is non-blocking, thus the application resource is released when the server is acquired. The order (release application, acquire server) could also be reversed. Finally Figure 3(d) shows a fully asynchronous service where the application is not involved in exploiting the service result.

3 Resource Context of an Operation

The Resource Context of an operation is defined as the set of resources that are held by the scenario during that operation, ordered in the order of acquisition. Figure 3 indicates resource contexts in two ways. First, it shows the contexts from the resource point of view, as a bold/dashed outline surrounding the Steps that have the resource in their context. This has value in indicating the Steps that are included in the holding time of the resource. Non-blocking and asynchronous service patterns are important for performance because they reduce the holding time of App.

It also shows the context of the scenario as it changes with time, with resources shown as strips which begin at acquisition and end at release. The resource context of a Step is the set of strips at the point corresponding to that Step. Thus in Figure 3(b) we see that the context of S2 is (Server, App).

3.1 Resource Context Nesting

In Figure 3(b) the holding time of Server is nested within the holding time of App, and this is a common case in client-server architectures. A non-nested holding pattern is shown for a buffer resource, in Figure 4.

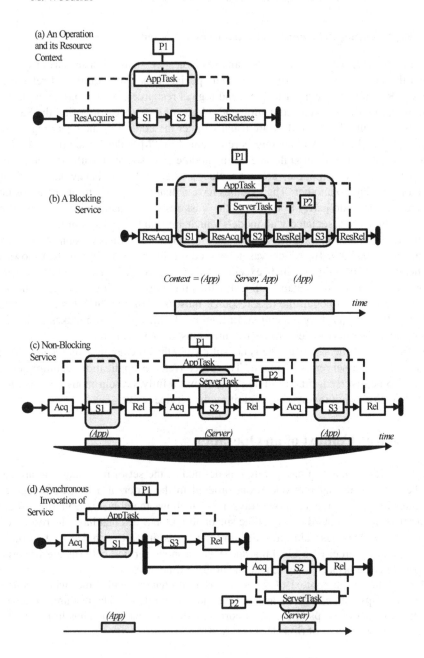

Fig. 3. Resource Context of an Operation

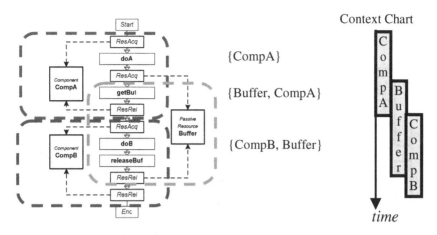

Fig. 4. Resource Contexts for a Buffer Handover

The buffer is acquired in the context of component CompA and released in another context (CompB), a common case for buffers.

Resource context nesting is a kind of structuring of resource usage, that in the following section provides a basis for a resource architecture.

Strictly Nested Resource Contexts:
Contexts are strictly nested if

(a) resources are always released in the reverse order to which they are acquired,
(b) the order of acquisition is the same in all scenarios. Thus, there is a partial order among the resources, such that every pair of acquisitions with no release between them satisfies the partial order.

Figure 5(a) shows a deeply nested example as a Context Chart, with a directed graph of the resources (which are all task resources) showing the partial order. A justification for using such a partial order is, that the tasks can never deadlock through a circular request chain.

3.2 Nearly-Nested-Context Cases

Many web-based and enterprise systems have simply nested contexts as just described. However nesting may constrain performance, and optimizations may break the nesting to a lesser or greater degree. In particular a resource may be released from the context before resources that were acquired after it. Contexts are Nearly Nested if they satisfy the order-of-acquisition condition above, but not the order of release.

A special case, if the second-last resource is released while the last is retained, is easily implemented as an early reply to a blocking request. That is, the active task releases the task that requested it before it is finished with execution of the request, and continues on concurrently. Examples are delayed writes in databases and file systems, and clean-up operations in servers generally. However the continuing task is the root of a new concurrent resource context, and can execute quite general operations.

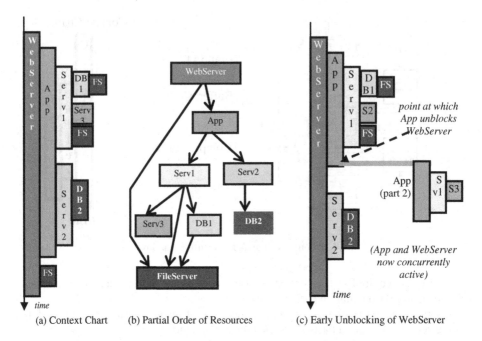

(a) Context Chart   (b) Partial Order of Resources   (c) Early Unblocking of WebServer

Fig. 5. A Deeply Nested Set of Resource Contexts: Context Chart, Graph of the Partial Order, and the Semantics of Early Unblocking

Figure 5(c) illustrates early unblocking of the WebServer thread by the application, and execution of the last operations of Application in its concurrent context. The concurrent context after the early release of WebServer is called here "part 2" of the resource context provided by Application. In this second case, the interaction for the acquisition of Serv1 by App in the architecture diagram in the middle is applied twice, to both part 1 and part 2 of the operation by App. Notice that after the end of part 1, WebServer is free to do concurrent operations.

Inspection of Figure 4(b) shows that the buffer handover can be modeled this way, with the operations of CompB in the second part of the buffer context.

3.3 An Embedded System Example

An example adapted from [15]0 illustrates a system with many resources and a variety of features in its resource contexts. It is a Building Security System first described as an example for the UML SPT Profile in [8], and analyzed further in [17], with resource contexts that were used to illustrate the CSM scenario language in [9, 10]. The deployment in Figure 6 shows a part for video surveillance of a building, including cameras, a part for controlling access to doors, and a common database. The details of behaviour are described in the references, but they lead to the scenarios and resource contexts shown in Figures 7 and 8.

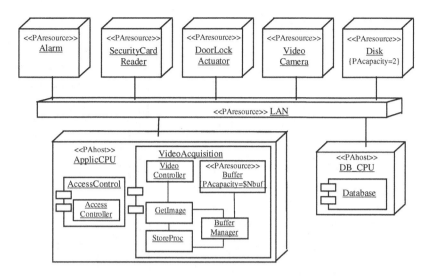

Fig. 6. The Building Security System

Figure 7 shows the door control scenario. The access control is initially nested while the requester waits, but at the decision point there is either an asynchronous message to the alarm task, or an early return to unlock the door (by Lock) while part 2 of the AccessController context logs the entry record in the database.

Figure 8 shows the video capture scenario. As previously discussed the buffer is not nested, only here it is more severe. Manager (M) acquires the buffer, GetImage (G) uses it, then passes it to StoreImage (S). The buffer context is shown as starting only after return from M, an approximation. Part 1 of the buffer context is associated to the operations by G after return from M, and part 2 is associated with the operations of S, allowing the controller V to be released early by G.

4 Resource Architecture

In the Resource Architecture [14]0, resources are first class entities, and all behaviour is represented as associated with some resource as a "resource operation". Interactions are requests to obtain a resource, while in a resource operation.

4.1 Resource Operations and Interactions

An interaction between two resources corresponds to a request made from a resource operation in a given resource context {R0, R1, ... Rn}, to obtain a new resource R and carry out some operation Op. The architectural interpretation:

1. considers every Step to be part of a Resource-operation by the last resource in its context,
2. considers each request for a resource R to be a request for an operation Op by R.

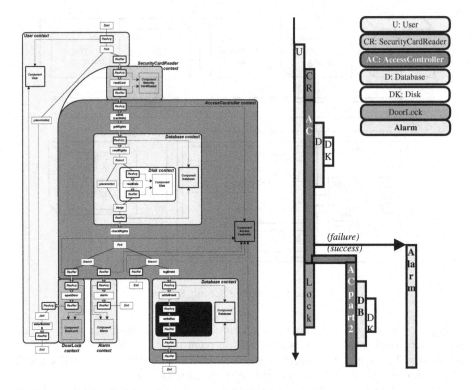

Fig. 7. Scenario for Door Access Control, with contexts shown as areas and as a Context Chart. The Access Controller has a part 2 to store the log of the access event.

3. The request for Op is an interaction between the current resource and operation, and resource R. It is a *synchronous* request if Op retains all of the previous resource context, and *asynchronous* if not.
4. Op is defined by the sequence of Steps following the acquisition of R, until R is released. Op includes any nested (synchronous) resource operations for additional resources.
5. If during Op the context changes to include only R, the operation after the change is defined as a continuation or *part-2* of Op.

Clearly a resource can have several different resource-operations, that do different things. A resource-operation and its interactions can be visualized as shown in Figure 9. Figure 9(a) shows two operations of resource ResA, with interactions with operations of ResB and ResC. Synchronous and asynchronous interactions are shown by arrow styles. The asynchronous interactions initiate a new resource context with just ResB, concurrent with the existing context including ResA. The synchronous interaction with ResC indicates that ResA (and any other resources) remain in the context for the execution of the operation at ResC.

Figure 9(b) interprets the scenario of Figure 3(b) as a resource architecture. The User-op includes App-op, which in turn includes S1, S3 and Server-op. Server-op

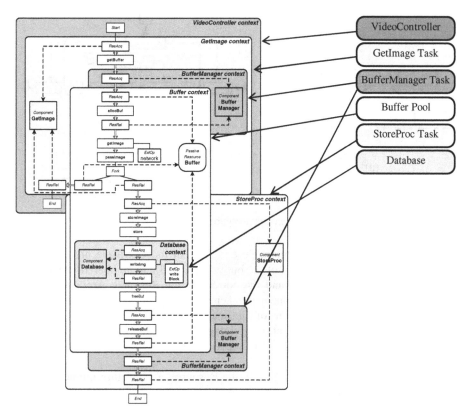

Fig. 8. Scenario and Resource Contexts (shown as shaded areas) for the Video Capture Scenario. A Context Chart is shown in Figure 10 below.

includes S2. The treatment of the processing resource is that each Step of each operation includes some number of processing sub-steps which acquire and release the processing resource, but the time detail is not part of the resource architecture. We keep track only of the total processor demand of the Step, and the processor that is used.

4.2 Separation of a Sub-operation

An operation by a software component may be divided into parts we will call sub-operations by the acquisition of logical resources. The part that begins after acquiring a logical resource (say, R1) is regarded in the Resource Architecture as an operation (say, Op1) of R1. Alternatively, since the operation is not really executed by R1, one can redefine this part as a separate operation (say, OpA) by a separate pseudo-component (say, CompA) derived from the original component, and invoked by Op1. To avoid introducing a spurious process resource, the resource multiplicity of CompA is made infinite. This approach is preferred because it makes the process context of the separated operation (OpA) traceable, and it accommodates a resource-operation that executes within multiple processes at different times.

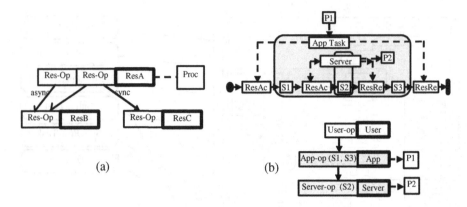

Fig. 9. Visualization of Resource Architecture: Resources, Resource-operations, and Interactions

Figure 10 shows the processOneImage operation of the GetImage process in the BSS, with the part after acquisition of the buffer separated into an operation getImage by a psuedo-process GetImage2, and the corresponding Resource Architecture. In Figure 10, the role of the Component is taken by GetImage, and the role of R1 is taken by the Buffer. The execution of GetImage after the acquisition of Buffer is separated out as the shaded operation getImage (in the role of OpA) of psuedo-component GetImage2 (in the role of CompA). Figure 11 shows the full Resource Architecture for the BSS.

As we can see by examining Figure 9, the Resource Architecture mimics exactly the Software Architecture if there are only process resources. However when logical resources are introduced as in Figure 10, they differ, because of the resource-operations of the logical resources.

4.3 Architecture in the Presence of Non-nested Resource Use

The architecture notation in Figure 9 was developed in the context of nested use of resources, which we may regard as "structured" resource use. One kind of non-nested behaviour has been incorporated easily, which is the "part 2" behaviour described above. Removal of all the earlier resources in the context list is modeled adequately this way. The earlier resources continue to be held by a concurrent scenario, so their holding times are unaffected.

In other non-nested behaviour some but not all of the earlier resources in the context list are removed during an operation. The operation should be divided into separate parts every time the context changes. The architectural notation for showing requests during an operation can be used, but must be augmented to also show releases; this is not considered here. The resource holding time would be the sum of the parts of the operation.

4.4 Performance Modeling

The purpose of a resource model is to support analysis of the resource usage, in particular the system performance. The view of resource architecture described here

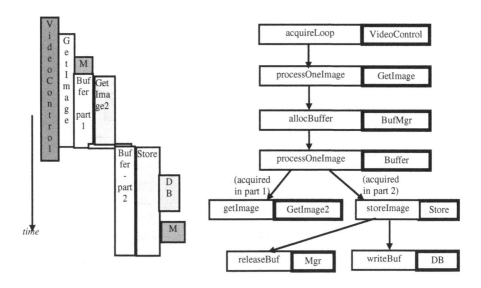

Fig. 10. The Buffer operation and the separation of getImage from processOneImage

corresponds to a form of performance model called Layered Queueing [3, 11]. Examples of layered queueing models are found in [5, 12]; tools and methods for solving them are described in [3, 11].

5 Using Resource Architecture to Reason About Performance

The value of resource architecture in reasoning about performance is, that it represents not only the causes of resource congestion, but also the flow of causality between congestion effects at different resources. Causality flows along blocking resource interactions, shown as arrows in the architecture. Waiting at a congested resource propagates to the invoking resource-operations (if the interactions are blocking), increasing their holding times and congestion levels also.

Resource architecture explains bottlenecks at logical and process resources ("software bottlenecks") and supports a root cause analysis [4]0. Because of the generality of the resource concept, it supports very general patterns and anti-patterns for performance [13]. Through root cause analysis it also helps to identify the most relevant performance improvements that can be made by

- code tightening
- latency masking, e.g. by pre-fetching,
- increased resources through replicas of processes and data, or larger thread or buffer pools, etc.
- reduced calls to a service, or batched calls,
- asynchronous and parallel operations (including the use of "second parts" of operations through early replies to a caller; this is discussed further in [2])

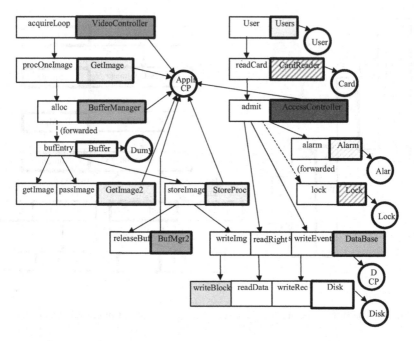

Fig. 11. The full resource architecture for the Building Security System

6 Continuous Performance Engineering

The above section points to the value of Resource Architecture in performance engineering at all stages and by all approaches. The broad goals of CPE are:

- management of performance expectations and risk
- early warning of problems through analysis by models derived from designs
- continuous assessment as design concepts evolve
- smooth handoff from early analysis to measurements and tests

Integration of the model approach with existing measurement techniques was argued in [16] to provide more realistic performance expectations, more efficient search for improvements, and more efficient measurements in the test phase. The elements of a process to integrate models and measurements included:

- performance prediction from architecture
- more detailed predictions tracking the design
- budgets for use of processing resources by operations, prior to coding
- unit tests on operations, designed from the model,
- end-to-end tests and field measurements, supported by test planning.

The resource architecture can play a central role in tying the actual system and its resources, to models for analysis and insight.

7 Conclusions

The concept of resource architecture has been discussed in detail to describe its similarities and differences from the corresponding software architecture. The central role of resource architecture in understanding or analyzing performance at any stage in software development, was identified. Additional details are found in the references.

References

1. Franks, G., Majumdar, S., Neilson, J., Petriu, D., Rolia, J., Woodside, M.: Performance Analysis of Distributed Server Systems. In: Proc. Sixth International Conference on Software Quality (6ICSQ), Ottawa, pp. 15–26 (1996)
2. Franks, G., Woodside, M.: Effectiveness of early replies in client-server systems. Performance Evaluation 36-37, 165–183 (1999)
3. Franks, G., Maly, P., Woodside, M., Petriu, D.C., Hubbard, A.: Layered Queueing Network Solver and Simulator User Manual, Real-time and Distributed Systems Lab, Carleton University, Ottawa (2005)
4. Franks, G., Petriu, D., Woodside, M., Xu, J., Tregunno, P.: Layered bottlenecks and their mitigation. In: Proc of 3rd Int. Conference on Quantitative Evaluation of Systems QEST 2006, Riverside, CA, USA, pp. 103–114 (September 2006)
5. Maly, P., Woodside, C.M.: Layered Modeling of Hardware and Software, with Application to a LAN Extension Route. In: Haverkort, B., Bohnenkamp, H.C., Smith, C.U. (eds.) TOOLS 2000. LNCS, vol. 1786, pp. 10–24. Springer, Heidelberg (2000)
6. Object Management Group, UML Profile for Schedulability, Performance, and Time Specification, OMG Adopted Specification ptc/02-03-02 (July 1, 2002)
7. Pender, T.: UML (TM) Bible. Wiley, Chichester (2003)
8. Petriu, D.C., Woodside, C.M.: Performance Analysis with UML. In: Selic, B., Lavagno, L., Martin, G. (eds.) UML for Real., pp. 221–240. Kluwer, Dordrecht (2003)
9. Petriu, D.B., Woodside, M.: An intermediate metamodel with scenarios and resources for generating performance models from UML designs. Software and Systems Modeling 5(4) (2006) DOI 10.1007/s10270-006-0026-8
10. Petriu, D.B., Woodside, M.: A Metamodel for Generating Performance Models from UML Designs. In: Baar, T., Strohmeier, A., Moreira, A., Mellor, S.J. (eds.) Proc. UML 2004. LNCS, vol. 3273, Springer, Heidelberg (2004)
11. Rolia, J.A., Sevcik, K.C.: The Method of Layers. IEEE Trans. on Software Engineering 21(8), 689–700 (1995)
12. Sheikh, F., Woodside, C.M.: Layered Analytic Performance Modelling of Distributed Database Systems. In: Proc. Int. Conf. on Distributed Computer Systems, pp. 482–490. Baltimore, U.S.A (May 1997)
13. Smith, C., Williams, L.: Software Performance Antipatterns. In: Proc. Second Int. Workshop on Software and Performance (WOSP2000), Ottawa, pp. 127–136 (September 2000)
14. Woodside, C.M.: Software Resource Architecture. Int. Journal on Software Engineering and Knowledge Engineering (IJSEKE) 11(4), 407–429 (2001)
15. Woodside, M., Petriu, D.C., Petriu, D.B., Shen, H., Israr, T., Merseguer, J.: Performance by Unified Model Analysis (PUMA). In: Proc. 5th Int. Workshop on Software and Performance (WOSP 2005), pp. 1–12 (July 2005)

16. Woodside, M., Franks, G., Petriu, D.C.: The Future of Software Performance Engineering. In: Briand, L., Wolf, A. (eds.) Proc. Future of Software Engineering 2007. IEEE Computer Society Order Number P2829, pp. 171–187 (May 2007)
17. Xu, J., Woodside, M., Petriu, D.C.: Performance Analysis of a Software Design using the UML Profile for Schedulability. In: Kemper, P., Sanders, W.H. (eds.) TOOLS 2003. LNCS, vol. 2794, Springer, Heidelberg (2003)

Reusable Architectural Decision Models for Enterprise Application Development

Olaf Zimmermann[1], Thomas Gschwind[1], Jochen Küster[1],
Frank Leymann[2], and Nelly Schuster[1]

[1] IBM Research GmbH
Zurich Research Laboratory, Säumerstrasse 4, 8803 Rüschlikon, Switzerland
{olz, thg, jku, nes}@zurich.ibm.com
[2] Universität Stuttgart, Institute of Architecture of Application Systems
Universitätsstraße 38, 70569 Stuttgart, Germany
frank.leymann@iaas.uni-stuttgart.de

Abstract. In enterprise application development and other software constructi-on projects, a critical success factor is to make sound architectural decisions. Text templates and tool support for capturing architectural decisions exist, but have failed to reach broad adoption so far. One of the inhibitors we perceived on large-scale industry projects is that architectural decision capturing is regar-ded as a retrospective and therefore unwelcome documentation task which does not provide any benefit during the original design work. A major problem of such a retrospective approach is that the decision rationale is not available to decision makers when they identify, make, and enforce decisions. Often a large, possibly distributed, community of decision makers is involved in these three steps. In this paper, we propose a new conceptual framework for proactive deci-sion identification, decision maker collaboration, and decision enforcement. Based on a meta model capturing reuse and collaboration aspects explicitly, our framework instantiates decision models from requirements models and reusable decision templates. These templates capture knowledge gained on other projects employing the same architectural style. As an exemplary application of these concepts to service-oriented architecture shows, reusable architectural decision models can speed up the decision identification and improve the quality of the decision making. Reusable architectural decision models can also simplify the exchange of architecture design rationale within and between project teams, and expose decision outcome as model transformation parameters in model-driven software development.

Keywords: Architectural decision, architectural knowledge, MDA, SOA.

1 Introduction

Having been neglected both in academia and industry for a long time, the importance of *architectural decision capturing* is now widely acknowledged [15][20][28]. How-ever, existing work focuses on capturing and representing decisions that have been made already. Little emphasis is spent on anticipating the required decisions based on

S. Overhage et al. (Eds.): QoSA 2007, LNCS 4880, pp. 15–32, 2007.

experience from previous projects, on recommending proven decision making techniques for these decisions, and on team collaboration aspects. In collaborative environments, decision making responsibilities are assigned to various team members; consensus must be found, and decision outcome communicated.

As a consequence, capturing architectural decisions remains a challenge for practicing architects. Reported inhibitors for capturing decisions include no appreciation from project sponsors, lack of time, and insufficient tool support [27]. Hence, intuition often is the only, but not always a suitable, decision driver; there is no systematic reuse of already gained knowledge. This lack of rigor leads to acceptance issues and quality problems with the software architectures under construction.

This paper aims to alleviate these problems by proposing a conceptual framework for three decision capturing steps we observed and practiced on our own enterprise application development projects [30][33]. We refer to these three conceptual steps as decision identification, making, and enforcement. As we will explain, today's practices support each of these steps only insufficiently. In our framework, reusable decision templates and semi-automatic decision model instantiation speed up the decision identification step. We aim to improve the quality of the decision making with decision dependency modeling, catalogs of decision drivers, and recommendations for decision making techniques. Finally, we propose decision injection into model transformations, code aspects, and configuration policies as an additional means of enforcing decisions in model-driven software development. A common meta model explicitly capturing reuse and collaboration aspects connects the three steps. Our reusable decision modeling framework is complementary to software engineering methodologies such as the Rational Unified Process (RUP) [19]; decision making can become a dedicated part of the work breakdown structure defined by the software engineering methodology of choice. The framework also is complementary to traditional component-and-connector modeling of software architecture design [3]; decisions explicitly refer to elements of design models such as logical components.

The remainder of this paper is structured in the following way: Section 2 introduces background and related work; Section 3 presents the requirements and the meta model for our conceptual framework for architectural decision modeling with reuse, and how the framework facilitates decision identification, making and enforcement. Section 4 applies our approach to the design of enterprise applications employing Service-Oriented Architecture (SOA) as their primary architectural style. Section 5 concludes with a summary and an outlook to future work.

2 Background and Related Work

Our work extends several recent contributions to software architecture research, which in turn are based on existing work in design decision rationale research. We also draw upon the rich architectural knowledge captured by the patterns community.

In [20], Kruchten et al. define an ontology that describes the attributes that should be captured for a decision, the types of decisions to be made, how decisions are made (i.e., their lifecycle), and decision dependencies. In their work, Kruchten et al. also focus on the visualization of the decisions. In [6], Falessi et al. present the decision, goal, and alternatives framework to capture design decisions. Their motivation is to increase the maintainability of a software system by identifying why a certain approach has been chosen, and which design decisions have to be updated when the system is changed. In our work we build on both of these approaches, especially the ontology put forward by Kruchten and the use cases identified by Falessi, and apply them to enterprise application development. Unlike existing work, we investigate proactive decision identification to ease the reuse of architectural rationale. We are particularly concerned with collaboration and automation aspects.

Jansen and Bosch [15] view a software architecture as a composition of a set of design decisions. Their model for architectural design decisions focuses on the time dimension, defining a dedicated entity representing architectural modifications occurring over the software lifecycle. Other decision capturing templates exist in industry and academia, which can also be viewed as informally specified meta models [1][28]. None of these models is rich enough to support decision identification in requirements models, and there is no genuine support for decision reuse and collaboration. We could not find an alignment of these works with software engineering methods and patterns; platform-independent concerns are not separated from platform-specific ones. Our work enhances the existing modeling ideas in these directions.

Design decision research in the 1990s [21] focused on facilitating the decision making step; explicit identification and enforcement steps are not present. For instance, Questions, Options and Criteria (QOC) diagrams [22] raise a design question, which points to the available solution options; decision criteria are associated with the options. Selecting an option can lead to follow-on questions. Many active and passive Decision Support Systems (DSS) have been proposed. Most of the existing work focuses on management decision support; however, Svahnberg et al. suggest a quality-driven multi-criteria decision support method for software architecture selection [26]. This method allows multiple team members to score already identified architecture candidates based on weighted quality attributes. The scores lead to a suggestion and stimulate a consensus discussion. However, identification and reuse of required decisions, available alternatives and relevant quality criteria are out of scope. QOC diagrams and DSS complement our work and can be leveraged during our decision making step.

In the patterns community, several schools of thought and many pattern templates exist [5][9][11]. Requirements linkage typically is informal and appears in textual *intent* or *forces* sections. Many pattern languages remain on an abstract, conceptual level; others specialize on a single problem or technology domain such as *enterprise application architecture* [7] or *process-driven SOA* [29]. Patterns for process-driven SOA describe how to automate the management of long-running business processes such as loan approval processing or order management along supply chains (problem domain) with workflow engines and communication middleware (technology domain). The activity flow in such processes can be specified using Business Process Modeling (BPM) tools and implemented as a network of communicating Web services [34]. In general, the relationship between architectural patterns and reusable decision models is synergetic. In this paper, enterprise application development serves as the sample domain; hence, SOA patterns appear as conceptual architecture alternatives in the reusable architectural decision model we introduce in Section 4.

3   A Conceptual Framework for Decision Modeling with Reuse

To overcome the limitations of the existing decision capturing approaches, we structure the architectural decision making process into three conceptual steps, decision identification, making, and enforcement.[1] *Decision identification* scopes the architecture design work on a particular software development project. Requirements and earlier decisions trigger the identification of individual decisions. During *decision making*, architects select alternatives according to certain decision drivers, which either are context-specific requirements or general software quality attributes [3][14]. This step is the core of the three-step process; making sound technical decisions on software development projects is what practicing architects are primarily responsible for. *Decision enforcement* deals with sharing the results of the decision making with the stakeholders and the project team, and getting them accepted. Figure 1 illustrates:

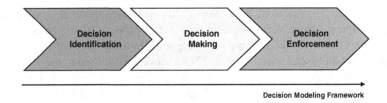

Fig. 1. Decision making steps

Each of the three steps has its own specific requirements, all of which have to be addressed by an underlying common meta model. In the remainder of this Section, we first investigate these requirements, then derive the required meta model elements from them and finally discuss how we support the identification, making, and enforcement steps.

3.1   Requirements

Having interviewed close to 100 practicing software architects, we identified the following design goals and use cases for our decision modeling framework.

Design goals. Supporting the decision identification, making, and enforcement steps requires extending existing practices for building up architectural knowledge, particularly if the decision making responsibilities are shared within and across teams. Therefore, providing *team collaboration support* is a mandatory design goal – architectural decision making is a team effort, and for budgetary and other reasons, software development projects today typically are carried out by geographically distributed teams. Furthermore, it should be possible to *harvest architectural decisions from completed projects*; a *small overhead* for capturing fresh decisions is desirable.

Use cases. In [6], thirteen general use cases for design decision rationale capturing are identified, covering a wide range of activities such as design problem detection,

---

[1] Finer grained models exist, for example in systems theory [10] and DSS research [26].

validation, documentation, coordination, and communication. With respect to our design goals, they lead to the following seven concrete primary use cases:

1. *Obtain architectural knowledge* from third parties, e.g., company-wide enterprise architecture groups or practitioner communities in consulting firms.
2. *Adopt and filter obtained decision knowledge* according to project specific needs: delete, update, and add architectural decisions and alternatives, and manage dependencies between decisions.
3. *Delegate decision making authorities* to subsystem architects and lead developers and support review activities with bidirectional feedback loops.
4. *Involve network of peers* in search of additional architectural expertise during decision making, requiring a common understanding of problem and solution space; hence, it is important to align terminology as much as possible.
5. *Enforce decision outcome* via pattern-based generation of work products, for example documentation and code snippets serving as architectural templates.
6. *Inject decisions* into design models, code, and deployment artifacts.
7. *Share gained architectural knowledge* with third parties such as the actors from use case 1, after having sanitized the project deliverables.

3.2 Meta Model Underpinning and Connecting the Framework Steps

To be able to support the use cases from Section 3.1 and automate parts of our three-step process, a common meta model is required. Figure 2 shows our proposal, which is inspired by previous research [1][15][20], the IBM e-business Reference Architecture Framework used in [28] and our own decision documentation practices [30][33]:

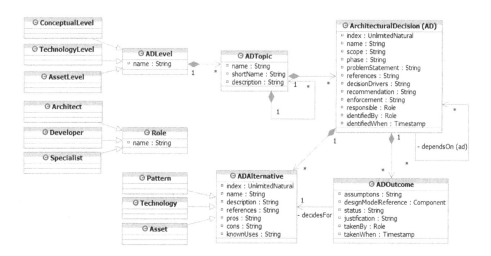

Fig. 2. Meta model in conceptual modeling framework for architectural decision reuse

There are three core domain entities, *Architectural Decision (AD)*, *ADAlternative*, and *ADOutcome*. In line with [15], we separate the outcome from the background information, in our case to facilitate reuse. AD and ADAlternative provide background information only; attributes such as *problemStatement* characterize an AD on an introductory level, while *references* and *knownUses* point to further information.

The rationale behind this modeling choice is that the same AD might pertain to many elements in a design model, e.g., business processes and Web service operations. The design model element types are referenced via the *scope* attribute in the AD. ADOutcome instances then can be created dynamically, and refer to design model element instances via a *designModelReference*. To give an example, an order management process model might state that five business processes have to be implemented as a set of composed Web services [30]; while attributes such as problem statement, references, and *recommendation* are the same for all five processes, the *justification* might differ, depending on the individual *decision drivers*. Decision drivers include project-specific non-functional requirements (including environmental issues such as skill availability) and general software quality factors. The patterns community uses the term *forces* synonymously.

Closely related ADs are grouped into *ADTopic*s, which can form a hierarchy. Each ADTopic hierarchy is assigned to one of three *ADLevel*s of abstraction, *ConceptualLevel, TechnologyLevel,* or *AssetLevel*. This novel structure is motivated by our observation that when designing enterprise applications, the technical discussions often circle around detailed features of certain vendor products, or the pros and cons of specific technologies, whereas many highly important strategic decisions and generic concerns are underemphasized. These discussions are related, but should not be merged into one. We therefore go through two refinements steps. This is good practice, e.g., Fowler [8] and RUP with its elaboration points recommend such an approach for UML class diagrams used as design models. We adopted this recommendation for decision models and made the three abstraction levels explicit in our meta model.

Several attributes such as *responsible*, *takenBy* and *status* model decision ownership and lifecycle in response to the collaboration use cases from Section 3.1. The *phase* attribute provides a link to general-purpose methodologies such as RUP. These and all other model attributes can queried, e.g., when looking for all open decisions to be made in the inception phase of an enterprise application development project.

Decision dependencies are explicitly modeled as associations between ADs. At present, we use a single *dependsOn* dependency type, but are in the process of adopting the taxonomy from [20]. To give an example, for our order management business processes, a conceptual decision for a PROCESS AUTOMATION PARADIGM is required: Should the processes be made executable in a WORKFLOW ENGINE, or be realized in traditional PROGRAMMING LANGUAGE CODE? If a workflow engine is decided for, a related technology decision is to agree on an EXECUTABLE WORKFLOW LANGUAGE, e.g., BUSINESS PROCESS EXECUTION LANGUAGE (BPEL) [23]. Once BPEL has been decided upon, a BPEL ENGINE can be selected, e.g., ACTIVE BPEL, IBM WEBSPHERE PROCESS SERVER or ORACLE BPEL PROCESS MANAGER.[2]

3.3 Step 1: Decision Identification

Let us now investigate state of the art and the practice for the first step in our framework, decision identification. Next, we discuss how our decision identification support can increase productivity and improve quality.

---

[2] In this and all further examples, we set ADs and ADALTERNATIVES in THIS FONT.

State of the art. Pattern languages [7][11], domain-specific plugins for software engineering methods [16], technical papers and vendor documentation can be studied to identify required technical decisions. In theory, these sources of information provide deep coverage of all design concerns. However, the consumability of the vast amount of information is a key issue. Architectural decisions are often hidden behind various other material not targeting architects and therefore not being presented appropriately.

Project reality. During our decision modeling work with practicing architects, it became apparent that ad-hoc decision identification solely based on personal experience is the state of the practice, as opposed to diligent literature studies, or systematic reuse of knowledge already gained in a community. As a consequence, much time is spent in early project phases (requirements analysis, high level design) to identify the critical design issues, invent potential solutions, and agree upon decision criteria, particularly if the team lacks experience. This time would be better invested in studying the business problem to be solved, and in the actual decision making.

Our approach. As Figure 3 shows, we propose the initial decision model for a project team to be instantiated from project-specific requirements models and reusable decision templates. *Reference architectures* play a key role here, providing a common technical vocabulary and architectural patterns for a certain domain [3]. Architectural decisions cannot live in isolation; they have to be bound to design model elements, which can be found in the reference architecture. We refer to this binding step as *decision scoping*. In contrast to the *pull* model employed in practice today, we *push* the initial to-do list to the architecture team. We expect this reuse approach to increase productivity significantly, and to have a positive effect on quality. The decision templates serve as a completeness check list which can be seen as an early, informal review of the architectural work.

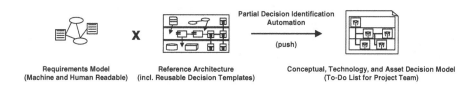

Requirements Model   Reference Architecture   Conceptual, Technology, and Asset Decision Model
(Machine and Human Readable)   (incl. Reusable Decision Templates)   (To-Do List for Project Team)

Fig. 3. Semi-automatic decision identification in requirements model and reference architecture

We do not aim to populate the entire design space; there will always be project-specific design issues worth capturing ad hoc. However, proactive decision identification works fine for many common design issues. For instance, in [34] we captured 26 architectural decisions dealing with WEB SERVICES as INTEGRATION TECHNOLOGY. These decisions cover interface design issues such as SELECTION OF INTERFACE DESCRIPTION LANGUAGE and MODELING STARTING POINT (BUSINESS REQUIREMENTS VS. EXISTING IT ASSET) These decisions were reused successfully on several Web services projects conducted by others [12].

3.4 Step 2: Decision Making

The actual decision making is the second step of our three-step framework.

State of the art. Architecture Tradeoff Analysis Method (ATAM) [3], Attribute-Driven Design (ADD) and Decision Support Systems (DSS), as well as many semi-formal techniques such as Strengths, Weaknesses, Opportunities, Threats (SWOT) tables can be used to support decision making. ATAM was originally positioned as an evaluation and review instrument, but can also be used during earlier decision making stages. Without customization, generic techniques such as ADD do not provide reusable, domain-specific advice. Many decision making techniques require information not yet available during the early elaboration stages or use the strategy to address one Non-Functional Requirement (NFR) at a time and hence do not take side effects caused by decision dependencies into account. As a consequence, not all techniques are equally suited for all decision types.

Project reality. Architectural decision making is often perceived as an art rather than part of an engineering process. Decisions makers often are biased; phrases like "this has always worked for me" or "this is the industry trend" justify decisions instead of sound technical judgment backed by tradeoff analysis activities or technical evaluations. Frequently, a single driver is overemphasized. For instance, we have seen architects use a simplistic "brain/heart/guts" model. In summary, personal experience, preferences, and intuition often are the main decision drivers; external forces such as vendor interests or strategic decisions motivated by potential future needs and synergies have a large, not always beneficial, impact on the decision making. Consequently, the technically best solution is not always selected. Such ill-motivated and -fated decision making often is a root cause for project failure as the quality of the produced software architecture degrades.

Our approach. Aiming to objectify the decision making, we integrate a collection of proven decision support techniques into our framework, which accompany and use the decision models created during the identification step. We also provide a list of decision drivers per decision, e.g., highlighting specific NFRs and software quality factors, but also non-technical factors such as political issues, license costs, and available skills.

Depending on the type of decision to be made, we select from a continuum of support techniques, e.g., simple recommendations, semi-structured SWOT tables, ADD [3], QOC diagrams [22], hands-on evaluations and formal alternative scoring algorithms [26]. A benefit of this approach is that it provides the decision makers with a technique well suited for a particular decision, as well as tangible advice that is aligned with requirements and background information (e.g., vendor best practices). Figure 4 illustrates.

In our opinion, it is neither feasible nor desirable to fully automate the decision making. The importance of tradeoffs in specific contexts and design drivers naturally makes full automation impossible; heuristic solutions are required. Matching of the requirements contexts and decision drivers is important when reusing architectural knowledge. In many circumstances, it is imperative to deviate from generic

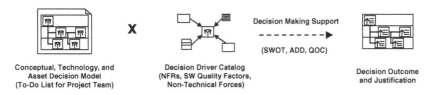

Fig. 4. Decision models, decision drivers and techniques for decision making

recommendations. Hence, the decision making support in our approach empowers the architects to make informed decisions based on collective insight.

To give an example, using DEEPLY NESTED XML SCHEMA TYPES as MESSAGE PARAMETER GRANULARITY was considered an anti-pattern in early Web services literature. Confronted with a rich core banking domain model, we still decided for this alternative in one of our projects [33]. We did so after having conducted a proof-of-technology to mitigate interoperability and performance concerns, which we had identified as key decision drivers. This decision justification became a reusable architectural recommendation at a later stage, due to the positive experience gained.

3.5 Step 3: Decision Enforcement

State of the art. Traditional software engineering processes like RUP [19] address decision enforcement through stepwise design refinement down to code. The agile community [4] emphasizes the importance of face-to-face communication. Maturity models such as the Capability Maturity Model Integration (CMMI) [25] and domain-specific governance models [13] also can be used to ensure that ADOutcomes find their way into running code. At build and deployment time, concepts such as code aspects and configuration policies can be used to express architectural intent explicitly. However, complexity and maturity concerns have limited a broad adoption of these two concepts so far.

Project reality. Coaching, architectural templates, and code reviews are the dominating decision enforcement approaches today. All of them are perfectly valid. However, applying these approaches takes time and depends on the coding and leadership skills of the decision makers. Personal architectural knowledge that remains tacit often is lost during the maintenance phase of the application lifecycle, e.g., when the team setup changes. Codifying architectural knowledge in design models is an additional option when following Model-Driven Architecture (MDA) principles. However, a key limitation of standard MDA is that model transformations often are not configurable and therefore hard to adjust to project-specific architectural decisions [32]. For example, many BPM-to-BPEL tools allow the user to make simple decisions, e.g., regarding activity naming, but use fixed values for key aspects, e.g., system transaction management settings. Consequently, development resources have to be invested for changing the default values to the settings required in the particular requirements context. Such disconnects and reconciliation problems between architecture and development tools and artifacts can be observed frequently.

Our approach. The existing practices work fine for many decisions, particularly those pertaining to micro design. As an additional option in our framework, machine-readable decision models can be interpreted by model transformations and code

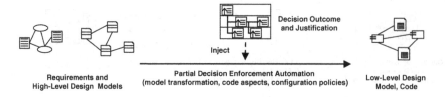

Fig. 5. Decision enforcement via injection into model transformations and code generation

generators. Figure 5 illustrates this *decision injection* concept, which can help to reduce unnecessary development efforts and ensure architectural consistency:

We have built a demonstrator for such an approach that uses Eclipse JET templates to codify key architectural decisions dealing with non-functional concerns regarding the implementation of executable business processes. For example, the demonstrator injects ADOutcome for TRANSACTIONAL POLICIES such as REQUIRESOWN and PARTICIPATES into the BPEL code generated by a BPM tool used to capture business requirements. In this example, the decision drivers are the logical business transaction boundaries, the physical resource protection needs, and the capabilities of the involved legacy systems. The BPM tool user, typically a domain expert (business analyst), can and should not be responsible for this architectural decision.

4   Application of Conceptual Framework to SOA Design

In this section, we describe how we applied the conceptual framework from Section 3 to enterprise application development and SOA design incrementally. First, we orga-nized the decision points encountered on our own SOA projects [30][33] according to the meta model from Section 3.2. As a second step, we factored in selected architectu-ral knowledge from projects technically led by peers, leveraging an IBM-wide SOA and Web services practitioner community with 3500 members. To verify that the con-cepts are not limited to SOA as the primary architectural style, we cooperated with architects specializing on information management, who documented their know-how about information integration and data-centric architectures using our concepts. The result is a reusable SOA decision model we refer to as *SOA Design Space*.

4.1   Requirements Model and Reference Architecture for SOA Design Space

In Section 3.3, we explained that we require a machine-readable requirements model to be able to partially automate the decision identification step. When constructing SOAs, *analysis-level business process models*, optionally annotated with NFRs, are well suited for this purpose [17]. Object-oriented analysis artifacts such as use case models also work well. Our minimum requirement for such models is that they have to list the processes and activities to be realized as software services; the decision identification support can then create *realization decisions* for these high-level functional building blocks.

In the SOA case, we use the abstract *SOA reference model* from [2] as our refe-rence architecture. It provides a conceptual, semi-strict layering scheme defining nine layers: consumer, process, service, component, resource, integration, Quality of

Service (QoS), information, and governance. It is possible to use other reference architectures, as long as these provide a layering scheme and allow associating a decision with the design model elements it pertains to. The selection of the concrete REFERENCE ARCHITECTURE is an executive-level architectural decision in its own right; making it is part of the project-specific adoption of the SOA Design Space.

If an analysis model has already been transformed into a high-level design model, e.g., with support from BPM and SOA tools, we can further improve the decision identification step because the business-level activities in the process model have already been refined into high-level design artifacts such as candidate services. Fewer decisions remain. An example for such a transformation is DATA CONTAINER ASSIGNMENT, producing typed service operations as output. Furthermore, un-necessary design points can be deleted. For example, if cycles have been removed from the business process automatically, DEALING WITH CYCLIC PROCESS MODELS is no longer relevant [17].

4.2 Organizing Principles in the SOA Design Space

To decompose the rather complex SOA design domain, we applied several proven structuring principles such as *separation of concerns* and *logical layering*. Figure 6 outlines the overall structure, resembling the ADLevel hierarchy from Figure 2:

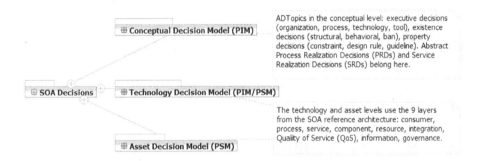

Fig. 6. UML packages for SOA Design Space and assignment to MDA levels

ADTopics are used as a fine-grained grouping mechanism on each MDA level. We aim for *high cohesion* within and *low coupling* between ADTopics. In the Conceptual Decision Model, we use the ontology from [20]. The reference architecture from [2] organizes the ADTopics. Table 1 lists selected conceptual ADTopic nodes with examples, comparing their identification, making, and enforcement characteristics:

Employing a *consistent naming style* for ADTopics, ADs, and ADAlternatives is another principle to make models comparable; all elements created according to the meta model from Section 3.2 have a unique identifier and a self-explaining short name. Our terminology takes inspiration from service modeling [2], enterprise archi-tecture [7] and SOA patterns [29] literature. By convention, alternatives are ordered from common and recommended to exceptional; if present, fallback alternatives such as CUSTOM CODING and OTHER appear last.

Table 1. Decision types in Conceptual Decision Model of SOA Design Space

Decision type (ADTopic) with examples	Identification (role, phase)	Decision Making Support (non-exclusive list)	Enforcement (now, future)
Executive Decisions, e.g., PLATFORM SELECTION, ARCHITECTURAL STYLE, GOVERNANCE	Enterprise architect, before project starts	SWOT analysis and other consulting techniques (high number of alternatives, incomplete data)	Now and future: Governance processes, limited tool support (personal productivity software)
Enterprise Architecture Decisions (EADs), e.g., existence decisions: TRANSACTION MANAGEMENT, SESSION MANAGEMENT, LAYERING, PERSISTENCE STRATEGY [7]	Lead architects and senior developers, during early project phases (solution outline, macro design)	Literature research (e.g., patterns books, online forums) and "if-then" best practices rules (often several valid choices, decision drivers semi-concrete)	Now and future: Architectural templates, coaching Future: pattern toolkits, configurable model transformations
Process Realization Decisions (PRDs), e.g., property decisions: MACRO VS. MICRO FLOW, INSTANCE CORRELATION, SYSTEM TRANSACTION BOUNDARIES, COMPENSATION [32]	Technical architects, lead developers, platform and technology specialists, during macro and micro design	Domain analysis and design (challenging NFRs and many other decision drivers), to be supported by QOC diagrams etc. (choices can be justified by concrete decision drivers)	Now: Manual coding, hard wired in MDA model transformations and code generators Future: Decision injection into code, aspects, policies
Service Realization Decisions (SRDs), e.g., MESSAGE EXCHANGE PATTERN, SERVICE GRANULARITY [32]	Same as PRDs, but different skill set	Same as PRDs, but often less alternatives because decisions on higher levels constrain choices	Same as PRDs

The SOA Design Space implements the abstract decision scoping concept from Section 3.2, using the process and service abstractions from the selected SOA reference architecture. PRDs have to be taken per process to be realized in software, SRDs once per process activity to be implemented as a software service.

Via *decision tagging*, ADs can be annotated with keywords to express crosscutting concerns, which then become additional dimensions in our SOA Design Space. For instance, we tagged all decisions dealing with transactionality across ADLevels and ADTopics so that they can be searched for.

There are many dependencies within and between the levels. To resume the example from Section 3.2, PROCESS AUTOMATION PARADIGM and deciding between abstract MESSAGE EXCHANGE PATTERNS such as REQUEST-REPLY and ONE WAY are architectural decisions in the Conceptual Decision Model. In the Technology Decision Model, concerns then are BPEL PROCESS DESIGN and SOAP MESSAGING VS. REPRESENTATIONAL STATE TRANSFER (REST) as MESSAGE EXCHANGE FORMAT; when integrating distributed components, the selection of a TRANSPORT PROTOCOL, e.g., HTTP or MESSAGING, is another technology decision. Vendor-specific issues appear in the Asset Decision Model. WEB SERVICE STACK SELECTION and deployment issues such as selection of an open source or commercial SOAP ENGINE (e.g., APACHE AXIS) and engine-specific BPEL configuration decisions such as LONG OR SHORT PROCESS LIFETIME and ACTIVITY TRANSACTIONALITY are examples for such decisions [31]. The dependencies between the levels are modeled explicitly.

4.3 Example: Ws-01, Service Provider Type

Figure 7 illustrates a single AD, the selection of the SERVICE PROVIDER TYPE. It is a screenshot of AD$_{kwik}$, a Web 2.0 collaboration front end implementing the concepts presented in this paper. We describe the user interface and knowledge engineering concepts of AD$_{kwik}$ in detail in [24].

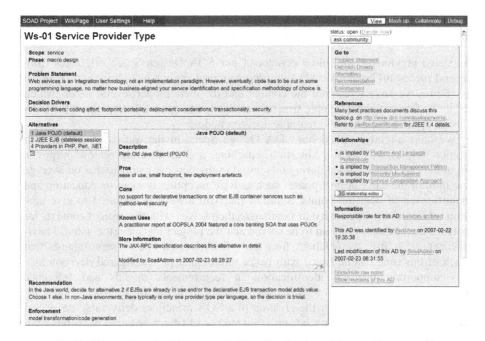

Fig. 7. Web services decision example: Ws-01, selection of SERVICE PROVIDER TYPE

The SERVICE PROVIDER TYPE decision is a SRD according to Table 1. On SOA projects, this decision has to be made for each service to be implemented, it can be identified in the analysis-level BPM model serving as input to the decision making process; therefore, this decision has a "service" scope (the scope attribute is defined in our meta model, see Figure 2). The phase attribute links the decision to a methodology. In this case, "macro design", a term from the method used by IBM Global Services, suggests that this decision should be taken during the early, overall architecture design. There is a problem statement motivating why this decision is needed. In this example, it is one paragraph paraphrasing the motivation for this decision found in the literature; in other cases, a simple question like "How to correlate incoming user requests to server-side session objects?" is more appropriate.

For this decision, the coding effort, the memory footprint, and several other general quality attributes are listed as particularly important decision drivers. The available alternatives are listed as well, along with their pros, cons and known uses. In the example, JAVA PLAIN OLD JAVA OBJECT (POJO), J2EE ENTERPRISE JAVA BEAN (EJB), and PROVIDERS IN PHP, PERL, .NET have been identified. The references field points to recommended reading, in this case two online resources. Dependencies to and from other decisions are modeled explicitly and shown as relationships. For example, the executive-level PLATFORM AND LANGUAGE PREFERENCES decision clearly has an impact: the non-Java alternatives are no longer relevant if using Java is imperative. As there are several WSDL-TO-JAVA CODE GENERATION WIZARDS, this decision then can be enforced via code generation, assuming that the selected wizard supports both POJO and EJB generation.

4.4 Initial Evaluation and Expected Benefits of SOA Design Space

As stated previously, the initial content of our SOA Design Space originates from several successful large-scale SOA development projects conducted since 2001. In the meantime, we have refactored the content and the meta model several times, which led to the fine-grained ADTopic structure outlined in Section 4.2. At present, the SOA Design Space consists of 160 reusable decision nodes.

We have already applied our SOA Design Space in the use cases specified in Section 3.1, as well as for education, coaching, and architecture review purposes. From the experience gained during this initial evaluation, we estimate that on average one third of the early project phases such as RUP inception is spent on education and identification of decision points. Some of that will always be required to give new team members an opportunity to familiarize themselves with the project context, for instance the business problem to be solved and the project logistics (tools, build environment, etc.). Still, the feedback from early SOA Design Space users suggests that much of this time can be saved with better tooling and pre-configured decision models supporting decision identification in requirements models and reference architectures.

In one case, the effort for the creation of a SOA principles deliverable decreased from eight to five person days because thirteen out of fifteen required decisions were present in the SOA Design space and could be reused. For instance, the architect on that project reused the decision node from Figure 7. The decision drivers listed in Section 4.3, particularly transactionality needs and ease of deployment, matched with the project requirements, so that our recommendation to use EJBs if leveraging the declarative EJB transaction model is adequate, and to use POJOs otherwise, was directly applicable. The architect also reported that he found several decisions in the SOA Design Space that he had not identified yet, but which turned out to be required: for instance, the decision for a SERVICE CATEGORIZATION SCHEME to distinguish technical utility services and logic-centric business services, which is described in [18] and [30], became a key element of his SOA design.

A rigorous decision making process is often seen as a prerequisite to achieve higher maturity levels, e.g., in CMMI [25]. Decision dependency modeling makes design errors visible and allows backtracking. A positive impact on software quality can be expected, for example when combinations that do not work are detected or disabled before the mistake is even made. These positive effects are hard to quantify; however, we have observed them on projects already.

Our decision enforcement approach leads to less manual reconfiguration and coding needs and simplifies the model-code reconciliation, faithful to the original vision of MDA. A positive impact on team communication and climate can also be expected. Decision capturing becomes a shared responsibility; decisions that are openly created, discussed, and justified often are easier to accept than dictated ones.

5 Conclusions and Outlook

In this paper, we presented a proactive approach to modeling and reusing architectural knowledge for enterprise application development. As discussed in Section 2, our approach extends existing proposals for retrospective architectural decision capturing. It facilitates reuse of design rationale and team collaboration, two issues particularly relevant in enterprise application development. In Section 3, we defined a conceptual framework facilitating collaborative decision making supported by an extended meta model. In this framework, three steps improve decision reuse and sharing of rationale:

- Semi-automatic decision identification, speeding up early project activities. In this step, we combine requirements models with reference architectures containing reusable decision templates to create an initial to-do list.
- More informed decision making via reusable collections of decision drivers, good practices recommendations and other supporting techniques. In this step, our framework promises to improve decision making rigor and quality.
- Improved decision enforcement in MDA via decision injection into parameterized model transformations and code generation, reducing development efforts and simplifying communication, governance, and maintenance.

As demonstrated in Section 4, our approach already has proven to be practical for BPM requirement models and SOA as architectural style; we compiled a SOA Design Space with 160 reusable decision nodes. We could observe initial effort savings and quality improvements on an early adoption project. Tool support is available.

The presented approach is generally applicable if several applications are built in the same or a similar context and if full decision automation is an illusion. We require the requirements model to be reasonably structured and at minimum one reference architecture for the selected architectural style to exist. Enterprise application development and SOA meet these applicability criteria.

The complexity of the solution space and keeping the content up-to-date, consistent, and easy to locate are key challenges for a broader adoption of the presented approach. In response to these challenges, we plan to investigate the integration of architectural design and decision models even further, to involve a broader practitioner community in future content engineering, and to leverage additional results from other fields, e.g., knowledge management and architectural patterns.

We envision several advanced usage scenarios for the SOA Design Space. Project managers can use it for planning and health checking purposes. Work breakdown structures and effort estimation reports can be created from the decision model, as open decisions correspond to required activities. If there are many, frequent changes, or many questions are still unresolved in late project phases, the project is likely to be troubled. Moreover, product-specific decision outcome can serve as input to software configuration planning. Product selection and operational modeling decisions define which software licenses are required, and on which hardware nodes the required software has to be installed. The SOA Design Space can also serve as an enterprise architecture communication vehicle; enterprise architects can maintain a company-specific instance of the SOA Design Space, consisting of a subset of decisions and alternatives to give freedom of choice to individual project teams without sacrificing overall architectural integrity. Finally, we plan to use the SOA Design Space as a prescriptive micro method for SOA construction, complementing service modeling methods.

Future research work includes exploring several advanced concepts, for example more expressive dependency modeling. Decision space pruning can rule out alternatives based on the outcome of other decisions. We also plan to investigate whether reusable architectural decision models can help improving the documentation of software products, for example packages and middleware with many variation points.

Acknowledgments. We would like to thank Davide Falessi, Jonas Grundler, Gregor Hohpe, Dirk Huppert, David Janson, Ed Kahan, Jochen Klein, Jana Koehler, Oliver Kopp, Petra Kopp, Philippe Kruchten, Einar Landre, Ralp Mietzner, Sven Milinksi, Frank Müller, Mike Papazoglou, Stefan Pappe, Cesare Pautasso, Willem-Jan van den Heuvel, Harald Wesenberg, and Uwe Zdun for their input, provided through many discussions and/or reviews of earlier versions of this paper.

References

[1] Abrams, S., Bloom, B., Keyser, P., Kimelman, D., Nelson, E., Neuberger, W., Roth, T., Simmonds, I., Tang, S., Vlissides, J.: Architectural Thinking and Modeling with the Architects' Workbench. IBM Systems Journal 45 (2006)
[2] Arsanjani, A.: Service-oriented modeling and architecture, IBM developerWorks (2004), http://www.ibm.com/developerworks/webservices/library/ws-soa-design1
[3] Bass, L., Clements, P., Kazman, R.: Software Architecture in Practice, 2nd edn. Addison Wesley, Reading (2003)
[4] Beck, K.: Extreme Programming Explained. Addison Wesley, Reading (2000)
[5] Buschmann, F., Meunier, R., Rohnert, H., Sommerlad, P., Stal, M.: Pattern-Oriented Software Architecture – a System of Patterns. Wiley, Chichester (1996)
[6] Falessi, D., Becker, M., Cantone, G.: Design Decision Rationale: Experiences and Steps Towards a more Systematic Approach. In: Workshop on Sharing and Reusing Architectural Knowledge, ACM SIGSOFT Software Engineering. Notes 31, 5 (2006)
[7] Fowler, M.: Patterns of Enterprise Application Architecture. Addison Wesley, Reading (2003)
[8] Fowler, M.: UML Distilled. Addison Wesley, Reading (2000)
[9] Gamma, E., Helm, R., Johnson, R., Vlissides, J.: Design Patterns – Elements of Reusable Object-Oriented Software. Addison-Wesley, Reading (1995)
[10] Hitchins, D.: Advanced Systems Thinking, Engineering, and Management. Artech House Publishers (2003)
[11] Hohpe, G., Woolf, B.: Enterprise Integration Patterns. Addison Wesley, Reading (2004)

[12] IBM Corporation: SOA and Web Services Best Practices, Academy of Technology Report (2004)

[13] IBM Corporation, SOA Governance and Management Method, http://www.ibm.com/software/solutions/soa/gov/method

[14] International Standards Organization (ISO), ISO/IEC 9126-1:2001, Software Quality Attributes, Software engineering – Product quality, Part 1: Quality model (2001)

[15] Jansen, A., Bosch, J.: Software Architecture as a Set of Architectural Design Decisions. In: Proceedings of the 5th Working IEEE/IFIP Conference on Software Architecture (Wicsa 2005), IEEE Computer Society Press, Los Alamitos (2005)

[16] Johnston, S.: RUP Plug-In for SOA V1.0, IBM developerWorks (2005), http://www.ibm.com/developerworks/rational/library/05/510_soaplug

[17] Koehler, J., Hauser, R., Küster, J., Ryndina, K., Vanhatalo, J., Wahler, M.: The Role of Visual Modeling and Model Transformations in Business-driven Development. In: Proceedings of the 5th International Workshop on Graph Transformation and Visual Modeling Techniques, Elsevier, Amsterdam (2006)

[18] Krafzig, D., Banke, K., Slama, D.: Enterprise SOA. Prentice-Hall, Upper Saddle River (2005)

[19] Kruchten, P.: The Rational Unified Process: An Introduction. Addison-Wesley, Reading (2003)

[20] Kruchten, P., Lago, P., van Vliet, H.: Building up and reasoning about architectural knowledge. In: Hofmeister, C., Crnkovic, I., Reussner, R. (eds.) QoSA 2006. LNCS, vol. 4214, Springer, Heidelberg (2006)

[21] Lee, J., Lai, K.: What's in Design Rationale?. Human-Computer Interaction 6 (3 & 4) (1991)

[22] MacLean, A., Young, R., Bellotti, V., Moran, T.: Questions, Options, and Criteria: Elements of Design Space Analysis, Human-Computer Interaction 6 (3 & 4) (1991)

[23] OASIS. Web Services Business Process Execution Language (WSBPEL), Version 1.1 (2003), http://www.oasis-open.org/committees/tc_home.php?wg_abbrev=wsbpel

[24] Schuster, N., Zimmermann, O., Pautasso, C.: ADkwik: Web 2.0 Collaboration System for Architectural Decision Engineering. In: Proceedings of the Nineteenth International Conference on Software Engineering & Knowledge Engineering (SEKE 2007), KSI (2007)

[25] Software Engineering Institute, Capability Maturity Model® Integration (CMMI), http://www.sei.cmu.edu/cmmi

[26] Svahnberg, M., Wohlin, C., Lundberg, L., Mattsson, M.: A Quality-Driven Decision Support Method for Identifying Software Architecture Candidates. International Journal of Software Engineering and Knowledge Management 13(5) (2003)

[27] Tang, A., Babar, M.A., Gorton, I., Han, J.: A Survey of the Use and Documentation of Architecture Design Rationale. In: Proceedings of the 5th Working IEEE/IFIP Conference on Software Architecture (Wicsa 2005), IEEE Computer Society Press, Los Alamitos (2005)

[28] Tyree, J., Akerman, A.: Architecture Decisions: Demystifying Architecture. IEEE Software 22 (2005)

[29] Zdun, U., Dustdar, S.: Model-Driven and Pattern-Based Integration of Process-Driven SOA Models, Internationales Begegnungs- und Forschungszentrum fuer Informatik (IBFI), Schloss Dagstuhl, Germany, http://drops.dagstuhl.de/opus/volltexte/2006/820

[30] Zimmermann, O., Doubrovski, V., Grundler, J., Hogg, K.: Service-Oriented Architecture and Business Process Choreography in an Order Management Scenario. In: ACM SIGPLAN International Conference on Object-Oriented Programming, Systems, Languages, and Applications (OOPSLA 2005), ACM Press, New York (2005)

[31] Zimmermann, O., Grundler, J., Tai, S., Leymann, F.: Architectural Decisions and Patterns for Transactional Workflows in SOA. In: Krämer, B., Lin, K.-J., Narasimhan, P. (eds.) ICSOC 2007. LNCS, vol. 4749, pp. 81–93 (2007)

[32] Zimmermann, O., Koehler, J., Leymann, F.: The Role of Architectural Decisions in Model-Driven Service-Oriented Architecture Construction. In: Proceedings of the OOPSLA 2006 Workshop on Best Practices and Methodologies in Service-Oriented Architectures, Unipub (2006)

[33] Zimmermann, O., Milinski, M., Craes, M., Oellermann, F.: Second Generation Web Services-Oriented Architecture in Production in the Finance Industry. In: ACM SIGPLAN International Conference on Object-Oriented Programming, Systems, Languages, and Applications (OOPSLA 2004), ACM Press, New York (2004)

[34] Zimmermann, O., Tomlinson, M., Peuser, S.: Perspectives on Web Services. Springer, Heidelberg (2003)

Using Planning Techniques to Assist Quality-Driven Architectural Design Exploration

J. Andrés Díaz-Pace[1] and Marcelo R. Campo[2]

[1] Software Engineering Institute
4500 Fifth Av. - Pittsburgh, PA 15213-3890, USA
`adiaz@sei.cmu.edu`
[2] ISISTAN Research Institute, Facultad de Cs. Exactas, UNICEN University,
Pje. Arroyo Seco - Campus Universitario, (7000) Tandil, Buenos Aires, Argentina
`mcampo@exa.unicen.edu.ar`
Also CONICET - Argentina

Abstract. A software architecture design captures the main decisions regarding the quality-attribute requirements for a system. When constructing these designs, the architect normally evaluates and combines solutions with different quality-attribute tradeoffs. This exploration of the design space can be seen as a searching problem, in which the architect's expertise is what directs the search towards a "good-enough" solution. Nonetheless, given complexity of this search, assisting the architect with adequate tool support becomes indispensable. In this context, we have investigated the utility of a planning-based tool approach called *DesignBots* to explore design alternatives. Specifically, the approach considers quality-attribute issues as goals achievable by combinations of architectural mechanisms, which are generated by a mixed-initiative and hierarchical planning engine. Our experiences with *DesignBots* show that the planning approach effectively helps architects to explore design alternatives productively.

Keywords: software architecture design, quality-driven mechanisms, artificial intelligence techniques, tool support.

1 Introduction

Architectural design is considered a critical activity within the software development process [4]. As usual, the most critical activities are also the most complex ones. A software architecture gives a blueprint with the main design decisions regarding the achievement of quality attributes (e.g., performance, modifiability, availability, security, etc.). The quality of these decisions is directly related to the architect's expertise. Therefore, capturing such an expertise, and providing tool support to help novice architects to take advantage of it, becomes a valuable contribution for the construction of good-quality designs. This field, however, is rather unexplored and there is little available knowledge about how to model the architect's rationale while creating designs.

S. Overhage et al. (Eds.): QoSA 2007, LNCS 4880, pp. 33–52, 2007.

Normally during architectural design, the architect applies her knowledge and good judgment to guide decision-making in a maze of different design solutions. A central objective in this activity is to obtain a reasonable balance among the quality attributes most relevant for the system. Unfortunately, these attributes often conflict with each other (e.g., performance versus modifiability, performance versus security, etc.). Looking closer at quality-attribute decisions, we have that the architect usually starts with a guess of the architectural solution, and progressively considers alternatives to improve this solution with respect to a set of quality goals. As decision-making proceeds, the architect gets involved in a complex process of exploration and composition of design alternatives. This process can be seen as a type of searching problem, in which the architectural knowledge serves to prune and direct the search of solutions. From a tool support perspective, it is certainly not realistic to try to automate the whole design process; however, we can develop "intelligent" tools able to assist the architect in the exploration of "promising" designs.

Over the last years, as part of different research projects, we have been working with a design approach focused on the interplay between quality-attribute issues and the architectural strategies used to satisfy quality [8]. This relies on that *qualities do not arise spontaneously from the architecture, but rather they are planned for by architects* [4]. In particular, quality is engineered through the articulation of specific architectural tactics and patterns. Therefore, among the spectrum of AI techniques available, we decided to investigate the utility of hierarchical planning techniques [19] as a computational support for an automated design assistant.

In this context, we have developed a tool approach called *DesignBots* to help architects to generate quality-driven design solutions. Basically, the architect feeds the *DesignBots* tool with an initial design, expressed in an architectural description language, as well as with a weighted list of quality-attribute scenarios for that design. Then, considering these scenarios as goals, a planning engine is able to propose alternative designs that improve the satisfaction of the scenarios, according to the importance of each quality with respect to the system. The alternative designs are constructed by applying basic "architectural" transformations on the initial architecture. These transformations are actually the planning operators for the engine, which is responsible for assembling them and produce a complex architectural transformation as output. Besides, as the engine is planning, the architect can be called for intervention to solve issues that cannot be automatically solved by the planner. The results of applying *DesignBots* have shown so far an important potential of planning to optimize the architectural design process. Essentially, the approach allows the architect to concentrate on the key design decisions for shaping the architecture, and delegate to the planner much of the routine work associated to the design alternatives derived from these decisions.

The rest of the paper is organized around 5 sections. In section 2, we explain how to model architectural design in terms of a hierarchical planning framework. Section 3 describes the general architecture that supports the *DesignBots* tool, explaining the steps and processing performed by the planning engine to generate design alternatives. In Section 4, we discuss the results of some case-studies. Section 5 covers related work. Finally, Section 6 gives the conclusions of the paper and analyzes lines of future research.

2 Architectural Design as a Planning Problem

Researchers in the field of automated design systems have long considered that the computational view of design activities is a *process of searching and planning* [10]. This view, however, has been little explored in the software development counterpart. Despite some limitations in the space of generic artifact designs, as discussed in [21], the application of planning for modeling the reasoning process in architectural design appears as an approach worthy to be investigated.

A premise of software architectures is that the achievement of quality attributes comes from applying specific patterns on the architecture. Architectural patterns are ruled by general design principles [7] (e.g., abstraction, information hiding, modularization, separation of concerns, coupling, and divide-and-conquer, among others), which have been recently codified under the concept of architectural tactics [4]. In summary, both patterns and tactics capture the usual mechanisms articulated by architects when designing an architecture that satisfies the stakeholders' concerns. It is common to express stakeholders' concerns in terms of scenarios [4]. From an operational point of view, we can see quality-attribute scenarios as the goals that drive the architect through a search for architectural transformations. Interestingly, several planning techniques for this kind of problems have been developed within the AI community [18, 22]. Furthermore, any architectural transformation can be traced to a network of design operations, in the context of predetermined tactics and patterns. Thus, this transformational process fits naturally with hierarchical planning [19].

Classical planning concentrates on how to construct sequences of actions for a given state that, when executed correctly, will make a system satisfy a set of goals [18]. In particular, hierarchical planning (also known as HTN planning) tries to produce a sequence of actions that perform the activities described by a network of goals. Essentially, HTN planning organizes plans in terms of hierarchies of tasks[1], called *hierarchical task networks*. These networks can be progressively refined in sub-plans, often nearly independent of each other. A sub-plan provides more details about the way an abstract task is achieved. Refinement of tasks is achieved in HTN either by means of *methods* or *operators*. The planning algorithm proceeds by applying methods that decompose each task into simpler tasks and resolving the conflicts among tasks, until a conflict-free plan consisting of primitive tasks is found. Primitive tasks are those that cannot be further decomposed, so they are executed over the current *state of the world* by means of operators.

There is a division between the *planning domain* (i.e., a collection of generic actions: HTN methods and operators) and the *planning problem* (i.e., the world state and the goals). For the purpose of *DesignBots*, three basic mappings are necessary in order to cast architectural design to HTN planning:

- Codify the knowledge about tactics, architectural patterns and mechanisms as the planning domain. HTN methods and operators are seen as "standard procedures" for tactics, architectural patterns and mechanisms. These tactics, patterns and mechanisms are the vehicles to address quality attributes.
- Convert the architectural description into the world state for the planning problem.

---

[1] The terms "goal" and "task" are used interchangeable in the HTN jargon.

- Process the quality-attribute scenarios for this architecture in order to get an initial task network for the planning problem. The tasks of this network are seen as goals of attainment for the planner.

Since the amount of knowledge needed for automation can be really large, some form of abstraction is needed within the planning domain. An advantage of HTN planning is that identifies strategic solutions for qualities at a general level, and then provides separately more details of the procedures to implement these solutions. For instance, let's suppose a task network with a modifiability goal that involves breaking a dependency between two components, and a tactic that tries to insert some component as an intermediary for the dependency. According to the type of dependency, let's also consider that this tactic could be materialized by different architectural patterns or mechanisms[2], namely: a virtual machine, a repository, a naming server, a publisher-subscriber schema, etc.

On the other hand, there are constraints (not directly related to quality-attribute issues) that affect the development of the planning process. The initial architecture, assumptions made by analysis models, architect's preferences, or component reuse, are examples of constraints that influence the selection of acceptable solutions by architects. For this reason, some degree of human decision-making must be taken into account, because not all the decisions and constraints can be automatically treated by the planning engine. The architect would answer some critical points of the solution, so that the remaining work would be reduced to routine issues solvable via planning. For instance, let's consider that a dependency between components is detected. Here, the planner could suspend itself and display a list of patterns to break the dependency, enabling the architect to choose the pattern of her preference, according to the specific design situation. After that, the planner would proceed to implement the details of the selected pattern. This modality of planning is called *mixed-initiative* [22], as it involves a construction of plans through dialogs between the architect and the planning engine.

3 The *DesignBots* Framework

The *DesignBots* framework divides the design knowledge into a set of specialized agents referred to as *designbots*. These agents are capable of working with architectural specifications and have competences on particular quality attributes. Regarding planning, each *designbot* is equipped with both quality-attribute knowledge and goals. On one side, the knowledge tells the agent how to apply a certain tactic for a general quality in order to derive an architectural transformation. This knowledge comes mostly from a "procedure for predictable architectural design" developed at SEI [3]. Each *designbot* is configured with adequate knowledge during tool setup. On the other side, the goals are the concrete quality-attribute issues that drive the agents in the elaboration of transformations. These goals are the result of

---

[2] Architectural patterns and mechanisms are seen as design elements with different levels of granularity that serve to make tactics concrete. An architectural mechanism is fine-grained and only implements a single tactic, while an architectural pattern is coarse-grained and usually encapsulates one or more tactics at the same time.

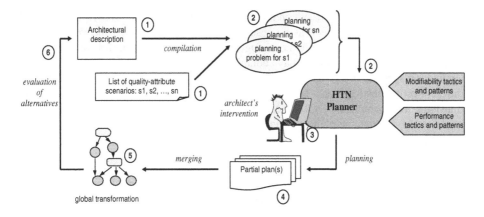

Fig. 1. Planning-based workflow for our architectural design tool

processing the quality-attribute scenarios stated for the initial architecture. Both the initial architecture and the scenarios are entered by the architect as a user of the tool. A general view of the approach is shown in Figure 1.

Since each *designbot* analyzes the architecture from the perspective of a single quality attribute, the planner will generate a collection of partial plans, each of which consisting of a sequence of architectural operations that intends to achieve a particular quality goal. For this reason, the *DesignBots* framework provides a procedure to combine the *designbots'* partial plans into a global transformation. The idea here is to prioritize the *designbots'* goals, balancing the effects of their plans on the re-design of the (initial) architecture. Once a set of candidate transformations is available, the architect can select any of them and modify her architecture. This exploration continues until the tool produces a design that satisfies the architect's expectations.

Basically, the *DesignBots* approach involves five main activities with different degrees of automation, namely: description of the input architectural model (step 1); allocation of quality-attribute scenarios to the *designbots* (step 1); analysis of individual scenarios to determine suitable tactics (step 2); execution of the planning process at the *designbots* (steps 3 & 4); and application of combined transformations on the architectural model (steps 5 & 6). In order to explain the steps of the approach, we will use a case-study about a battlefield control system (BCS) adapted from [17]. BCS involves a central commander and a network of army units (e.g., troops, tanks, planes, sensors, maps, etc.). The commander is assigned to a series of missions, which can be accomplished by controlling the movement, strategy and operations of their units. As the initial BCS architecture, we have a central repository with information from the battlefield, as well as a number of fighter and sensor nodes. Both types of nodes can submit information to the repository. The fighter nodes are also able to execute orders from the commander.

3.1 The Architectural Model and the Quality-Attribute Goals

For representing architectural models, we chose a custom architectural description language that allows us to specify systems as graphs of interacting components. This language, called *ADLite*, is based on the *component-and-connector viewtype* (C&C) [4]. Actually, *ADLite* can be seen as a subset of ACME [14] in which the vocabulary of components and connectors has been augmented with responsibilities, properties and templates[3]. The components may contain responsibilities that serve to capture application-specific functions. Besides, it is possible to annotate *ADLite* elements with different properties (e.g., data for quality-attribute analysis). The tool provides a special translator that compiles *ADLite* specifications to a Prolog-like representation, as the world state on which the planning engine will perform its computations. Figure 2 shows the initial BCS architecture in *ADLite*, and Figure 3 shows the HTN script generated for this architecture.

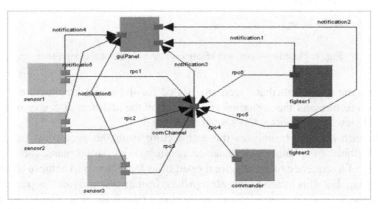

#	Main Quality	Scenario Description	Estimated Measure
1	Modifiability	A new type of sensor is added to the network by the system administrator, and the architecture should take account of it.	average cost change = 55 %
2	Performance	The number of fighter and sensor nodes increase, and the system should keep the level of service bounded	average throughput = 10 % average latency = 0.65 msec.

Fig. 2. The initial BCS architecture and some quality-attribute scenarios for it

The input architecture is accompanied by a list of quality-attribute scenarios. Each scenario must involve a single quality and a level of response (e.g., throughput or latency for performance, cost of components affected by a change for modifiability, etc.). Two particular scenarios elicited for BCS are included at the bottom of Figure 2. The architect determines a ranking for the list of scenarios, based on which of them are most influential for the architecture. Once ranked, the scenarios are distributed among the *designbots* according to their target quality. At this point, the *designbots* are ready to begin with the analysis activities.

The analysis of scenarios employs scopes and reasoning frameworks. An *architectural scope* sets apart the region of the architecture affected by a scenario.

---

[3] For simplicity, a number of features of ACME such as: families, types, connector roles, or attachments were deliberately taken out in *ADLite*, because they do not provide essential information at this stage of the research and could be incorporated later quite easily.

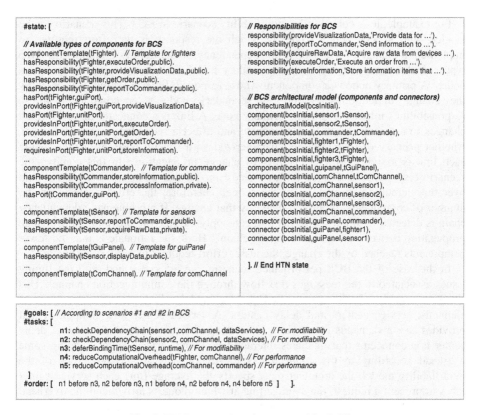

Fig. 3. HTN state and goals generated for BCS

This is desirable for two reasons: each *designbot* can better focus its analysis to derive pursued goals, and additionally, the searching state for the planner gets narrowed. The identification of scopes needs some cooperation of the architect. First, she has to extract the main responsibilities implied by the scenario. Then, she must execute algorithms provided by the tool that traverse the architectural model and create a view (i.e., the scope) with those elements related to the extracted responsibilities. After obtaining a scope, the *designbot* is able to apply a reasoning framework on it. A *reasoning framework* [5] is a technique for estimating a response measure for a quality attribute, given a base architecture. In general, *DesignBots* considers quality-attribute frameworks as "black-box" tools that can be replaced in the future by more elaborated analysis models to compute scenario responses. Currently, the prototype supports two frameworks, namely: a queuing model for analyzing performance, and a dependency chain model for analyzing modifiability. The last column of the table in Figure 2 gives estimations of the architecture fitness regarding the two BCS scenarios. Once instantiated on the scope, a reasoning framework also establishes a number of goals for the *designbot*. Specifically, the processing of goals is based on Prolog rules, which look at scenario information and manipulate the reasoning framework parameters to control its response as needed [3].

For example, let's consider the modifiability scenario in BCS. This scenario can be tackled with a dependency model in which the response is the effort required to implement a change. Very briefly, our dependency model defines a graph with three types of elements: primary nodes, secondary nodes and links among the previous nodes. A primary node is a component whose responsibilities are directly affected by the change under consideration. A secondary node is a component whose responsibilities interact with some primary node. A link is a connector through which changes in a primary node may propagate and affect a secondary node. Each node, whether primary or secondary, is characterized with several costs of change, while each link is assigned to a probability of change propagation[4]. In this context, the scenario response is estimated through a cost model that computes a weighted sum over the elements participating in the scope. Therefore, the effort depends on the number of components directly affected by that change. If a problematic dependency chain is detected within a scope, the tool can apply the rule of "preventing the change propagation between components in that chain". Here, the rationale is that the fewer components reached by the change, the lesser effort required to support the change.

In the case of the BCS performance scenario, we are concerned with the timing issues associated to the messages that flow through the communication channel. This situation is analyzed with a simplified queuing model, which identifies two types of elements: service centers and delay centers. A service center is a component that provides and/or demands for services, processing different types of requests. A delay center is a connector that mediates interactions among service centers, adding some overhead according to the connector type. Analogously to the properties of the modifiability model, the architect must specify the average time each service center takes to process a request, the average rate at which requests arrive, and the overhead of requests in delay centers. The scenario responses are the latency and throughput of the scope, which can be estimated either using equations or through discrete simulation. To improve the actual responses of the scenario, the tool could follow the rule of "keeping the latency of communications under certain values". Here, the rationale is that a controlled shared channel improves the communications of nodes flowing through the channel. Some goals inferred by the tool for the two scenarios are listed at the bottom of Figure 3. Due to space reasons, the whole analysis process through which the *designbots* infer goals is omitted (see [13] for more information).

3.2 The Tactics, Architectural Patterns and Mechanisms

The *designbots* rely on a body of architectural patterns and mechanisms, which can range from basic actions (e.g. creation/deletion of components or allocation of responsibilities) to more complex ones (e.g. delegation of responsibilities or insertion of a blackboard as intermediary). Some scripts for basic architectural mechanisms are shown in Figure 4a. They give a base for writing more elaborated mechanisms and patterns on top of them. Moreover, a "higher level logic" is needed to organize the application of mechanisms and patterns. This logic captures abstract design strategies known as *architectural tactics* [4]. Each tactic gives directives for improving a single

---

[4] These costs have default values assigned initially by the tool, but the architect may modify the values of particular elements when necessary.

quality attribute. For example, the tactic of "breaking the dependency chain" is relevant for modifiability, and the tactic of "balancing resource allocation" is applicable for performance. In general, tactics admit different implementations in terms of architectural patterns and mechanisms. There is also a causal connection between reasoning-framework analysis and tactics, because the tactical directives are obtained by looking at the reasoning-framework parameters.

```
#method: addComponent( ?name, ?creation ) ->
        #pre: [ equal(?creation, new), not(component(?name, ?anyTemplate) ]
        #body: [
            #tasks: [
                n1: #eval: @getInput ("Provide template for component: "+ ?name, ?template),
                n2: createComponent(?name, ?template)    ]
            #order: [ n1 before n2 ]    ] #end-method.

#operator: createComponent( ?name, ?template ) ->
        #pre: [ not(component(?name,?template), componentTemplate(?template), architecturalModel(?current) ]
        #add: [ component(?current, ?name, ?template) ]
        #delete: [] #end-operator.

#operator: createComponent( ?name, ?template ) ->
        #pre: [ not(component(?name,?template), not (componentTemplate(?template)), architecturalModel(?current) ]
        #add: [ componentTemplate( ?template), component(?current, ?name, ?template) ]
        #delete: [] #end-operator.

#operator: moveResponsibility( ?responsibility, ?target, ?source ) ->
        #pre: [ component(?target,?someTemplate), component(?source, ?otherTemplate), architecturalModel(?current) ,
            hasResponsibility(?responsibility, ?someTemplate, ?any1), not(hasResponsibility(?otherTemplate, ?responsibility, ?any2)) ]
        #add: [ hasResponsibility(?otherTemplate, ?responsibility, ?any2) ]
        #delete: [ hasResponsibility(?someTemplate, ?responsibility, ?any1) ] #end-operator.
...
```

Fig. 4a. HTN domain with basic architectural mechanisms

As an example, a HTN script for the tactic "breaking the dependency chain" is given in Figure 4b. In particular, this tactic is targeted to the goal schema *checkDependency(?primaryChanged, ?rippled, ?typeOfDependency)*. The first two goals of the task network at the bottom of Figure 3 (from scenario #1 in BCS) are instances of that schema. The tactic proceeds as follows. First, the task *checkDependency()* verifies if the architect really wants to effect on the dependency between two designated components. To do so, there are special tasks, called *user-query tasks* that permit to gather information at planning time (e.g., *@selectOption()*, *@warning()*, *@getInput()*, etc). In the case of *@selectOption()*, it displays a GUI panel and asks the architect for a decision.   Then, we have two alternatives for achieving the task *checkDependency()*. If a positive answer is entered by the architect, the next task is to effectively break the dependency by means of an intermediary. If not, a warning message is sent to the GUI panel. Following the thread of the tactic, we have again various options for implementing the intermediary. The first option proposes the replacement of the actual connector with a new one that softens the component coupling, while the second option refers to directly inserting a new component to bridge between the components. If the latter option is selected, one of the paths to materialize the tactic is the *ForwarderReceiver* pattern [7]. This pattern provides transparent inter-process communication (IPC) for systems with a peer-to-peer interaction model. In Figure 4b, the arrangement of roles for forwarders and receivers as well as the responsibilities for them are specified by the top-level method:

applyForwarderReceiver(), plus the sequence of tasks: *defineForwardersForPeer(),*
defineReceiversForPeers() and *updateInteractionsOfPeerWithRest()* (for simplicity,
the details of their possible implementations are skipped in the figure).

Note that the tasks in the body of HTN methods are not ordered in a sequence, but
rather they present a partial order. Having partially-ordered task networks fit well
with design activities, because the architect has freedom to decide the tasks to work
on, and the planner only enforces task precedence when this is really necessary.

```
#method: checkDependency( ?primary, ?secondary, ?dependency ) -> // Starting method for applying the tactic
    #pre: [ primaryComponent(?primary), secondaryComponent(?secondary), equal(?dependency, dataServices),
            someDependency(?primary, ?secondary) ]
    #body: [
        #tasks: [
            n1: #eval: @selectOption("Can the dependency: "+?primary+" - "+?secondary+" be (further) broken?", [yes,no], ?yesno),
            n2: breakDependency(?primary, ?secondary, ?dependency, ?yesno)    ]
        #order: [ n1 before n2 ]    ] #end-method.

#method: breakDependency( ?primary, ?secondary, ?dependency, ?break ) ->
    #pre: [ equal(?break, no) ]
    #body: [
        #tasks: [
            n1: #eval: @warning("Breakup of dependency: "+?primary+" - "+?secondary+" may not be achieved?")    ]
        #order: [ ] ] #end-method.

#method: breakDependency( ?primary, ?secondary, ?dependency, ?break ) -> // Alternative method for task "breakDependency"
    #pre: [ equal(?break, yes) ]
    #body: [
        #tasks: [
            n1: #eval: @selectOption("What strategy is better for you?", [lowerCouplingConnector,intermediaryComponent], ?option),
            n2: insertIntermediaryFor(?primary, ?secondary, ?option), // Using an intermediary to break the dependency
            n3: checkDependency(?primary, ?secondary, ?dependency)    ]
        #order: [ n1 before n2, n2 before n3 ]    ] #end-method.

#method: insertIntermediaryFor( ?primary, ?secondary, ?strategy ) ->
    #pre: [ someDependency(?primary, ?secondary), equal(?strategy, intermediaryComponent) ]
    #body: [
        #tasks: [
            n1: #eval: @selectOption("What kind of communication in: "+?primary+" should be tackled ?, [send,receive,both], ?ptype),
            n2: #eval: @selectOption("What kind of communication in: "+?secondary+" should be tackled ?, [send,receive,both], ?stype),
            n3: applyForwarderReceiver(?primary,?ptype, yes), // Materializing the tactic with a forwarder-receiver pattern
            n4: applyForwarderReceiver(?secondary,?stype, yes)    ]
        #order: [ n1 before n3, n2 before n4 ]    ] #end-method.

method: applyForwarderReceiver( ?peer, ?variant, ?continue ) ->
    #pre: [ component(?peer), equal(?variant, send), equal(?continue, yes) ]
    #body: [
        #tasks: [
            n1: #eval: @selectResponsibilities("Responsibilities for sending data/services in peer: "+?peer, ?list),
            n2: defineForwardersForPeer(?peer, ?list, yes),
            n3: defineReceiversForPeer(?peer, ?list, yes),
            n4: updateInteractionsOfPeerWithRest(?peer, ?list)    ]
        #order: [ n1 before n2, n1 before n3, n2 before n4, n3 before n4 ]    ]    #end-method.
...
```

Fig. 4b. HTN domain with a tactic and an architectural pattern

3.3 Planning for Design Alternatives with Mixed-Initiative

The evaluation of possible tactics is driven by the results of the scope analysis. In
particular, each *designbot* chooses the tactic that better fits with the current reasoning
framework, and then yields control to the planner. This way, the planner starts to
consider different HTN methods/operators for the tasks until arriving to a solution
plan. In general, as the planner decomposes a task network, we have that the most
abstract tasks will typically capture design decisions (embodied by tactics) without

concrete effects on the architectural model, while the tasks at the intermediate and lowest levels of the decomposition will involve actions that modify the architectural model. The final solution is composed of many architectural operations, which are grouped as an architectural transformation and returned to the architect by the *designbot*. The tool evaluates these transformations with respect to their original reasoning frameworks, and if the responses are satisfactory, the architect can decide to apply some of them on the architecture. Although the HTN algorithm was originally designed to proceed forward and avoid backtracking [19], we have provided some points of backtracking in our algorithm, so that the planner can evaluate alternative paths of decomposition if necessary. The main backtracking points are: generation of a network of goals for a tactic, execution of a task from the list of tasks without predecessors within the network, and selection of an HTN method/operator whose preconditions hold in the world state. These points can be selectively enabled or disabled at configuration time.

The planning process is managed by the architect through a GUI console that controls the HTN algorithm, as outlined in Figure 5. According to the mixed-initiative metaphor, the presence of user-query tasks makes the planner suspend their execution

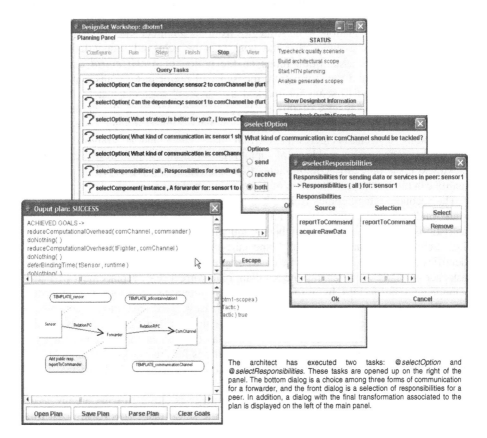

Fig. 5. Snapshot of the mixed-initiative planning interface

and consider instead other tasks within the network. The algorithm may temporarily halt if the partial order precludes other tasks to be available (because they depend on pending user-query tasks). On the GUI side, the architect can opportunistically pick user-query tasks that she judges relevant to the current design and answer them. As long as the planner finds tasks ready for execution, it resumes the planning and tries to address them. Figure 5 depicts a typical interaction between the planner and the architect, while planning for the modifiability goals given in Figure 3 under the tactic of inserting an intermediary (several user-query tasks are listed in the central panel, which corresponds to the main planning console).

So far, we have considered how individual *designbots* can take quality-attribute scenarios and produce transformations for their scopes. This is appealing in the sense that each *designbot* pursues one quality attribute at a time. However, interesting architectural decisions have to do often with multiple quality attributes. Therefore, it is necessary to handle the goals and transformations from a unified perspective. This problem is commonly referred to as *multi-goal planning* [23]. Currently, the *DesignBots* framework provides two strategies to approximate multi-goal planning and coordinate the *designbot*'s plans: (i) order the goals and solve them linearly, and (ii) merge groups of partial solutions to goals into a joint transformation. Since the planning theory behind these strategies is out of the scope of this paper, we have preferred a short explanation of the strategies from the architect's perspective.

The first strategy assumes that the goals can be achieved sequentially in any arbitrary order. This assumption relies on the notion of *architectural drivers* [4]. Thus, when selecting a transformation, the tool will prefer those plans generated by *designbots* associated to scenarios marked as "drivers" over the rest of the plans. Figure 6a shows the results of this strategy in BCS. Although the application of architectural operations is not always commutative, this strategy based on the prioritization of scenarios performs well in many cases and is straightforward to implement. The main problem of applying solutions sequentially (even with backtracking) is that early commitments to a solution strongly focused on a specific quality can hinder the consideration of better solutions later on.

The second strategy comes from a heuristic for plan merging [23]. Depending on what kinds of interactions occur among the tasks of the *designbots*' plans, the heuristic is able to construct a number of equivalence classes and derive a joint plan (i.e., architectural transformation). A special type of interaction called task-merging identifies "composite tasks" capable of accomplishing the "useful" effects of a set of tasks across plans while leaving the resultant plan correct (e.g., replacement of 1-to-1 component relationships by n-to-1 relationships, removal or insertion of facades, cancellation of unnecessary connectors, compression and separation mechanisms, etc.). The construction of the right list of interactions is domain-specific. Basically, the architect is initially asked to select plans as candidates for merging, then the *mediator* analyzes the plans and suggests interactions for their tasks, and the architect finally decides which of these interactions should be processed by the heuristic.

Figure 6b shows the BCS architecture after merging the modifiability and performance solutions. Note that this second strategy is closer to what architects do when faced with tradeoffs among solutions, in the sense that tradeoffs are cast to a number of "optimizations" over the plans for individual qualities. As drawbacks, the

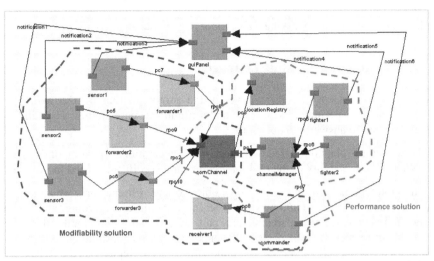

a) The mediator has imposed first a *forwarder-receiver* for the modifiability scenario, and then a *pool-of-connections* with a *resource-scheduler* for the performance scenario.

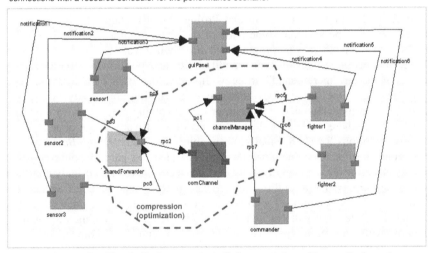

b) Here, the functionality of *locationRegistry* was mixed with the one of *channelManager*, the forwarders were collapsed into a single *sharedForwarder* for all the sensors, and the *commanderReceiver* was assimilated to the commander. These groupings follow a "compression criterion", which intends to reduce the number of components in order balance performance against modifiability.

Scenario	Initial Estimations	Sequential Transformation	Merged Transformation
1	average cost change = 55 %	average cost change = 38 %	average cost change = 42 %
2	average throughput = 10 % average latency = 0.65 msec.	average throughput = 12 % average latency = 0.61 msec.	average throughput = 18 % average latency = 0.45 msec.

Fig. 6. Application of modifiability and performance plans: a) sequentially b) merged

heuristic is quite complex to implement, and it does not produce always a successful combination of plans. In practice, if two tasks present a harmful interaction that cannot be solved (e.g., *a* before *b* in *plan1*, and *b* before *a* in *plan2*), it will not be possible to merge the corresponding plans. In that case, sometimes the mediator can replace one of the plans by asking a *designbot* to generate an alternative plan.

4   Evaluation and Lessons Learned

As a proof-of-concept, we have developed a prototype tool of *DesignBots* and conducted some experiments with small and medium-size case-studies. The validation mainly pointed to answer two questions:

1. How useful is planning-based assistance in the generation/evaluation of designs?
2. What is the scalability of the tool for architectural specifications and knowledge?

The prototype is built on top of a Java object-oriented framework, which supports the construction of *designbots* with different capabilities regarding architectural design and planning. For the architectural part, we have an *ADLite* toolkit that allows the architect to visually edit design elements such as: responsibilities, components, connectors, and scenarios. For the planning part, we have implemented a SHOP2-like algorithm as given by [19]. The original algorithm was extended with user-query tasks, backtracking, and undo/redo of steps. Our algorithm is based on *JavaLog* [1], a seamlessly integration between Java and Prolog. An advantage of *JavaLog* for the *DesignBots* prototype was that some parts of the planning processing were specified in Prolog and some others were programmed directly in Java.

Three architectures with different modifiability and performance scenarios were studied, taking an "incremental" strategy. Initially, the BCS case-study served to deploy and tune the *DesignBots* infrastructure. Having this ready, we applied *DesignBots* to a moderate-size classroom project involving a home alarm monitoring system (HAS), where we had graduate students of a software design course produce alternative solutions for HAS. Finally, in the third case-study, *DesignBots* was tested in the context of a telecommunications project [13], as part of some consulting activities made for the company Delsat Group. We considered two usually conflicting types of *designbots*: modifiability-centered and performance-centered agents. Each type of *designbot* was equipped with assets such as: a reasoning frameworks, tactics and related architectural patterns and mechanisms. After reproducing various design situations with the prototype, we performed an empirical comparison of the *designbots'* alternatives against the human designs. The experiments were executed on a Pentium IV computer with 1 GB RAM running Windows OS.

As a sample, results of the HAS case-study are summarized in Table 1. This case-study comprised 3 modifiability and 3 performance scenarios, which were assigned to 6 different *designbots*. Among the transformations undergone by the initial architecture, we can mention: support for adding new sensor types, easy configuration of reactive and diagnosis functionality, timing issues for reactive actions, and personalization of action rules. In Table 1, we show the architectural mechanisms specified for the planning domain, and which of these mechanisms were actually selected by the *designbots* to generate solutions for the scenarios. Symbols +, - and +/- reflect the relative variations in the scenario responses when applying two solutions, using the sequential and merged strategies respectively.

Table 1. Analysis of the alternatives generated for BCS

Scenarios	Main design issue	Architectural tactics and mechanisms available to the designbots	HTN Planning System			Response Analysis	
			Supported	Suggested	Choice	Sequential Solution	Merged Solution
M1	Support adding new types of sensors within the device layer	1. Separate the sensor interface from its implementation	Yes	Yes	Within option 2 , the first mechanism was selected	+	+
		2. Insert an intermediary between the devices and the data they produce or consume - *AbstractDataRepository* - *DataIndirection* - *PublisherSubscriber*	Yes	Yes		tradeoff	
M2	Configuration of reactive and diagnosis functionality should be easy for the user	1. Provide customization of devices and their interactions - *PublisherSubscriber* - *Façade* - *ClientDispatcherServer*	Yes	Yes	Within option 1 , the first mechanism was selected	+	+/-
		2. Defer binding time - *ConfigurationFiles* - *UniformProtocol*	No	No		tradeoff	
M3	New configuration rules should be made available for the devices	1. Provision of some kind of interpreter - *RuleBasedEngine*	Yes	Yes	Option 1 was the only available	+/-	-
P1	Fulfill the deadlines associated with the production and consumption of data	1. Define scheduling policy - *PriorityBasedDispatcher* - *RoundRobinScheduling*	Yes	Yes	Within option 1 , the first mechanism was selected	+/-	+
						tradeoff	
P2	The level of response should be kept bounded	1. Define scheduling policy - *PriorityBasedDispatcher* - *RoundRobinScheduling*	Yes	Yes	Within option 1 , the first mechanism was selected	+/-	+/-
		1. Manage event rate - *NotificationDispatcher*	Yes	No		tradeoff	
P3	The vocabulary of notifications can be updated, but maintaining the above level of response	1. Define scheduling policy - *PriorityBasedDispatcher* - *RoundRobinScheduling*	Yes	Yes	Within option 1 , the first mechanism was selected	+/-	+

Overall, these three case-studies gave us interesting material to approximate "real" software design situations with *DesignBots*. Although more experimental studies are necessary, some findings and conjectures are shortly discussed below.

Architectural modeling (question #2). The choice of *ADLite* had expected pros and cons. Having a compact architectural language was beneficial for experimentation, because it allowed us to move easily from quite informal architectural descriptions to *ADLite* specifications. However, *ADLite* restricts the architectural representation to a single view (C&C viewtype), and this affects the kind of analyzes and transformations derived from it (e.g., dynamic creation of components, operations involving processes, scheduling or deployment issues). The property annotations alleviated the

C&C limitations, and they actually worked well to capture the parameters of the analysis models used in the case-studies. However, *ADLite* does not support information about architectural styles that could help to check some design rules over the architecture and its derived alternatives.

Planning support (questions #1 & #2). Deciding what is the best way of writing tactics and architectural patterns for the *designbots* was a central concern we faced at this stage. In general, the HTN writing style admits many alternative implementations of the same concepts. This depends on issues such as: modularity, level of architect's intervention, or default values, among others. Since a clear task decomposition helps to visualize the relationships of architectural tactics with patterns/mechanisms, we preferred to codify the planning domain as modular as possible. Furthermore, opportunities of architect's intervention were included only when this would avoid extra work in the planner. We also observed that, due to the limited GUI offered by the tool and the lack of design rational about what the planner was doing, the planning work sometimes demanded intellectual efforts from the architects to understand the important aspects in the re-design of the case-studies. The prototype proved to be useful for recording alternative plans of action or variants for a base solution the architects were familiar with. The "constructive schema" supported by the planning paradigm and the possibility of backtracking were the two factors that enabled this kind of assistance. As another issue worth of mentioning, the architects recognized that the alternatives built by the *designbots* had clear influences from the quality-attribute analyses used to establish the *designbots*' goals. These relationships between architectural structures and qualities were not always well reflected in the designs produced by humans. Since tactics and patterns are at the core of the planning domain, *DesignBots* makes these issues more visible in the resulting designs.

Accuracy and scalability of solutions (question #2). On the other hand, from the perspective of design assistance, the alternatives recommended by the *designbots* showed structural similarities with those developed by people. A 70% of the patterns applied by the *designbots* were considered correct by the architects that participated into the projects. Some differences were observed in the configuration of components when compared to those arranged manually by the architects. Analyzing the HAS and DELSAT case-studies, we found that the *designbots* elaborated more valid solutions for the HAS architecture, and they provided fewer and flawed solutions for the DELSAT architecture, when comparing these solutions with those developed by the DELSAT architects. An explanation for this tendency is that in the first case-study the design was carried out by novice designers, while in the second one the design was produced by expert architects. This effect is interesting in two senses. First, we envision the possibility of helping in teaching software architecture design. Second, even when equipping the *designbots* with sufficient tactics and patterns, the planner is not always capable of emulating design experience. The heuristic knowledge used by expert humans to select among alternatives should be also modeled and applied in order to improve a solution. This feature could additionally serve to prune the search space and make the treatment of large designs more efficient. Along this line, the scalability of the approach gets compromised depending on the way knowledge is mapped to planning operators and methods.

5 Related Work

Considerable research has been done in the area of design support, although few approaches have explored the links between architectural design and artificial intelligence. Interesting approaches are: rule-based systems [3], goal-feature graphs [11, 12], system reconfiguration [2, 6, 15], and multi-objective optimization [9, 16].

The *NFR-Framework* used by Chung et al.[11] treats quality attributes as a graph of potentially synergistic or conflicting goals. The knowledge related to satisfaction of quality attributes is codified into methods and correlation rules. Methods are used in the decomposition and achievement of goals, similarly to what happens in the HTN model, while correlation rules somehow help with the analysis of tradeoffs among alternatives. The alternatives are linked to the leaves of the graph, according to their contributions to specific goals. Then, there is a special procedure that calculates the effects of decisions on the graph. Unfortunately, the alternatives reported are still very general regarding architectural structure. A later work by deBruin et al.[12] overcomes this problem, proposing a feature-solution graph that connects requirements with solutions fragments at the architectural level. Here, the developers can build architectures by recursively composing designs based on use-case maps into a reference architecture. When compared to *DesignBots*, the graph barely considers guidelines for exploring alternatives, and the features do not reflect well tradeoffs.

On the other hand, many researchers have tried to represent design knowledge using rule-based blackboard architectures. The first experiments can be traced in the *Programmer's Apprentice* project at MIT [20] to build a CASE environment with automated support for requirements, design and implementation. Unfortunately, much of that work failed due to the weak support given by the representation formalism and the inherent complexity associated with the generation of operational programs from requirements. In the last years, the Software Engineering Institute has developed a tool called *ArchE* [3] as a rule-based expert system to help architects to quickly explore design alternatives. Based on the philosophy of the ADD method [4], the approach is focused on designing software architectures in such a way they can predictably achieve quality-attribute requirements. Nonetheless, there are still open issues such as: the considerable amount of data generated during normal design activities, the aspects of interaction with the architect, and the management of quality tradeoffs. Current *ArchE*[5] efforts are oriented to improve the searching capabilities of the tool using a combination of planning with other AI techniques.

In the domain of dynamic configuration management, the Arshad's work [2] proposes the use of temporal planning to reconfigure distribute systems, where plans are derived from basic architectural elements and operations. The state, goals and operators are all expressed by means of scripts. This schema works quite well as long as the configurability situations can be anticipated by the developer. The planning results reported by the approach concur with our observations about domain writing and planning scalability to practical cases. A more flexible tool is given by Garlan et al. [15], which make architectural information explicit at runtime and provide a mapping between architecture and code. This tool detects when the system behavior

---

[5] http://www.sei.cmu.edu/architecture/arche.html

falls outside of acceptable range and modifies the configuration of components and connectors accordingly. Although still based on rules, the reconfiguration applies many of the analyses/strategies used by *DesignBots*.

The *DeSiX* approach [6] provides a set of tools for component-based systems on multi-processor architectures that allow for design space exploration. Scenario-based analysis for performance, reliability and cost properties serve to focus the design on particular static/dynamic architectural configurations. The developer can map usage profiles to simulation tasks, and then visualize the resulting architectures using Pareto curves. These curves are practical for investigating optimal alternatives with respect to component deployment. A drawback of *DeSiX* is that it does not support yet automated search, and the developer has to manually select configurations to be evaluated by the tool. Regardless its bias to system architectures, however, *DeSiX* confirms the arguments of *DesignBots* (and other approaches in this section) about the central role of quality attributes as drivers in the exploration process.

Other researchers have argued for a view of software engineering as a search framework [9], in which automation is supported by optimization techniques such as hill-climbing, evolutionary algorithms and constraint-based solvers. An important requirement of this view is a well-defined mapping from software concepts to elements supported by an AI search technique. Several early results have been collected by Clarke et al.[9]. Nonetheless, these results are not based on a consistent architectural design theory, nor do they explore "constructive" techniques like planning. Very recently, Grunske [16] has applied evolutionary algorithms in the optimization of architectures related to satellite domains. Having an architectural specification that fulfills its functional requirements as the initial solution, a special tool tries to find solutions with better tradeoffs between reliability and cost requirements. Case-studies have been carried out for very limited problem/solution spaces. Overall, it still remains to be seen whether this kind of techniques can handle complex solution spaces in acceptable time and with a good diversity of solutions.

6 Conclusions

In this paper, we have described how architectural design can be cast to a planning system in order to provide tool support for the generation of design alternatives. Moreover, we have built a *planning-based design assistant* that basically considers quality-attribute goals as drivers for the architecting process, and then systematically applies patterns and tactics in function of these goals. Although several abstractions used by *DesignBots* have been developed elsewhere, the main contribution of our work is that of approaching architectural decision-making from a planning perspective. We have shown that hierarchical and mixed-initiative planning fits well with architectural design, because the HTN methods/operators can be seen as the "operating procedures" that an architect would normally use to deal with quality-driven design issues. As a tool for exploratory design, the benefits of *DesignBots* are twofold. First, the architect is less likely to overlook the options, variants and details associated with the generation and evaluation of designs, although she is still in control of the principal architectural decisions. Second, the *DesignBots* framework is flexible enough to consider updates of the base of design knowledge (e.g., other quality-attribute models, new tactics and architectural mechanisms, etc.).

In general, the prototype has managed to work well for the qualities of performance and modifiability, with limited architectural knowledge about tactics and mechanisms. In exchange for the efforts spent in the *DesignBots* setup, we were able to represent basic architectures and plan alternatives for them. Even though the results are preliminary, they are good indicators of the potential of this tool approach. Nonetheless, there are still problems and limitations that should be addressed in further research. A first limitation is the C&C viewtype. Currently, *ADLite* specifications are being replaced by UML2 component diagrams and Use-case-Maps, which will permit structural and behavioral architectural views. A second limitation is the specification of architectural knowledge, which we foresee as a time-consuming and error-prone activity. Another problem is that the potential combination of operations to examine by the planner may grow huge to be managed in reasonable response times. Therefore, better control strategies/heuristics are needed to direct the selection and instantiation of architectural patterns/mechanisms. Regarding tradeoffs, we are investigating how the *designbots* could reason about the implications of their plans and negotiate counterproposals at planning time. A possible extension for task networks is to record information about the decisions behind decompositions and revaluations. With such information, a decision-driven backtracking schema could help to search for better alternative plans, using predefined patterns according to actual tradeoff conditions and decisions previously made.

Finally, *DesignBots* has reinforced the argument that the design of architectures driven by quality-attribute issues can be (partially) tractable by automated means. To make this approach industrial-strength, more quality attributes, design strategies and case-studies will be necessary. Provided this support, we believe that the combination of guidelines for articulating the design knowledge (e.g., like those of "predictable architecture design") with AI techniques constitutes an encouraging research direction on proactive tools for architectural design.

References

1. Amandi, A., Campo, M., Zunino, A.: JavaLog: A Framework-based Integration of Java and Prolog for Agent-oriented Programming. In: Ledley, R.S. (ed.) Computer Languages, Systems and Structures, Elsevier Science, Amsterdam (2004)
2. Arshad, N., Heimbigner, D., Wolf, A.: Deployment and Dynamic Reconfiguration Planning for Distributed Software Systems. In: Proceedings ICTAI 2003, pp. 39–46 (2003)
3. Bachmann, F., Bass, L., Klein, M.: Preliminary Design of ArchE: A Software Architecture Design Assistance. Technical Report CMU/SEI-2003-TR-021 (2003)
4. Bass, L., Clements, P., Kazman, R.: Software Architecture in Practice, 2nd edn. Addison-Wesley, Reading (2003)
5. Bass, L., Ivers, J., Klein, M., Merson, P., Wallnau, K.: Encapsulating Quality Attribute Knowledge. In: Proceedings WICSA 2005, pp. 193–194 (2005), ISBN 0-7695-2548-2
6. Bondarev, E., Chaudron, M., de With, P.: Quality-Oriented Design Space Exploration for Component-Based Architectures. Computer Science Reports. TUE Department of Mathematics and Computer Science. Eindhoven University of Technology, Eindhoven, The Netherlands (February 2006)

7. Buschmann, F., Meunier, R., Rohnert, H., Sommerlad, P., Stal, M.: Pattern-Oriented Software Architecture. In: A System of Patterns, Wiley & Sons, Chichester (1996)

8. Campo, M., Díaz-Pace, A., Zito, M.: Developing Object-oriented Enterprise Quality Frameworks using Proto-frameworks. In: Software: Practice and Experience, vol. 32(8), pp. 837–843. Wiley, Chichester (2002)

9. Clarke, J., Dolado, J., Harman, M., Hierons, R., Jones, R., Lumkinm, M., Mitchell, B., Mancoridis, S., Rees, K., Roper, M., Shepperd, M.: Reformulating Software Engineering as a Search Problem. In: Software, I.E.E. (ed.) Software IEE Proceedings, vol. 150(3), pp. 161–175 (2003), ISSN: 1462-5970

10. Coyne, R.: Design Reasoning Without Explanations. AI Magazine 11(4), 72–80 (1990)

11. Chung, L., Nixon, B., Yu, E.: Using Non-Functional Requirements to Systematically Select Among Alternatives in Architectural Design. In: Proceedings 1st International Workshop on Architectures for Software Systems, Seattle, pp. 31–43 (April 24-28, 1995)

12. de Bruin, H., van Vliet, H.: Quality-Driven Software Architecture Composition. Journal of Systems and Software 66(3), 269–284 (2003)

13. Diaz-Pace, A.: A Planning-based Approach for the Exploration of Quality-driven Design Alternatives in Software Architectures. PhD. Thesis. UNICEN University, Faculty of Sciences, Tandil, Argentina (2004)

14. Garlan, D., Monroe, R., Wile, D.: ACME: Architectural Description of Component-based Systems. In: Foundations of Component-based Systems, Cambridge Press (2000)

15. Garlan, D., Cheng, S., Schmerl, B.: Increasing System Dependability through Architecture-based Self-repair. In: de Lemos, Gacek, Romanovsky (eds.) Architecting Dependable Systems, Springer, Heidelberg (2003)

16. Grunske, L.: Identifying "Good" Architectural Design Alternatives with Multi-Objective Optimization Strategies. In: International Conference on Software Engineering (ICSE), Workshop on Emerging Results, Shanghai, ACM 1-59593-085-X/06/0005, pp. 849–852 (May 20-28, 2006)

17. Kazman, R., Klein, M., Clements, P.: ATAM: Method for Architecture Evaluation. Technical Report CMU/SEI-2000-TR-004 (August 2002)

18. Long, D., Fox, M.: Progress in AI Planning Research and Applications. Upgrade/Novatica 159. III (5), 10–25 (2002)

19. Nau, D., Au, T.-C., Ilghami, O., Kuter, U., Murdock, J.W., Wu, D., Yaman, F.: SHOP2: An HTN planning system. Journal of AI Research 20, 379–404 (2003)

20. Rich, C., Waters, R.: The Programmer´s Apprentice. Addison-Wesley, Reading (1990)

21. Smith, G., Gero, J.: What does an agent mean by being "situated"? Design Studies 26, 535–561 (2005)

22. Wilkins, D., desJardins, M.: A Call for Knowledge-based Planning. In: AI Magazine, vol. 22(1), Springer, Heidelberg (2001)

23. Yang, Q.: Intelligent Planning: A Decomposition and Abstraction based Approach. Springer, New York (1997)

Customizing Traceability Links for the Unified Process

Patrick Mäder, Ilka Philippow, and Matthias Riebisch

Software Systems/Process Informatics Group
Technical University of Ilmenau, Germany
{patrick.maeder,ilka.philippow,matthias.riebisch}@tu-ilmenau.de

Abstract. Traceability links are generally recognised as helpful means for improving the effectiveness of evolutionary development processes. However, their practical usage in analysis and design is still unsatisfying, especially due to the high effort required for creation, maintenance and verification of the links, and due to lacking or missing methods and tools for their management.

In this paper a concept for the systematic management of traceability is introduced, adapted for the and integrated into the Unified Process as one of the widely accepted software development methods. As an extension, requirements templates are applied to facilitate a tool supported analysis of natural language texts in use case descriptions. Template-based analyses enable a determination of types of terms and a check of their correct application as well as a recognition of implicit connections between development artefacts. A rule set is defined as a first step towards a powerful support of traceability handling. In the ongoing project the rule set is enhanced by heuristics and semantic-based rules to a whole framework of methods and rules.

Keywords: Traceability Link, Traceability Model, Evolutionary Development, Requirements Engineering, Object-Oriented Methods, Requirements Templates, Unified Process, Glossary.

1 Introduction

Complex, business critical software systems have to adapt to frequently changing needs. Evolutionary development processes have been developed to enable short responses to changes. In complex settings changes bear high risks, such as incomplete implementation, misunderstood dependencies, missing comprehension and lacking coverage. To manage these risks, the concept of traceability has been developed and introduced to the most development process standards. However, we have to state that traceability is poorly used in practice, and their usage is mostly limited to requirements engineering. Even in research, traceability is more discussed for requirements.

However, traceability links are needed in the areas of design and implementation as well. They facilitate design decisions and change impact analysis, they support program comprehension and they enable completeness checks for changes, if

S. Overhage et al. (Eds.): QoSA 2007, LNCS 4880, pp. 53–71, 2007.

they can be maintained in a correct and complete state. For a comprehensive support of such design activities, traceability links have to be defined at a fine-grained level. Unfortunately, the maintenance of the links for such a way of design traceability requires an extremely high effort because a high number of links has to be managed, and many link maintenance tasks have to be carried out manually. Two major open research questions have to be addressed: to master the amount and the complexity of traceability information, and to maintain and update the links. A tool support would be very helpful, but would require a traceability link update into development methods. Even if most design methods claim to support the concept of traceability, their definitions of artefacts, relations and activities are too imprecise to define traceability link update techniques.

As discussed earlier, our vision is the integration of traceability link management and maintenance into development methods and tools [1]. One of the challenges on this way consists in the refinement of the description of the major development methods. Detailed development activities are then extended by update activities for traceability links. The developer's activities are enriched as well, e.g. by describing the reasons and decisions for that activity. To meet the needs of the industrial practice it is necessary to perform this refinement for concrete development methods that are widely used in industry. In this paper we have chosen the Unified Process UP [2] for the definition of a process-specific model of traceability links. Although, Letelier showed in [3] the application of his metamodel for the UP, his definitions are not detailed enough to derive rules for traceability links. The UP description by its authors offers traceability as one of its features, but there is no detailed description of how and between which artefacts the traceability links should be established. Furthermore, works are necessary to define traceability links syntactically and semantically.

The contribution of this paper consists in an analysis and classification of UP artefacts concerning to traceability aspects. Based on that, all required links between the artefacts of the UP activities of requirements engineering and design are defined. Additionally, a syntactic and semantic definition of traceability links is established customized to the UP's methods. This definition has been developed and validated in practical projects and case studies. These results constitute a milestone and provide a basis for further works towards our vision e.g., empirical investigations for rules concerning the suitable level of detail for traceability links, or for rules how far to follow traceability links during the impact analysis of a change.

The analysis of the UP and the customisation of the traceability concept are performed during practical development projects. As results of these works, guidelines for the level of detail and rules for the verification of traceability links have been established.

2   Traceability

Traceability is the ability to follow and recover the development steps of a system based on the connection between inputs or stimuli of every development step with its products. These products are the inputs of next development steps. This leads to a graph of dependencies, which shows the realization of the systems requirements within the developed system.

The following concepts and definitions are based on the related works mentioned in section 4 as well as on our experiences from practical projects in the Automotive domain.

2.1   Categories of Traceability

Implicit Traceability. Implicit traceability results from existing associations between elements of the system model. For example, the use of the same identifier in an analysis and a design artefact expresses a dependency between both. The creation of this traceability link does not cause any additional effort.

Explicit Traceability. Explicit Traceability results from the establishing of connections between two artefacts during the software development process by a developer. It can be considered as an enhanced form of traceability [4], enabling the storage of additional information with the link. This information for example could be decisions made during analysis and design. By using explicit traceability links, program comprehension and changes of the system are facilitated.

The creation of explicit traceability requires additional effort of the developer. If one or both of two linked artefacts are changing, there is a risk that the traceability link is becoming inconsistent or invalid. It is necessary, to check explicit traceability links between changed artefacts, before they are used.

In contrast to explicit traceability implicit traceability describes references between two model elements, without any additional properties. It is possible to search for implicit connections, to store them and make them explicit. Thus, the benefits of adding additional information are given. But, in this case it is necessary to verify the correctness of the link, before using it.

2.2   Traceability Links

Components of Traceability Links. In the following we define the components of an explicit traceability link. This definition is driven by the goal of (semi)automatic support for link establishment and maintenance and focuses on getting the highest possible benefit from the usage of traceability. It provides the required data e.g. for the conservation of design decisions and for performing an impact analysis. This definition was established based on an analysis of the related works mentioned in section 4 and by our experiences from projects in the Automotive domain. An explicit traceability link consists of:

- a unique identifier for its recognition and to avoid ambiguity,
- a start element as source of the link, including type and context of this element (e.g. a class of the analysis model)
- an end element as destination of the link, including type and context of this element

- the type of the link
- the development decision connected with the link, including the goal of the decision, alternatives, rating of the alternatives and the choice

The link can contain additional information:

- the link status concerning the certainty of correctness (e.g. after changes of one or both of the connected elements),
- the creator of the link and
- a priority, which shows the importance of the link and allows to check only high prioritised links after changes of elements (according to [5]).

A traceability link is syntactical defined in Backus-Naur-form as follows: This

```
Traceability Link::=  <ID> <Start element> <End element> <Type> <Decision>
                      [ <Status> ] [ <Developer> ] [ <Priority> ]
Start element::=      <ID>
End element::=        <ID>
Type::=               refine | realize | verify | define
Decision::=           <Goal> <Alternatives> <Choice>
Status ::=            0 | ... | 100 "%"
Developer::=          <Text>
Priority::=           0 | 1
Goal ::=              <Text>
Alternatives::=       <Alternative> | <Alternative> <Alternatives>
Choice::=             <Alternative.ID>
Alternative ::=       <Alternative.ID> <Text>
Alternative.ID::=     <Number>
```

definition of a link provides all information required for the link establishment and update as well as for the traceability goals mentioned above. It conforms to the UML metamodel [2].

Types of Traceability Links. The traceability link type shows the relationship between two connected elements and/or the development activity for the generation of the destination element from the source element. A reduction of the number of types of traceability links aims at a minimization of the necessary number of rules for establishing and checking of links. Several authors use different types of links for different concepts: The link types of UML [2] and its extension SysML [6], by Letelier [3] and in the link metamodel of Ramesh and Jarke [7] differ in its concepts and categorisation. Based on the analysis of theses works of related works (sect. 4) and on our experience from projects and case studies, the following four basic types of traceability links have been identified:

- Refinement («refine») – in accordance with the level of detail of the connected objects (e.g. between an analysis and a design object),
- Realization («realize») – the dependent object represents a part of the solution to the problem described with the independent object (e.g. between a use case and an analysis class),
- Verification («verify») – of behaviour and properties of the developed solution or its parts (e.g. between a use case and a test case) and
- Definition («define») – of objects (e.g. between a glossary item and its usage in one of the models).

Representation. In the UML traces are defined as a special kind of dependency. Therefore, the same graphical representation is used: a unidirectional arrow, enhanced with the stereotype «trace». For a simple dependency the arrow is directed from the dependent (destination) to the independent (source) element e.g. an analysis object is connected toward a use case. The graphical direction of the traceability link does not exclude its usage in both directions, forwards and backwards.

3   Software Development Processes and Methods

Software development processes consist of activities and artefacts leading from requirements to the systems implementation. The handling of traceability links can be the more automated the more the acts of a developer correspond to the activities of a method. It is possible to apply traceability rules to these activities. The better and fine-grained the process description is the easier is the defining of rules for creation and updating of traceability links. Therefore, the approach for traceability proposed in this paper is presently focused on one concrete process, the Unified Process.

3.1   The Unified Process UP

In the UP several ancestor methods like Object-Oriented Software Engineering OOSE [8] have been combined based on best practices and experiences. The UP is available as commercial and as open-source version. The UP process model, the activities of the method and the composition of the artefacts are described detailed enough for the aimed level of support. The UP can be customized and concretised to particular projects and companies needs. The UP is an incremental and iterative process; it is based on use case and architecture centric development of software. The incremental, iterative approach can be seen as a two-dimensional scheme as described in [2]. For establishing traceability links especially the requirements activities of the UP have to be more detailed and enhanced. For this purpose text templates akin to those in [9] are integrated into the process.

3.2   Describing Requirements by Text-Templates

Chris Rupp et al. describe in [9] the requirements development as a three-step process, consisting of formulating, analysing and successive improving requirements by rules. A concept of so-called requirements patterns is introduced to accelerate this process. Rupp characterises it as a general concept to construct natural language requirements based on formal defined elements, which are verifiable and can be modelled. A pattern consists basically of one or more generic, syntactic requirements templates. Furthermore it consists of a semantic definition of important parts of the template, of logical operators to combine conditions and of rules to define test criteria's. Using the templates supports the definition of test cases and the identification of objects.

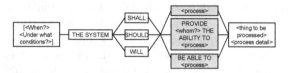

Fig. 1. Requirements Templates for all Three Kinds of Requirements

In [9] Rupp et al. categorize requirements into three types: independent system activity, user interaction and interface requirement. Figure 1 shows the elements of all three types of requirements combined into one graphic. Each requirement is based on a functionality, which is described by a so-called process word. A process word is strictly a verb defined in a process word list. From top to bottom the grey shaded boxes correspond to the introduced three types. If the requirement is of type user interaction an actor has to be filled into the template. The legal classification can be chosen by using one of the words: shall, should or will. To complete the requirements expression an object and its enhancements and optional logical and time constraints have to filled into the template.

In addition to the advantages of well formulated, verifiable requirements, the usage of requirements templates offers some more benefits. Requirements templates support traceability. Rules can be defined based on the type of the requirement, its elements and the position of these elements within the sentence. Eventually this supports the consistency between different model elements. A detailed explanation of this support is given in the next chapter.

The Rupp text templates can effectively support the structured description of use cases according to [10]. For enabling the definition of activities in use case descriptions we have coupled the text templates closely to the development glossary: all terms filled into the template have to be defined in the glossary. The actors of the user activity have to be the same as these specified in the field actors of the use case description.

```
User Activity    <actor> <process> <thing to be processed and details>.
System Activity  The System [shall/should/will]
                 <thing to be processed and details> <process>.
```

3.3   Traceability Relevant Artefacts in the UP

In this section traceability relevant artefacts of the UP are introduced. We focus mainly on the workflows requirements and analysis/design, as these contain the traceability relevant activities and artefacts.

Artefacts of the Requirements Workflow

Requirements. Requirements describe properties or features of the system that has to be developed. In the UP they are not hierarchically ordered instead they represent different views for different groups of stakeholders.

The Vision Document contains Needs, describing informally what the stakeholders expect of the system and Features, describing informally what the system offers to fulfil these needs.

The Software Requirements Specification (SRS) consists of Software Requirements, which are commonly divided in functional and non-functional requirements and constraints. The UP centralizes these requirements in two artefacts: the Use Case Model, consisting of all functional requirements and the Supplementary Specification, consisting of all non-functional requirements and constraints expressed as declarative statements.

Glossary. The glossary lists terms of the project domain and gives a definition to each of them. The strict usage of defined glossary terms in all development phases enables automated generation of connections between the same terms used in different artefacts. Every special term from the very beginning of a project has to be defined in the glossary. Only defined terms are allowed to be used during the development process. That means, that the identifier of all model elements consist only of defined terms. Also the elements of the before introduced requirements templates have to be defined in the glossary. Glossary items can be categorised into type groups, according to Rupp [9] in three types: actor, object and process. By using additional information about the type of a term, rules can be identified for suggesting a special term while naming an object or writing a requirement. These rules can also be used to support the verification of the right usage of terms in the model.

Domain Object Model (DOM). The DOM represents glossary items as classes in UML class diagrams. The usage of equal names in both artefacts realizes a connection as implicit traceability links.

Interface Description. Interfaces are described, depending on their kind as e.g., prototypes of graphical user interfaces, drawings or textual descriptions.

Artefacts of the Object-Oriented Analysis

Analysis Class. Analysis classes define the necessary structure for the realization of a use case in the system. Class identifier must be meaningful and domain specific and have to be defined in the glossary.

Package. Packages organize model elements and diagrams in groups.

Use Case Realization-Analysis. Use case realizations consist of a set of diagrams describing a use case specification. For visualisation of the structure a class diagram is used. Interaction diagrams describe the communication between these classes.

Relation Between Analysis Objects. Relations visualize functional or structural dependencies. The following relations can occur between analysis objects: Association, Generalization, Dependency and Hierarchy.

Analysis Model. An analysis model consists of all artefacts, developed during the analysis workflow.

Architectural Description. An architecture description is a short textual summary of architecture relevant aspects of the system.

Artefacts of the Object-Oriented Design

Design Class. Design classes are refined and detailed classes, suitable and ready for implementation.

Use Case Realization-Design. Use case realizations-design describe the collaboration of several design objects for use case realization.

Subsystem and Component. Subsystems and components result from decomposing complex systems into smaller, easier manageable parts of the system.

Design Model. A design model is a refinement of the analysis model and is enhanced with more details and particular technical solutions. The elements of the design model have to be specified as far, that they can be implemented.

3.4   Development Activities and Relations Between Model Elements

In this section a model of useful traceability links for the UP is proposed. At first the UP development activity is named and then, related to it, traceability links between the developed artefacts are introduced. For illustration, every step is explained by a simple example, for a wiper control. The activity chart in Fig. 2 contains only those activities necessary for the establishment of traceability links. It has to be pointed out that a sequential representation of activities is used for better visualisation. However, in practice the activities are carried out incrementally in several iterations.

Development Activities During the Requirements Workflow

Elaboration of the Vision Document. Based on a natural-language text document of stakeholder requirements (needs), the system features have to be defined. The needs and the realizing features are connected by explicit traceability links of the type «

Creating the Glossary and the Domain Object Model. Parallel with the vision document the glossary elaboration has to be started by defining and entering all domain-relevant terms. Each new term identified during an activity must be defined, before it can be used. The developer has to ensure that there is not already another term defined for the same issue. If the new term has relations to other terms it has to be modelled in the DOM as well. Additionally, every term has to be categorized by one of the following types: actor, object or process. These categories refer to the type of term used within the before introduced templates and for the naming of model elements. By knowing the type of a term, it is possible to verify its correct usage within a text template or within an identifier of a model object.

In our example three terms have been identified based on the feature definition: wiping speed, interval time and single wipe. They have to be defined and listed in the glossary. These terms and those for the next development activities are defined in Table 1. realize»(see Fig. 3).

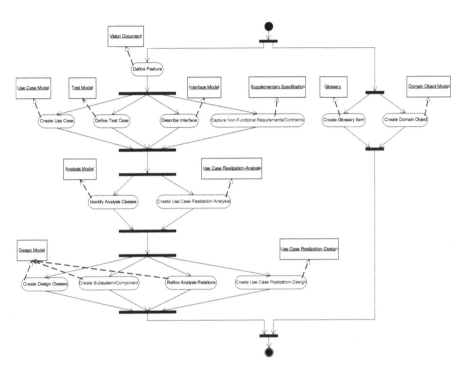

Fig. 2. Development Activities of the Unified Process Workflows: Requirements and Analysis/Design

Development of the Use Case Model. As first step the border of the system and the interacting actors must be specified. The actors have to be defined in the glossary as well (Table 1). The next step is to find use cases for the before defined features. Between use cases and features m:n relations can exists, that means that several use cases can refine one feature or that several features are refined by one use case. Features and use cases are connected by an explicit traceability link of type «refine». The association between an actor and a triggered use case

For the example, the following needs are known:	Based on the needs, the following
The wiper control of a car shall be developed. It shall be possible to:	features could be identified:
• *choose different wiping speeds,* ◄--«realize»---	• *Adjustable wiping speed*
• *to trigger a single wipe and* ◄--«realize»---	• *Single wipe*
• *to adjust the time between wipes in interval mode.* ◄--«realize»---	• *Adjustable interval time*

Fig. 3. Traceability Links between Needs and Features for the Wiper Control Example

Table 1. Glossary of the Wiper Control Example

	Term	Definition	Type
1	Driver	Person who drives a car	Actor
2	Clamp 15	An electrical connection, which is getting active when ignition is switched on.	Object
3	Steering Column Switch	Switch to choose the wiping speed with the positions off, interval, slow and fast.	Object
4	Wiping Speed	Speed of the wiping blade	Object
5	Interval Time	Time between to wipings in interval mode	Object
6	Wiping	Moving the wiper blade from its start position to its end position and back.	Object
7	Single Wipe	Manually triggered single wiping	Object
8	Choose	The user selects one or more elements from a finite set of elements.	Process
9	Set	The system logically chooses the value of a certain figure, according to selection criteria from a finite set.	Process
10	Trigger	The user starts by a certain action a process of the system.	Process

can lead to an implicit traceability link. The use case specification should be enhanced with test case specifications for the verification of its realization. Use cases and test cases have to be connected by an explicit traceability link of type «verify». The relation is of m:n multiplicity. For the description of use cases, text templates akin to Rupp [9] are used (see section 3.2).

In the example the following three use cases have been identified: Set Wiping Speed, Choose Interval Time, and Trigger Instant Wipe. These use cases are connected to the before defined features by explicit traceability links of type «refine» (see Fig. 4).

Table 2. Example Description of the Use Case "Set Interval Time"

	Name	Choose Interval Time
	Description	This use case allows the driver to set a new interval time, which is waited between two wipes.
	Actors	Driver
	Rationale	Steering column switch has been set to position interval.
	Precondition	Clamp 15 is active and the steering column switch has position OFF.
	Normal Flow	1	The driver switches the steering column switch to position INTERVALL.
		2	The driver switches the steering column switch to position OFF.
		3	The driver switches the steering column switch after not more than 30s to position INTERVALL.
		4	The system has to set the new interval time as the time the steering column switch has been in position OFF.
	Altern. Flow	no
	Postconditions	no

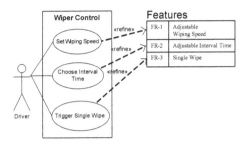

Fig. 4. Traceability Links between Features and Use Cases for the Wiper Example

Development of the Interface Description. Textual documents, GUI-prototypes or models can be used for interface descriptions. The description of an interface contains associations between actors and use cases, in which an interface is used, represented by an explicit traceability link of type «refine». In the example there is only one interface between driver and system, the steering column switch of the car (see Fig. 5).

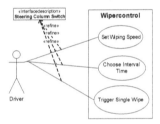

Fig. 5. Example of an Interface Description

Development Activities of Object-Oriented Analysis

Identification of Analysis Classes. In the analysis phase classes and packages are used for modelling the structure of the system. In the UP analysis classes are distinguished as interface, entity or control class. There are different approaches for finding analysis classes. The examination of nouns and verbs in use case descriptions is a widely accepted technique. Nouns are candidates for classes or attributes and verbs are candidates for responsibilities or methods. Another way to find classes is the CRC-card method. The particular choice for a method is determined by the project. Every use case is connected by explicit traceability links to the analysis classes, which realize its flow. Each class can be connected to several or only one use case and vice versa. That means a class can realize more than one use case.

In the example three analysis classes are defined for the three use cases (see Fig. 6). All use cases are triggered by the driver using the same interface (see

Fig. 5. Therefore all use cases are connected by traceability links with the interface class Steering Column Switch. The use cases Set Wiping Speed and Trigger Instant Wipe are realized by the class Wiper Control and the use case Choose Interval Time is realized by the class Interval Reader. All these development activities are traceable through the corresponding links.

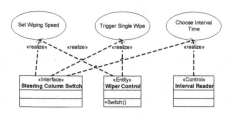

Fig. 6. Identified Analysis Classes to the Wiper System

Performing of Use Case Realizations-Analysis. In this step the cooperation between the different analysis classes has to be described by UML interaction diagrams. For each use case at least one diagram is modelled, representing communication and messages between instances.

The interaction diagrams have to be connected with the related use case, using an explicit traceability link of type «realize». It is also possible to connect them implicitly by using consistent diagram names. By drawing messages between classifiers in interaction diagrams an implicit connection between the corresponding classes is established. This connection can be used to verify associations in the class model between these classes. The sequence chart in Fig. 7 specifies the necessary communication between the analysis classes, to realize the use case Choose Interval Time from the example.

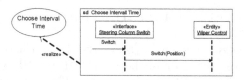

Fig. 7. Example of a Use Case Realization

Development Activities During Design

Creation of Design Classes (Design Class Model). The design model is a refinement of the analysis model. As a first step all elements of the analysis model have to be copied. The copied elements are considered as initial design model. It is possible to connect analysis and design elements automatically while copying them by explicit traceability links of type «refine».

During the design phase almost all elements of the initial design model are detailed, enhanced and refined step by step. Doing this the traceability links between elements have to be changed or extended. Newly added design elements have to be connected to analysis elements. Eventually, every analysis package has to be connected to one or more design subsystems, each analysis class has to be connected to one or more design classes and/or interfaces and each use case realization-analysis hast to be connected to a use case realization-design.

Refinement of Analysis Relations. During design the relations established between analysis objects have to be further refined and adopted to the chosen programming language. It is necessary to connect the original relation in the analysis model and the replacing elements in the design model by explicit traceability links of the type «refine». If an analysis class is realized in the design model by an attribute of a class or vice versa, this activity has to be documented by a traceability link as well. The replacement e.g. of a bidirectional association by two unidirectional associations is shown in Fig. 8.

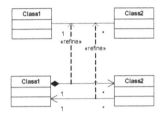

Fig. 8. Refining Analysis Relations to be able to Implement Them

Establishment of Subsystems and Components. The functional decomposition of the system into packages is started in the analysis phase and completed during the design phase. The parts of the system, separated by subsystems and their components communicate only using defined interfaces. Subsystems refining an analysis package are connected to this package by explicit traceability links of the type «refine». Newly introduced components and subsystems in the design model to fulfil non-functional requirements or constraints are connected by traceability links of the type «realize».

Establishment of Use Case Realizations-Design. During analysis the use case realizations are used to answer the question, what the system has to do to realize a use case. During design these diagrams are further refined to show how it is to do. The design diagrams have to be connected by explicit traceability links of type «refine»with the corresponding diagram in the analysis model. Additionally established diagrams have to be connected by traceability links of the type «realize»with the related use case.

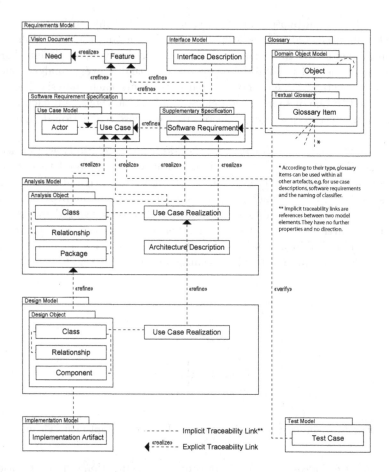

Fig. 9. Traceability Links between Artefacts of Requirements Analysis, Object-Oriented Analysis and Design

Activities of Implementation. The design model is transformed into executable code during implementation. If it is possible to generate the source code automatically or a developer has to implement it, depends on the level of detail of the design model. If the source code is generated automatically, no additional traceability is necessary. The used tool usually offers all functions necessary to follow a design object into implementation. If a developer is doing the transformation manually, it is possible to use implicit traceability by consistent naming of the implementation objects otherwise explicit traceability links have to be used. Traceability links are stored in the source code as annotations.

Flow Description by Activity Diagrams and State Machines. Activity diagrams and state machines allow the modelling of processes without a predefined structure of the system. Activity diagrams are especially used to describe flows, e.g. use cases, information flows between use cases (as interaction diagram) or methods and algorithms in the design model. State machines allow to model reactive objects, like classes, use cases, subsystems or whole systems. Both diagram types can be used in various situations within the development process, that's why they are discussed separately.

If an activity diagram or a state machine is used to describe a use case, a class or another model element, then both, the diagram and the model element have to be connected by an explicit traceability link of the type «refine». Alternatively, a consistent naming of the diagrams and the corresponding model element can be used for implicit traceability.

3.5 Tailoring of the Traceability Model

The introduced traceability links are summarized in Fig. 9. The presented traceability model has been developed based on experiences, exploration of the UP and best practices in software engineering. The traceability links allow following essential development activities. However, tailoring is possible and sometimes necessary depending on the complexity of the project, the expected results by using traceability and the available resources to establish traceability. There are two possible ways to tailor the traceability model to meet special needs:

1. omitting or adding traceability connections of the model and
2. enhancing or decreasing the level of granularity of defined links.

The first point is reasonable in the case that at the same time corresponding development activities are omitted or added. Examples for such scenarios are:

- software development without object-oriented analysis for very small and short-living projects or
- requirements analysis without feature definition.

The second point, the change of the level of granularity, refers in particular to traceability links between use cases and analysis objects and between analysis and design objects. Here a high number of traceability links has to be established, but at the same time a higher level of granularity can support the developer with valuable information, e.g. if traceability links between use cases and analysis classes are used. It is possible to connect artefacts with a higher or lower level of detail at both sides of the traceability link, then described in our model before. In the case of use cases, more detail means to link parts of the use case descriptions and less detail means to link to features instead of use cases. For analysis classes more detail means to connect to methods and attributes and less detail means to connect to the package, which contains the class. Figure 10 shows three examples of possible traceability links. The level of detail is rising from left to right.

It has to be pointed out, that while using a higher level of detail, the traceability links of fewer detail are included implicitly. That means by connecting a use case action with an operation of an analysis class, there is also an implicit connection between use case and class.

In principle it is possible to increase or lower the level of detail only at one connection side, but without real advantage because the resulting information is not more precise. An advantage is only reached by a corresponding change on both sides of the connection.

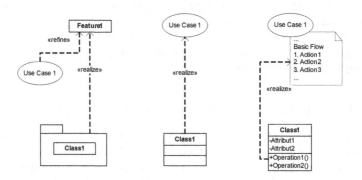

Fig. 10. Example of the Level of Traceability between Use Cases and Analysis Objects

3.6   Verification of Traceability Links

Defined traceability links have to be verified for completeness and correctness. Only thus the usability can be assured and a decay of traceability information after changes of the connected models can be avoided. In the following rules for validation are defined. Presently this set of rules is a first step for validating only the pure existence of traceability links. For reaching this aim the analysis of terms used in identifiers, the evaluation of relations in the class model or the analysis of use case descriptions is necessary. E.g. one of the rule set introduced in the list below is: each use case has to be realized by at least one analysis class. This rule verifies the existence of at least one traceability link between both model elements. But it is not sufficient for the verification of correctness. Approaches for further validations offer the usage of terms in the model and the validation of plausibility between diagrams. For example, the analysis of terms means to search for glossary items of type object in the use case description and try to relate them to the identifier of the linked analysis classes and their attributes. Differences between both should lead to a notice for the developer.

Plausibility check between different diagrams means, that for each use case triggered by an actor, an analysis class of type interface has to be defined. Another case considering use case realizations, the classes of all instances within the use case realization have to be linked to the use case, because they realize it. In the Table 3 the so far known rules are listed.

While applying the defined rules, one has to keep in mind that the UP is an incremental and iterative process. That means these rules will raise warnings as long as the model is not fully completed. However it is possible to check all chains of artefacts to the last existing artefact and all loose artefacts. An example for

Table 3. Verification Rules for Traceability Links

Need ←«realize»– Feature (m:n)	
1.	Each need is realized by at least one feature.
2.	Each feature is realizing at least one need.
Feature ←«refine»– Use Case (m:n)	
1.	Each feature is refined by at least one use case.
2.	Each use case is refining at least one feature.
Use Case/Actor-Assoc. ←«refine»– Interf. Descript. (m:n)	
1.	Each association between a use case and an actor is refined by at least one interface description.
2.	Each interface description is refining at least one association between use case actor.
Actor – – – – – Use Case (m:n)	
1.	Each actor is associated to at least one use case.
2.	The associated actor(s) are the same as the actors used in the description of the use case.
Use Case ←«refine»– Suppl. Software Requirement (m:n)	
1.	Each software requirement (non-functional requirement, constraint) is refining at least one use case.
Use Case/Suppl. Softw. Req. ←«verify»– Test Case (m:n)	
1.	Each software requirement is verified by at least one Test Case.
2.	Each Test Case is verifying at least one use case or software requirement.
Glossary – – – – – DOM (1:0,1)	
1.	Each domain object is defined in the glossary.
Use Case ←«realize»– Analysis Class (m:n)	
1.	Each use case is realized by at least one analysis class.
2.	Each analysis class is realizing at least one use case.
Use Case ←«realize»– Use Case Realization-Analysis (1:n)	
1.	Each use case realization is realizing one use case.

a loose artefact is a use case, which is realized by an analysis class, but does not refine any feature. This should lead to a warning for the developer.

The rule set is going to be expanded during the next steps of the project towards powerful support for developer.

4   Related Work

A comprehensive description of research topics, results and open issues in the field of traceability was given in a former publication [11]. In this paper according to the specific topic, three studies concerning traceability frameworks has to be pointed out in particular.

Based on the analysis of industrial software development projects Ramesh and Jarke [7] define two metamodels for traceability. The authors differentiate low-end and high-end users of traceability. Correspondingly they explain a simplified and a full version of their metamodel. Further they give a predefined standard set of link types. The authors focus especially on project management and organizational needs of traceability. They do not give answers to the problem how traceability should be established in analysis and design.

Spence and Probasco [4] discuss several alternatives for traceability between requirements. The paper is focused on the UP. They do not give answers to the question how the transition to analysis and design and the on-going work should be traced.

Letelier [3] offers a metamodel for requirements traceability in UML-based projects. He gives an example of the usage in a UP project. The author is focusing on a general traceability model and gives advise on how to customize it using UML mechanisms. By keeping the model general useable, it is not possible to define rules and activities for the creation, verification and the update of links, which could be carried out (semi)automatically by a tool.

5   Conclusions and Future Work

In this paper the general activities of a software process model have been enhanced by the establishment of traceability links to reduce the effort and to enable tool support. Traceability links improve the maintainability and support evolutionary development processes e.g., by recovering former development activities, especially for the case of changing requirements. A model for traceability links has been introduced which can be tailored if necessary. Based on the development activities and artefacts, a set of rules for the verification of the traceability links has been developed.

As a part of ongoing work, the developed traceability link model is currently completed and refined towards a complete coverage of the methodical activities, to facilitate appropriate tool support for the creation, update and verification of the traceability links with a minimum interaction with the developer. For refining the model, architectural development methods like Qasar [12] are investigated and integrated.

Other development methods and processes like Fusion [13] and Refactoring [14] are currently investigated aiming towards a generally usable traceability model. For the realization of tool support we have started the implementation of plug-ins for existing UML tools. The plug-ins will support the developer by the establishment of traceability links in the background while modelling and by maintaining the consistency of existing links during changes of artefacts. However, a consequent application of the rules of the development method in all modelling activities constitutes a precondition for such a support.

Acknowledgments. This work is partly funded by a grant from the German Research Foundation (Deutsche Forschungsgemeinschaft DFG) under id Ph49/7-1.

References

1. Riebisch, M.: Supporting evolutionary development by feature models and traceability links. In: Proceedings 11th Annual IEEE International Conference and Workshop on the Engineering of Computer Based Systems (ECBS 2004), Brno, Czech Republic, pp. 370–377 (May 2004)
2. Arlow, J., Neustadt, I.: UML 2 and the Unified Process. In: Practical Object-Oriented Analysis and Design, 2nd edn., Addison-Wesley, Reading (2005)
3. Letelier, P.: A framework for requirements traceability in UML-based projects. In: Proceedings of 1st International Workshop on Traceability in Emerging Forms of Software Engineering, Edinburgh, UK (September 2002)

4. Spence, I., Probasco, L.: Traceability strategies for managing requirements with use cases. Rational Software White Paper TP166, IBM (2000), http://www-306. ibm.com/software/rational/info/literature/whitepapers.jsp

5. Cleland-Huang, J., Chang, C.K., Christensen, M.J.: Event-based traceability for managing evolutionary change. IEEE Trans. Software Eng. 29(9), 796–810 (2003)

6. Weilkiens, T.: Systems Engineering mit SysML/UML. dpunkt.verlag (2006)

7. Ramesh, B., Jarke, M.: Toward reference models of requirements traceability. IEEE Trans. Software Eng. 27(1), 58–93 (2001)

8. Jacobson, I.: Object-Oriented Software Engineering: A Use Case Driven Approach. Addison Wesley, Reading (1992)

9. Rupp, C., et al.: Requirements-Engineering und Management. Carl Hanser Verlag (2007)

10. Cockburn, A.: Using goal-based use cases. JOOP 10(7), 56–62 (1997)

11. Maeder, P., Riebisch, M., Philippow, I.: Traceability for managing evolutionary change. In: Proceedings of 15th International Conference on Software Engineering and Data Engineering, Los Angeles, USA, ISCA, pp. 1–8 (2006)

12. Bosch, J.: Design and Use of Software Architectures: Adopting and evolving a product-line approach. Addison-Wesley, Reading (2000)

13. Coleman, D.: Object-Oriented Development: The Fusion Method. Prentice-Hall, Englewood Cliffs (1994)

14. Fowler, M.: Refactoring: Improving the Design of Existing Code. Addison Wesley, Reading (1999)

Architecture Recovery and Evaluation Aiming at Program Understanding and Reuse

Aline Vasconcelos[1,2] and Cláudia Werner[1]

[1] Federal University of Rio de Janeiro
COPPE/UFRJ – Systems Engineering and Computer Science Program
P.O. Box 68511 – ZIP 21945-970 – Rio de Janeiro – RJ – Brazil
[2] CEFET Campos - Federal Center for Technological Education of Campos
Dr. Siqueira, 273 – ZIP 28030-130 – Campos dos Goytacazes – RJ- Brazil
{aline, werner}@cos.ufrj.br

Abstract. Organizations use to have implemented systems that represent a large effort and budget invested in the past. These systems are evolved and adapted over time in order to accommodate technological and business changes. Moreover, big companies often develop similar systems within the same domain. This has been motivating them to migrate to reuse approaches, such as domain engineering and product line. However, existing systems in general don't have up-to-date architectural documentation that can help in their maintenance and reuse. Considering this scenario, this paper presents an approach to architecture recovery and evaluation that aims at extracting knowledge from existing systems to help in their understanding and reuse. This extracted knowledge is represented through a recovered application architectural model composed by architectural elements that represent domain concepts traced to implemented functional requirements, which may help in generating reusable artifacts. In order to evaluate the approach feasibility, an experimental study was performed.

Keywords: Architecture recovery, dynamic analysis, data mining, architecture evaluation, software inspection, program understanding, software reuse.

1 Introduction

There is a large number of reverse engineering approaches in the literature to recover documentation from existing systems. Many approaches of software clustering and remodularization [2, 16], or more specifically of architecture recovery [3, 7, 13, 20] reconstruct documentation from system available artifacts, such as source code and executable. These approaches are motivated by the fact that existing systems, which have been developed many years ago (i.e. legacy systems), usually don't have up-to-date documentation that can help in their understanding. These systems represent a great investment made by the organizations and incorporate business knowledge that sometimes cannot be obtained in any other source of information. Moreover, big organizations tend to develop applications in the same or similar domains along the years. This motivates the reuse of the whole or parts of existing systems in new developments, mainly in domain engineering and product line approaches. However,

S. Overhage et al. (Eds.): QoSA 2007, LNCS 4880, pp. 72–89, 2007.
© Springer-Verlag Berlin Heidelberg 2007

existent reverse engineering approaches, in general, are not focused on reuse and on the generation of abstractions that can be mapped to domain concepts. Moreover, they use to be based on criteria that are domain or implementation specific.

In the last years, architecture recovery approaches have been receiving attention from the reverse engineering community since the architecture communicates high-level knowledge about the system, facilitating its comprehension and reuse. Architecture recovery can be defined as a reverse engineering activity that aims at obtaining a documented architecture for an existing system [9]. Many definitions to software architecture are given in the software engineering literature since this field has not consolidated concepts and representation models yet. Among the accepted definitions, we adopt the one from Bass *et al.* [6], in which software architecture is defined as the structure, or structures of a system that comprises software elements (i.e. architectural elements), the externally visible properties of those elements, and the relationships among them. The architectural element we recover in this work stands for a group of functionally cohesive classes that implement a domain concept. Concerning architectural structures or views, our approach recovers a static and a dynamic architectural representation. However, it is not the focus of this paper to describe the dynamic view recovery. Further details about this view can be obtained in [23].

Our goals in this work are: (1) to contribute to software reuse by clustering functionally cohesive classes to compose architectural elements that represent domain concepts and possibly reusable artifacts; (2) to cope with program comprehension, through the reverse engineering of an application architectural model, with meaningful names given to architectural elements; and (3) to provide an architecture recovery approach that can be reused across different domains and implementations.

Our approach of architecture recovery, named ArchMine, is integrated to the Odyssey environment [18], which is a reuse infrastructure based on domain models that supports both: development for reuse, through a Domain Engineering process; and development with reuse, through an Application Engineering process. ArchMine is integrated to the Application Engineering context and aims at generating artifacts that can possibly be reused in a Domain Engineering process.

In order to be reusable, we must ensure that the recovered architectural elements are cohesive and consistently represent domain concepts. To this end, we adopt an architectural evaluation model based on inspection, ArqCheck [5], extended to evaluate architectural elements reusability.

Finally, in order to extract knowledge from existing systems that can help in their comprehension, we base our architecture recovery on use case scenarios and data mining. Use case scenarios represent application usage scenarios that guide application execution during dynamic analysis. The result of the dynamic analysis is a set of execution traces, i.e. method executions, each set related to a specific use case scenario. They translate the application functional requirements and represent a means to map functional requirements to system entities (i.e. classes). Data mining, in addition, is employed to mine the gathered execution traces and discover related classes based on the functionality they implement. Our approach is semi-automated and human-guided. We argue that, in contrast to fully automated approaches, by incorporating human knowledge to architecture recovery we can extract models that are rich of information and directed to user goals, e.g. software reuse.

This paper is organized as follows: section 2 presents meaningful related work in architecture recovery and architecture evaluation; section 3 presents our approaches for architecture recovery and evaluation, i.e. ArchMine and ArqCheck; section 4 describes an experimental study performed to evaluate these approaches; and section 5 concludes the paper presenting its contributions, limitations, and future work.

2 Related Work

Concerning architecture recovery, works on software clustering and remodularization, besides architecture recovery itself, have many points in common. In [3], an architecture recovery approach based on clustering classes by name similarity is presented. Reinforcing the conclusions they had in a previous work [2], name similarity shows to be a good approach to architecture recovery. Bojic and Velasevic [7] apply dynamic analysis to architecture recovery, like the work presented in this paper, but using a formal concept analysis technique to recover architectural elements. However, there are no experimental studies to confirm the validity of their approach, as we do in our work. In [21], dynamic analysis is also employed, but in this case to map low-level system events into more abstract architectural operations or connectors. Mappings are formally defined using Colored Petri Nets. Although, proposing a language to define the mappings and relying on regularities in system implementation, these mappings are very implementation dependant. In order to achieve more generality, our approach is not based on implementation patterns.

Kazman and Carrière [13] present a semi-automated approach to architecture recovery performed with the support of the Dali workbench. In their approach, criteria to classes clustering into architectural elements are application-dependant, while in our approach they are general to object oriented (OO) applications from different domains. Sartipi [20] also employs data mining to architecture recovery, but in his work data mining is used to derive relations among entities based on their static structural properties, instead of their dynamic behavior as in our approach.

Mitchell and Mancoridis [16] present an automatic approach to architecture recovery that analyzes the static graph extracted from source code and clusters its entities based on the evaluation of their coupling. They apply a sub-optimal function that tries to maximize the connectivity inside architectural elements, while minimizing the connectivity among architectural elements. Architectural element names are derived randomly by selecting the name of one of their constituent classes. This problem of not automatically attributing semantic names to architectural elements is general in reverse engineering approaches, with the exception of few works as the one in [22].

To the best of our knowledge, current reverse engineering approaches don't provide a systematic means to evaluate the recovered architectures, being informally evaluated by system experts. In order to fulfill this gap, we adopt an extended version of ArqCheck [5] to evaluate the architectures recovered by ArchMine. ArqCheck is a generic and simple approach to architecture evaluation. Some architecture evaluation methods, like the ones based on scenarios - e.g. ATAM [14] and SAAM [12], may require a great effort, and others are specific to some architectural representations – e.g. SAEM [10].

3   Approach for Architecture Recovery and Evaluation

In this section we present our approach for architecture recovery and evaluation. First, as shown in Fig. 1, architecture recovery sub-process takes place, which encompasses information extraction and architectural views reconstruction, performed through the ArchMine approach. The architecture evaluation sub-process main goal is to evaluate the reusability of architectural elements and is based on an extended version of the ArqCheck approach [5]. Fig. 2 and Fig. 6 detail these sub-processes, which are described in the following sub-sections. The processes are modeled following OMG SPEM (Software Process Engineering Metamodel) notation. They jointly derive knowledge about the application to help in its understanding and reuse.

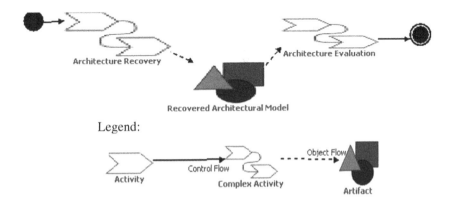

Fig. 1. Architecture recovery and evaluation process

3.1   Architecture Recovery Sub-process

In order to reconstruct architectural elements, we cluster classes based on relations among them derived by means of dynamic analysis and data mining. Dynamic analysis involves gathering application execution traces, i.e. sequences of methods that implement application functionalities. We apply a data mining algorithm inspired on Apriori [1] to mine execution traces and indicate related classes based on the functionalities they implement.

The approach is application and implementation independent and can be applied to OO applications from different domains. However, our supporting tool set was designed to analyze Java applications. ArchMine has been refined since 2005 [24] through its application in 5 case studies, involving systems of different sizes and domains. The 5th case study is presented in section 4, describing the application of ArchMine and ArqCheck approaches.

The remainder of this section explains the architecture recovery sub-process activities, together with its tool set and an accompanying example. The example presents a real case study, i.e. ArchTrace [17] partially recovered artifacts. ArchTrace is a traceability links evolution system which reads an architecture description and the related source code, establishing and maintaining traceability links between them.

Static Structure Extraction. *Static Structure Extraction* and *Use Case Scenarios Definition* can be performed in parallel, as shown in Fig. 2. *Static Structure Extraction* reconstructs a UML class model (i.e. static structural model) from source code. This task is fully automated by applying the Odyssey static reverse engineering tool, Ares. Ares is a plug-in to Odyssey [18] that reads Java source code and reconstructs a UML class model. This class model is at a low-abstraction level and classes are further clustered into architectural elements. Fig. 3 depicts a partial view of the class model recovered from ArchTrace source code, which is at a very low-abstraction level.

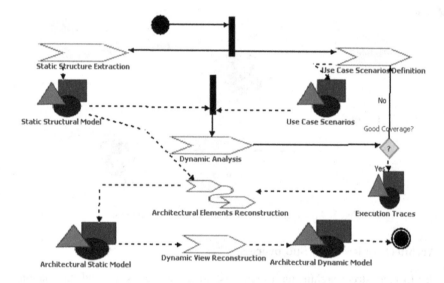

Fig. 2. Architecture recovery sub-process

- **Use Case Scenarios Definition.** This activity aims at determining usage scenarios to guide application execution for dynamic analysis. A use case (*uc*) is a description of sequences of actions, including variants, that an entity (e.g. a system) performs to produce an observable result of value to an actor [8]. It represents a functional requirement (*fr*) of a system, denoted by *uc* $\Leftrightarrow$ *fr*. Each sequence of actions in a *uc* is called a use case scenario and represents one means for obtaining that *fr* [8]. Moreover, user inputs (e.g. menu option selection, button pressed, mouse pressed, mouse released) trigger system actions that lead to the execution of use case scenarios, generating concrete scenarios. Each use case scenario may have one or more associated concrete scenarios, representing execution paths inside the application that lead to the execution of that use case scenario.

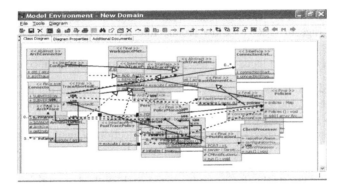

Fig. 3. ArchTrace partial class model in the Odyssey environment

Table 1 lists the manually defined use case scenarios for the ArchTrace application. For example, the use case scenario "Configures Architecture" can be performed through an application menu option or through a toolbar button (i.e. concrete scenarios).

Table 1. ArchTrace use case scenarios

ArchTrace Use Case Scenarios	
1. Configures preferences.	8. Removes traceability links from old file versions.
2. Configures architecture.	9. Traceability to immutable arch. element.
3. Configures repository.	10. Executes Data Mining policy.
4. Configures policies.	11. Updates traceability links when new file versions are committed.
5. File save.	12. Help about.
6. Traceability links to different file versions.	13. Traceability link to file when already exists a link to the directory.
7. Removes traceability links from files when a traceability link to the directory is created.	14. Suggests traceability links to the most recent file versions.

ArchMine defines some guidelines to help in the definition of use case scenarios, namely: derive 1 use case scenario for each application main menu and pop-up menu option; in case of nested menu items, choose the one in the last level of the hierarchy; tool bar buttons may derive use case scenarios; panel buttons that are not trivial, such as Ok, Cancel, Next etc., may also derive use case scenarios; tabs in tabbed panes may derive use case scenarios or make part of a greater scenario; for concrete scenarios that represent the same use case scenario, only define one scenario; fill in all the input data in the scenarios in order to exercise the most parts of the system as possible. These guidelines were derived through the case studies in which the approach was applied.

In addition to the guidelines, user manuals; test cases; or available stakeholders (e.g. users, developers, maintainers) may be accessed in order to facilitate comprehending the use case scenarios and system functionality. Use cases and their scenarios are informally specified in the Odyssey environment. ArchMine does not require 100% of use case scenarios coverage in order to allow architecture recovery. However, the higher the coverage achieved in use case scenarios definition concerning all the application use case scenarios, the higher tends to be the quality of the recovered architectural model.

Dynamic Analysis. It involves application execution and monitoring for the specified use case scenarios, and gathering execution traces that are related to the realization of an application functionality or use case scenario. We instrument the bytecode of Java applications through AspectJ [4], allowing the detection of methods execution with related information, i.e. class, instance and thread. It is performed with the support of our Tracer tool [23], which takes as input the jar file and classPath of Java applications, and inserts the tracing code around each method execution. The output is a set of XML trace files (Fig. 4), in which methods are ordered and indented by control flow hierarchy. Through static filters, Tracer tool eliminates from the execution traces the classes belonging to libraries (e.g. Java API), which are not relevant to comprehend the application architecture.

The tag "Label" indicates the executed use case scenario (e.g. Fig. 4, "Configures architecture"). Since the Tracer tool allows enabling and disabling tracing, it is possible to delimit a set of method executions belonging to a given use case scenario.

```xml
<?xml version="1.0" encoding="ISO-8859-1" ?>
<Label name="Configures architecture">
<Method class="edu.uci.ics.archtrace.gui.ArchTraceTreeModel"
    instance="@64" method="getChildCount" thread="AWT-
    EventQueue-0" time="24 de Março de 2006 14h34min57s BRT">
  <Method class="edu.uci.ics.archtrace.model.ArchTraceElement"
    instance="@64" method="getChildCount" thread="AWT-
    EventQueue-0" time="24 de Março de 2006 14h34min57s BRT"/>
  </Method>
...
```

Fig. 4. An excerpt of a hypothetical XML execution trace

In order to evaluate classes coverage by dynamic analysis, the classes in the execution traces are compared to the ones extracted in the static model. Classes that were not monitored are shown to a system expert (e.g. a programmer, a developer, a designer) who indicates scenarios that still need to be executed. As shown in Fig.2 there is an iteration between *Dynamic Analysis* and *Use Case Scenarios Definition*.

Architectural Elements Reconstruction. It is a complex activity, composed of a series of tasks, namely: classes clustering, architectural elements names generation, and architectural elements dependencies computation. We apply a data mining algorithm inspired on Apriori [1] to mine execution traces and detect high-level relations among classes that implement common functionalities in the system. They are clustered into architectural elements. In order to make clear how we apply an Apriori-like algorithm, some Apriori concepts are defined:

- Apriori discovers association rules among items of database transactions.
- *Association rule* is an implication of the form: X $\Rightarrow$ Y, where X and Y are items of the database and X $\cap$ Y = $\varnothing$. X is the *antecedent* of the rule, while Y is its *consequent*. Our rules have one *antecedent* and many *consequents*.
- Apriori requires two threshold values: *minimum support* and *minimum confidence*. *Support* "s" means that s% of the transactions in the database contain X and Y. *Confidence* "c" implies that c% of the transactions that contain X also contain Y. Given a set of transactions τ, the problem of mining association rules is to generate all rules that have support and confidence equals or greater than the user specified *minimum support* and *minimum confidence*.

In order to mine association rules, some concepts from the database domain are mapped to the dynamic analysis context. These mappings are presented in Table 2.

Table 2. Mapping of concepts for mining association rules

Data Mining Concepts	Mapping to Dynamic Analysis
Transaction	A use case scenario, represented by an execution trace.
Data Item	A class, in the execution trace, implementing the use case scenario.
Support	Percentage of use case scenarios implemented by a class.
Minimum Support	The minimum percentage of use case scenarios in which the classes in an association rule must appear together.
Confidence	Percentage of use case scenarios of class X in which a class Y also appears.
Minimum Confidence	The minimum percentage of use case scenarios of class X in which a class Y must also appear for the association rule between X and Y to be valid.
Antecedent	The class that is used as input to discover the association rules.
Consequent	The classes that are associated to the antecedent with support and confidence greater or equals to the minimum values.

Mining is supported by our TraceMining tool, that reads the gathered execution traces and generates architectural elements in the Odyssey environment Instead of detecting large itemsets and then deriving association rules, as in the original Apriori algorithm, TraceMining queries specific antecedents, which are randomly chosen by the tool. The mining and architectural elements reconstruction process is guided by some heuristics, which are explained in the following.

- *H1*: Minimum support must be low, since the most monitored classes that can be clustered into architectural elements along the mining process, the higher tends to be the quality of the recovered architecture.
- *H2*: Minimum confidence must be tuned along the mining process by the user. This tuning may be performed with a system stakeholder (i.e. programmer, designer, developer), if possible. The user that guides the mining process must try to balance architectural elements size, i.e. composing

not too large, neither too small clusters. Architectural elements size is impacted by minimum confidence: the higher the minimum confidence, the smaller the clusters will be.

- *H3*: Classes must be mined and grouped from higher to lower support values. Higher support value classes are the most general ones, providing services required by many others. They compose more general architectural elements that might implement infrastructure services or some core functionality of the application.

- *H4*: Classes that participate in a few number of use case scenarios tend to compose business architectural elements, which are more specific. They are the last mined and clustered ones. It is important to state that in the same support value boundary, classes must be randomly chosen as antecedents for the mining process.

- *H5*: Groups already formed must be filtered from subsequent mining cycles, otherwise it shouldn't be possible to distinguish between more general and more specific architectural elements.

- *H6*: Whenever intersections are observed among the mining results, they must be prioritized in the composition of architectural elements, since they tend to reveal strongly related classes, that together participate in some association rules.

- *H7*: Some superclasses and interfaces may not be monitored during dynamic analysis. Therefore, they must be grouped in the architectural element to which they are closest. Closeness, in this case, is evaluated by measuring the number of subclasses per architectural element for each superclass and the number of implementing classes for each interface. These classes are highly dependant on the superclass or interface specification.

This heuristic set was derived through the case studies in which the approach was applied. It doesn't intend to be an exhaustive list, although these heuristics proved to provide good results along the case studies. In order to illustrate some of the described heuristics, Table 3 depicts some classes of the ArchTrace application and the corresponding scenarios that they implement. Use case scenarios numbers are extracted from Table 1. Table 4 presents the structure of some resulting architectural elements with the corresponding association rules and heuristics that originated them.

The minimum support adopted was 0% (H1), since the goal was to cluster all the monitored classes. Minimum confidence used was 60% (H2), since this value generated the best balanced sizes for architectural elements, i.e. from 2 to 8 classes. The first mined antecedent was ArchTraceWindow (H3), the class that had the highest support value in the example. CheckBoxTreeCellEditor was the only class that had confidence higher than 60% for ArchTraceWindow, generating the first element.

The second mined class was DenyImmutableAETracePolicy, because according to heuristic H5 classes already grouped must be filtered, and, therefore, 30% was the next support value in the scale. In this support value boundary, DenyImmutableAE-TracePolicy was randomly chosen as antecedent (H3 and H4). According to heuristic

Table 3. ArchTrace classes x use case scenarios

Classes - support	Use Case Scenarios
ArchTraceWindow – 57%	6, 7, 8, 9, 10, 11, 13, 14
CheckBoxTreeCellEditor – 50%	6, 7, 8, 9, 10, 13, 14
TraceAbortedException – 30%	6, 9, 13, 14
DenyImmutableAETracePolicy – 30%	4, 6, 9, 13
ArchTraceException – 30%	6, 9, 13, 14
DenySubCITracePolicy – 22%	4, 6, 13
SuggestRelatedTracesPolicy – 15%	10, 4
SuggestionDialog, SuggestionListModel – 15%	10, 4, 14
DataMiner, MinedElement, MinedElements – 7%	10, 4

Table 4. ArchTrace partial recovered architectural elements

Architectural Element Name/Heuristics	Association Rules	Classes
GUI-6 / H2, H3	ArchTraceWindow⇒CheckBoxTreeCellEditor-confidence=87,5%	CheckBoxTreeCellEditor, ArchTraceWindow
PRE-TRACE POLICIES-7/ H2, H3, H4, H5	DenyImmutableAETracePolicy⇒ ArchTraceException, DenySub-CITracePolicy, TraceAbortedException – confidence=75%	DenyImmutableAETracePolicy, ArchTraceException, DenySubCITracePolicy, TraceAbortedException
SUGGESTION-MINED-4 / H1, H1, H2, H3, H4, H5	SuggestionDialog⇒ SuggestionListModel-confidence=100% SuggestionDialog⇒DataMiner, MinedElement, MinedElements,, SuggestRelatedTracesPolicy-confidence=66,7%	DataMiner, MinedElement, MinedElements, SuggestionDialog, SuggestionListModel, SuggestRelatedTracesPolicy

H2, the classes ArchTraceException, DenySubCITracePolicy, and TraceAbortedException were the ones that had confidence (i.e. 75%) greater or equal to the specified minimum confidence (i.e. 60%). Following the support scale, as shown in Table 3, the next randomly selected antecedent was SuggestionDialog, with support value of 15%. It was grouped with DataMiner, MinedElement, MinedElements, SuggestionListModel, and SuggestRelatedTracesPolicy in the same architectural element.

Reconstructed architectural elements are exported to Odyssey by the TraceMining tool, restructuring the static structural class model already extracted (e.g. Fig. 3) and leading it to a higher-abstraction level (e.g. Fig. 5). During exporting, architectural element names are derived based on the most common substrings in their class names, providing semantics to their names. Therefore, class names are broken down into substrings, which start by a capital letter or after an underscore symbol. TraceMining establishes a ranking among the substrings, by counting their occurrence in architectural element class names, and composes architectural element names by concatenating the best ranked ones. Architectural element names also contain a sequential number, to avoid redundancies in generated names. Whenever the system expert doesn't agree with

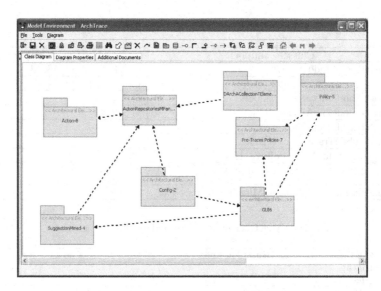

Fig. 5. ArchTrace architectural model after applying the mining heuristics

architectural element names, they can be changed. This situation occurred in some re-covered elements for ArchTrace.

Besides deriving architectural element names, TraceMining also computes depen-dencies among architectural elements based on the relationships among their classes. In the Odyssey environment, derived architectural elements and their classes are traced to the use case scenarios that they implement.

Dynamic View Reconstruction. It aims at representing interactions among architec-tural elements, showing how the system behaves to perform the selected use case scenarios. The dynamic view is represented through UML sequence diagrams and its reconstruction is performed with the support of the Tracer and Phoenix tools. Further details can be obtained in [23].

3.2 Architecture Evaluation Sub-process

The recovered architecture is evaluated by applying an extended version of ArqCheck. ArqCheck is an inspection method that uses a checklist as the defect de-tection technique. It was chosen to architecture evaluation due to the following fac-tors: it is simple and it requires less effort to architecture evaluation than other meth-ods, like the ones based on scenarios [13, 14]; it can be configured to the architectural representation at hand; its feasibility was evaluated through two experimental studies; and it has been developed in the same academic environment as the work presented in this paper, facilitating its extension.

The questions in the checklist employed by ArqCheck are divided into three evalua-tion categories: architectural representation consistency, conformance to functional requirements, and conformance to non-functional requirements. For the non-functional requirements, the checklist questions are based on the knowledge available in architectural tactics [6], covering Availablity, Performance, Modifiability, Usability, Security, and Testability. The checklist was extended in this work to evaluate architectural elements Reusability. Since there aren't architectural tactics to evaluate Reusability, the questions were formulated based on the knowledge available in Component-Based Development (CBD) literature [19, 25], which aims at defining self-contained and cohesive software artifacts. The applied extensions were evaluated through a case study, confirming their feasibility.

Moreover, in order to describe non-functional requirements, quality scenarios are adopted, representing an information set that allows characterizing a non-functional requirement that facilitates its understanding [6]. Quality scenarios describe non-functional requirements like use case scenarios describe the functional ones. Quality scenarios in the checklist must be instantiated any time it is applied according to the non-functional needs of the current system.

The inspection process adopted by ArqCheck is adapted from the traditional inspection process described in [11] and is presented in Fig. 6.

Three roles participate in an inspection process, namely: the moderator, who manages the process execution; the inspected artifact author; and the inspector, who identifies defects on the artifact. The process activities are detailed in the following and exemplified in the next section through the described experimental study.

Inspection Planning. This activity involves identifying the moderator for the inspection, who selects the inspectors and distributes the inspection material. It also involves configuring the checklist of ArqCheck, that includes: analyzing the questions of the checklist to adapt the concepts to the architectural representation employed; classifying questions in applicable or not, according to the architectural representation and non-functional requirements of interest; and instantiating quality scenarios for the selected non-functional requirements. It generates the configured checklist.

Presentation and Detection. *Presentation* involves presenting the material to be inspected by the author and training inspectors in applying ArqCheck. During the *Detection*, selected inspectors individually review the recovered architectural model, identifying discrepancies, that can be classified as defects or false-positives (i.e. discrepancies that are not defects in fact) during the Inspection Meeting. These identified discrepancies are registered in the discrepancy reports of ArqCheck. Each inspector generates one discrepancy report.

Inspection Meeting. In the *Inspection Meeting*, the moderator, inspectors and document author debate about the discrepancies identified in the discrepancies reports, classifying them in defects or false-positives. The final decision about a discrepancy classification is the moderator's responsibility. Defects correction discussion is not the goal of the meeting, but a list of defects is generated as a result.

Rework and Follow-up. In the *Rework* activity, the document author corrects the defects identified by the inspection, generating a Restructured Architectural Model.

Follow-up involves re-evaluating the quality of the inspected material, after correction, in order to decide whether a new inspection over the inspected artifact must occur or not.

In the next section, an experimental study applying ArchMine and ArqCheck is presented and obtained results including some lessons learned are discussed.

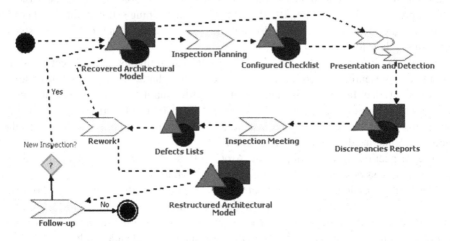

Fig. 6. Architecture evaluation sub-process

4   Empirical Study

Experimentation represents the core of a scientific process, being the unique way to evaluate a new theory. It offers a systematic, disciplined, computable, and controlled approach to evaluate new methods, techniques, languages, and tools. In [26], three kinds of empirical studies that can be carried out in software engineering are presented, i.e. surveys, case studies, and experiments. The choice among them depends on factors such as the proposal and conditions to the evaluation.

In order to evaluate ArchMine and ArqCheck, we conducted a case study with an application of industrial use. Its goals, hypothesis, metrics, planning, execution, and results along with lessons learned, are discussed in this section.

4.1   Experimental Study Goals and Definition

ArchMine had been evaluated through 4 case studies before this one, through which it has been refined, according to the lessons learned. It proved to be feasible. However, one important issue identified was that the evaluation of the architectures recovered was ad-hoc, requiring a huge human effort, and not assuring that the quality of the recovered architecture was improved after evaluation.

In order to improve this evaluation, an extended version of ArqCheck was adopted. Therefore, the goal of this experimental study is to evaluate if the extended version of ArqCheck reduces the evaluation effort and allows improving architectural quality for reuse, concerning the architectures recovered with ArchMine. The experimental study outline is presented as follows, according to the notation proposed in [26]:

Analyze the evaluation of the architectures recovered by ArchMine
through the extended version of ArqCheck
For the purpose of characterization
With respect to architecture evaluation effort reduction and architecture
reusability improvement
From the point of view of software engineers
In the context of the recovery of an object oriented framework, written in
Java, and in use in an industrial context

4.2 Experimental Study Hypothesis and Metrics

This experimental study intended to reject two null hypotheses, namely: (HO_1) – the incorporation of an extended version of ArqCheck to evaluate the architectures recovered by ArchMine doesn't reduce the evaluation effort; and (HO_2) – the quality of the recovered architecture, concerning its reuse, is not improved by incorporating an extended version of ArqCheck to architecture evaluation.

In order to test these hypotheses, some metrics were established, namely: M1 - average time spent to architecture evaluation by the inspectors; M2 - number of inspectors who found it difficult to apply extended ArqCheck; M3 – number of inspectors who found that the quality of the architecture, concerning reuse, had improved. Metrics M2 and M3 were derived by counting the answers given by the inspectors in a post-evaluation form.

4.3 Experimental Study Planning and Execution

The architecture of the CSBase framework [15], that manages resources in a distributed grid environment and was developed in a partnership between the academy and the industry, was recovered following the heuristics defined for ArchMine (section 3.1). It has 720 classes. Use case scenarios were defined by the researcher with a system expert, following the guidelines of ArchMine (section 3.1). 129 use case scenarios were monitored. The architecture was recovered by the first author of this paper.

As soon as the architectural model has been recovered, the inspection process took place. The researcher, in the role of moderator and document author, planned the inspection process by configuring the checklist to evaluate CSBase recovered architecture. Although it is the moderator's responsibility to choose the inspectors, in this special case the inspectors were selected by the CSBase manager. The checklist was configured by classifying the questions in applicable or not, changing some architectural terms to the architectural representation adopted, and by instantiating the quality scenario for the non-functional Reusability requirement. Table 5 presents an excerpt of the checklist used in this study. In order to classify the questions in applicable or not, in some cases, the moderator needed the help of the system experts. Question 8, for example, was not applicable in this study because CSBase didn't have a previous documented requirements model.

Reusability quality scenario instantiated to evaluate CSBase recovered architecture is presented in Table 6. It is accompanied by a Context Identification Guide, which indicates how to look for the elements that must be evaluated for Reusability.

Table 5. Excerpt of the checklist used in the experimental study

N°	Items that Evaluate Architectural Representation Consistency	Yes	No	NA
1.	In the diagrams, is there any architectural element that doesn't have relationships, being isolated from the others?			
2.	All the architectural elements, identified by their names, were represented by the same abstraction in the different diagrams?			
N°	**Items that Evaluate the Conformance to Functional Requirements**	**Yes**	**No**	**NA**
8.	All the functional requirements, or quality attributes or other requirements, created by the architectural decisions, is being satisfied by any architectural element?			x
N°	**Items that Evaluate the Conformance to Non-Functional Requirements (Reusability)**	**Yes**	**No**	**NA**
9.	The responsibilities of the internal modules (i.e. classes) of a reusable element belong to the same context, i.e. they intend to achieve the same goal or are used in the same use case scenarios?			
10.	Is it possible to identify groups of reusable architectural elements with similar responsibilities or that share some common implemented functionalities that should be grouped to compose a component?			
11.	From the point of view of the concept that the reusable architectural element represents, are there modules (i.e. classes) that should be allocated in it, considering their responsibilities or functionalities, but that are allocated in another architectural element?			
12.	Are there couplings between a reusable architectural element and other elements that hinder its reuse?			
13.	Considering the coupling among reusable architectural elements, are there couplings that justify their clustering in one component?			

After configuring the checklist, the moderator presented the recovered architecture and the checklist to the inspectors, training them in applying ArqCheck. They were also given a discrepancies report, to be filled anytime they found that an answer in the checklist indicated a defect in the architecture.

Inspectors were also asked to fill some evaluation forms informing the difficulty degree in applying ArqCheck and the quality of the architecture for reuse, before and after correction. Once the inspectors concluded discrepancies detection, the moderator

Table 6. Reusability quality scenario for CSBase recovered architecture

Reusability requirement: the recovered CSBase architectural elements must be reused in the specification and development of other applications in the distributed grid management domain.	
Reusability Scenario	
Stimulus source	Domain Engineer
Stimulus	Reuse of the recovered architectural elements in domain design.
System Context	Domain Engineering process
Artifact	Recovered CSBase architectural elements, represented through packages in the Odyssey structural view.
Answer	Domain models generated.
Answer Measure	--------
Context Identification Guide: according to the reusability requirement, identify the reusable elements that must be evaluated. Reusable elements are mainly identified through the stimulus and artifact described in the reusability scenario. In order to answer reusability questions, evaluate their internal structure, relationships with other architectural elements, and traced use case scenarios.	

consolidated the discrepancies list, by eliminating redundancies. The final defects list was generated after the inspection meeting. Based on this list, the moderator conducted the rework activity, contacting system experts, whenever he had difficulties to correct the architecture. The restructured architectural model was presented to the system experts (i.e. inspectors), who evaluated its final quality.

4.4 Experimental Study Results and Lessons Learned

Concerning the null hypotheses of the experiment, there were evidences to reject only the first one. Architecture evaluation effort was not reduced in comparison to our previous studies, according to the values of metrics M1 and M2. However, in order to confirm this result, it would be necessary to run the study again with two evaluation approaches (i.e. ad-hoc and ArqCheck) applied to the same application. Concerning the second hypothesis, the system inspectors agreed that ArchMine recovered architectural concepts for CSBase and that the quality of the architecture for reuse had improved after inspection, according to the values of metric M3. After discussing the results of the study with the system experts, some lessons learned were outlined:

- CSBase is client-server and since the client and the server were separately monitored, some interface components were not adequately captured.
- Architectural element names, in general, adequately reflected CSBase domain concepts, which indicates that names derivation strategy is a good contribution of ArchMine when compared to other reverse engineering approaches (e.g. Bunch [16]).
- The minimum confidence used was 60%, a value that was tuned along the previous case studies, demonstrating to be a reasonable value. Minimum support was 0% in order to cluster all the monitored classes.
- The effort required to apply ArqCheck is also due to limitations of the Odyssey environment in the manipulation of the recovered model.

5 Conclusions

In this paper we presented ArchMine, an architecture recovery approach based on dynamic analysis and data mining. ArchMine recovers architectural elements that represent functionally cohesive groups of classes, describing domain concepts and possibly reusable artifacts. Recovered architectural elements are evaluated by applying ArqCheck. The main contributions of our approach are: (1) the recovery of functionally cohesive architectural elements, traced to the implemented functional requirements, that can possibly be used for reuse and program understanding; (2) a general approach to recover the architecture of OO applications; (3) the recovery of an application architectural model, with meaningful names given to architectural elements, that can be used to comprehend its domain concepts; (4) the incorporation of an evaluation method that makes architectural evaluation a more systematic and controlled activity than in other reverse engineering approaches – e.g. [13, 16, 20].

However, we identify some limitations of the approach, such as the impact of the selected use case scenarios, minimum support, confidence and antecedents chosen for the mining process in the quality of the recovered architecture. These limitations are minimized by the heuristics and guidelines proposed in ArchMine. These guidelines and heuristics may be iteratively refined as the approach is applied in new case studies, although the current ones proved to provide good results. As future work, it is important to evaluate the divergences in the recovered architectures by varying these values in the recovery process.

Our final goal is to generate a reference architecture for the domain. We are currently working in the detection of variability among the recovered architectures, which requires recovering the architectures of at least three systems in the same domain. This approach will be useful for organizations that develop similar applications and intend to migrate to domain engineering or product line approaches.

References

1. Agrawal, R., Srikant, R.: Fast Algorithms for Mining Association Rules. In: 20th Very Large Databases Conference, Santiago Chile, pp. 487–499 (1994)
2. Anquetil, N., Fourrier, C., Lethbridge, T.C.: Experiments with Hierarchical Clustering Algorithms as Software Remodularization Methods. In: Working Conference on Reverse Engineering, Pittsburgh PA USA, pp. 235–255 (1999)
3. Anquetil, N., Lethbridge, T.: Recovering Software Architecture from the Names of Source Files. Journal of Software Maintenance: Research and Practice 11, 201–221 (1999)
4. Aspectj: Eclipse Project, AspectJ 1.5.3. (2007), http://eclipse.org/aspectj/
5. Barcelos, R., Travassos, G.H.: Evaluation Approaches for Software Architectural Documents: A Systematic Review. In: Ideas 2006 - 9° Workshop Iberoamericano de Ingenieria de Requisitos y Ambientes de Software, La Plata Argentina, vol. 1, pp. 433–446 (2006)
6. Bass, L., Clements, P., Kazman, R.: Software Architecture in Practice, 2nd edn. Addison-Wesley, Reading (2003)
7. Bojic, D., Velasevic, D.: A Use-Case Driven Method of Architecture Recovery for Program Understanding and Reuse Reengineering. In: 4th European Software Maintenance and Reengineering Conference. Zuriq Swiss, pp. 23–31 (2000)
8. Booch, G., Rumbaugh, J., Jacobson, I.: The Unified Modeling Language User Guide, 1st edn. Addison-Wesley, Reading (1998)
9. Deursen, A.V., Hofmeister, C., Koschke, R., Moonen, L., Riva, C.: Symphony: View-Driven Software Architecture Reconstruction. In: Fourth Working IEEE/IFIP Conference on Software Architecture (WICSA 2004). Oslo Norway, pp. 122–132 (2004)
10. Duenas, J.C., De Oliveira, W.L., De La Puente, J.A.: A Software Architecture Evaluation Model. In: 2nd International ESPRIT ARES Workshop, Las Palmas de Gran Canaria Spain, pp. 148–157 (1998)
11. Fagan, M.E.: Design and Code Inspection to Reduce Errors in Program Development. IBM Systems Journal 15(3), 182–211 (1976)
12. Kazman, R., Bass, L., Abowd, G., Webb, M.: SAAM: A Method for Analyzing the Properties of Software Architectures. In: International Conference on Software Engineering (ICSE). Sorrento Italy, pp. 81–90 (1994)
13. Kazman, R., Carrière, S.J.: Playing Detective: Reconstructing Software Architecture from Available Evidence. Technical Report CMU/SEI-97-TR-010. Pittsburgh PA USA (1997)
14. Kazman, R., Klein, M., Clements, P.: ATAM: Method for Architecture Evaluation. Technical Report CMU/SEI-2000-TR-004 CMU/SEI. Pittsburgh PA USA (2000)

15. Lima, M.J.D., Ururahy, C., Moura, A., Melcop, T., Cassino, C., Nery, M., Silvestre, B., Reis, V., Cerqueira, R.: CSBase: A Framework for Building Customized Grid Environments. In: Third International Workshop on Emerging Technologies for Next-generation GRID (ETNGRID 2006), Manchester Reino Unido, pp. 187–192 (2006)

16. Mitchell, B.S., Mancoridis, S.: On the Automatic Modularization of Software Systems Using the Bunch Tool. IEEE Transactions on Software Engineering 32(3), 193–208 (2006)

17. Murta, L.G.P., Van Der Hoek, A., Werner, C.M.L.: ArchTrace: Policy-Based Support for Managing Evolving Architecture-to-Implementation Traceability Links. In: International Conference on Automated Software Engineering (ASE), Tokyo Japan, pp. 135–144 (2006)

18. Odyssey.: Software Reuse Environment based on Domain Engineering (2007), http://reuse.cos.ufrj.br/odyssey

19. Sametinger, J.: Software Engineering with Reusable Components. Springer, New York (1997)

20. Sartipi, K.: Software Architecture Recovery based on Pattern Matching. In: International Conference on Software Maintenance, Amsterdam the Netherlands, pp. 293–296 (2003)

21. Schmerl, B., Aldrich, J., Garlan, D., Kazman, R., Yan, H.: Discovering Architectures from Running Systems. IEEE Transactions on Software Engineering 32(7), 454–466 (2006)

22. Tzerpos, V.: Comprehension-Driven Software Clustering. PhD Thesis. Department of Computer Science University of Toronto (2001)

23. Vasconcelos, A.P.V., Cepêda, R.S.V., Werner, C.M.L.: An Approach to Program Comprehension through Reverse Engineering of Complementary Software Views. In: 1st International Workshop on Program Comprehension through Dynamic Analysis, Pittsburgh PA USA, pp. 58–62 (2005)

24. Vasconcelos, A.P.V., Werner, C.M.L.: Towards a set of Application Independent Clustering Criteria within an Architecture Recovery Approach. In: 5th IEEE/IFIP Working Conference on Software Architecture - Software Architecture Evaluation and Analysis Working Session, Pittsburgh PA USA, pp. 235–236 (2005)

25. Vitharana, P., Jain, H., Zahedi, F.M.: Strategy-Based Design of Reusable Business Components. IEEE Transactions on Systems, Man, and Cybernetics – Part C: Applications and Reviews 34(4), 460–474 (2004)

26. Wohlin, C., Runeson, P., Höst, M., Ohlsson, M.C., Regnell, B., Wesslén, A.: Experimentation in Software Engineering: An Introduction. Kluwer Academic Publishers, Boston (2000)

Factors Influencing Industrial Practices of Software Architecture Evaluation: An Empirical Investigation

Muhammad Ali Babar[1], Len Bass[2], and Ian Gorton[3]

[1] Lero, University of Limerick, Ireland
Muhammad.Alibabar@ul.ie
[2] Software Engineering Institute, Carnegie Mellon University, USA
ljb@sei.cmu.edu
[3] Pacific Northwest National Laboratory, USA
ian.gorton@pnl.gov

Abstract. To support software architecture evaluation practices, several efforts have been made to provide a basis for comparing and assessing evaluation methods, document various best practices, and report the factors that may influence industrial practices. However, there has been no study to explore the experiences and perceptions of architects for determining the factors that influence architecture evaluation practices in a wide range of organizations. Hence, there is little empirically founded knowledge available on the factors that influence the industrial practices of software architecture evaluation. The goal of this paper is to report the results of an empirical study aimed at gaining an understanding of different factors involved in evaluating architectures in industry. The results of this study shed light on the factors that influence architecture evaluation practices based on the experiences and perception of architects who regularly evaluate architectures of various sizes of applications. It also discusses some of the strategies that practitioners apply to deal with the influence of the identified factors.

1 Introduction

Recently, it has been recognized that quality attributes (such as maintainability, usability, and performance) of large software systems are largely constrained by the systems' software architectures [1-3]. Since architecture plays a significant role in achieving system wide quality attributes, it is very important to evaluate a system's architecture with regard to desired quality requirements as early as possible. The principle objective of evaluating architecture is to assess the potential of a proposed architecture to deliver a system capable of fulfilling required quality requirements and to identify any potential risks. Architectures are assessed either informally as an inherent part of the design process or formally as a requirement of organizational software development processes. Formal evaluation requires appropriate methods and processes to be used in order to perform architectural evaluation as objectively as possible. Architecture evaluation has its origin in design reviews. The major difference between design reviews and architecture evaluation is the level of abstraction and the criteria used; software architecture of a system is evaluated against business goals [1, 4].

S. Overhage et al. (Eds.): QoSA 2007, LNCS 4880, pp. 90–107, 2007.
© Springer-Verlag Berlin Heidelberg 2007

There are two broad categories of approaches to evaluating software architecture: qualitative analysis and quantitative measures [5]. The former category includes techniques like scenarios, questionnaires, and checklists. The latter category consists of metrics and simulation. The software architecture community has proposed several evaluation methods such as Scenario-based Architecture Analysis Method (SAAM) [6], Architecture Tradeoff Analysis Method (ATAM) [7], and Architecture-Level Modifiability Analysis (ALMA) [8]. These are scenario-based methods, a category of evaluation methods considered quite mature [9, 10].

Several studies have also critically analysed these methods and proposed several feature-based criteria to compare and assess these methods [10, 11]. An international working group on Software Architecture Review and Assessment (SARA) has produced a report summarizing architecture evaluation best practices [12]. Others have also made efforts to report architecture evaluation best practices in [5, 13].

Since there can be several technical and non-technical factors that may influence the use of a particular practice in a certain context, there have also been attempts to identify and understand the factors that may influence software architecture evaluation practices in the real world [4, 13]. Though these factors have been identified by senior researchers and practitioners based on their extensive experiences and knowledge of evaluating software architectures for many large scale systems, there has not been an attempt to provide empirical evidence for these factors. Rather, they have been reported based on anecdotal evidence from mainly the telecommunication and defence domains.

Hence, there is a vital need to explore the experiences and perceptions of architects with diverse industrial backgrounds to determine the factors that influence architecture evaluation practices of a wide range of organizations. Such an effort can not only provide empirically supported knowledge about the factors that influence architecture evaluation practices in industry, but can also help reveal the similarities and differences between the factors previously identified by senior researchers and practitioners (as mentioned above) and found by this study.

The goal of this paper is to report the results of such an empirical study aimed at identifying different factors that may influence software architecture evaluation practices in industry. The results of this research shed light on architecture evaluation practices based on the experiences and perception of architects who regularly evaluate software architectures of various sizes of applications.

As such, the objectives of this study were:

- To determine the factors that influence industrial software architecture evaluation practices and to reveal any similarities and differences between the factors identified in this study and those reported by researchers and practitioners with extensive experience of software architecture evaluation (e.g., [4, 13]).
- To gain an understanding of the challenges posed by the identified factors to architects in evaluating software architectures of varying sizes of systems in both small and large organizations.
- To identify and discuss different approaches to dealing with these challenges used by practitioners and /or reported in literature.

The paper makes following contributions to the software architecture evaluation research and practice:

- It presents the design and results of an empirical study on software architecture evaluation practices in varying sizes of organizations.
- It provides information about how practitioners think about different aspects of software architecture evaluation and what challenges they face while evaluating software architectures.
- It provides an empirical validation of previously identified factors influencing architecture evaluation practices as well as identifying additional factors such as system integration, vendor involvement, training and governance frameworks.
- It clusters the identified factors into five categories so managers and evaluators can study and comprehend the influence of one category's factors together rather than considering each factor individually.
- It discusses some of the approaches, described by the participants or recommended in the literature, for dealing with the challenges in software architecture evaluation caused by the identified factors.

This paper is organized as follows. Section 2 provides the details of the methodology used for this research. Section 3 presents and discuses the results of data analysis. Conclusions and future work finish the paper in section 4.

2   Research Methodology

This section describes the methodology and data analysis approach and procedures used for the reported research.

2.1   Focus Group

Our approach to collecting data was a focus group, which is considered a proven and tested technique to obtain the perception of a group of selected people on a defined area of interest. Focus group studies are carefully planned and structured discussions involving 3 to 12 participants. Focus group discussion is largely free-flowing, but discretely guided by an experienced moderator, who is responsible for keeping the group discussion focused on relevant topics and make sure that everyone has an opportunity to participate. Focus group discussion enables a researcher to explore the way people feel and think about the issues to be studied.

The participants of a focus group study are usually selected based on some pre-defined criteria, which ensures that the participants have certain individual characteristics and professional background as related to the discussion topic. The group discussion allows the participants to build on the responses and ideas of the others, which increases the richness of the information gained. Focus group sessions produce mainly qualitative information about the objects of study.

Compared to other qualitative research methods (e.g., interviews), focus group research can generate candid and insightful information inexpensively and faster. However, focus group research also has several weaknesses such as subjective self-reported data based on personal opinion and interpretation of a particular event/situation, biased moderation, and small sample size, which makes generalizing the results difficult [14, 15]. In the following sections, we describe the objectives, logistics, and data analysis process of this study according to the five steps involved in the focus group research method.

2.2 Define the Problem

This step is aimed at defining the research problem that needs to be studied by using the focus group research. The focus group research method is usually suitable for gathering initial information about some ideas rather than testing a hypothesis or making a final decision. This study started with the identification of the research goal, which was to gain an understanding of the challenges of evaluating software architecture and obtain insights into the factors that influence architecture evaluation practices. Furthermore, we also wanted to know how practitioners deal with the challenges caused by those factors.

2.3 Plan Focus Group

Planning includes setting criteria for selecting participants, deciding the session length (i.e., usually 2 to 3 hours) and preparing documents to provide the participants with the study background, objectives, and protocols. The objective of our study was to gain an understanding of the formal and informal approaches used to evaluate software architectures by practitioners. We were particularly interested in knowing the factors that influence the organisational practices of architecture evaluation.

2.4 Select Participants

This step is aimed at selecting participants according to the criteria devised during the planning stage. In order to gain insights into the dimensions of industrial practices in software architecture evaluation, it was vital to invite participants with a certain level of experience in software architecture design and evaluation. It was also deemed necessary to invite participants from various sizes of organisations within a broad range of industries. Hence, the selection process of selecting participants for our focus group was governed by the following criteria:

- At least 5 years of experience of architecture design and evaluation in different industrial domains such as finance, medicine, education and retail.
- Availability and willingness to commit needed time and effort.
- Knowledge and expertise of the issues of architecture evaluation; and
- Willingness to share their experiences and candid opinion of different dimensions of software architecture evaluation in their organisations.

It was also ensured that the participants were invited from in-house software development companies, software vendors, and consultancies. According to the selection criteria, our study needed responses concerning a very specific set of practitioners, basically software architects with several years of experience. Such practitioners usually have time constraints and are not likely to respond to invitations from unfamiliar sources. That was why a random sampling was not viable.

Consequently, it was decided to use a non-probabilistic sampling technique, called availability sampling. Availability sampling operates by seeking responses from those people who meet the inclusion criteria, if defined, and are available and willing to participate in the research. The major drawback of non-probabilistic sampling is that the results cannot be considered statistically generalizable to the target population [16]. However, given the abovementioned constraints, it is believed that the sampling technique was reasonable. We used two means of contacting potential respondents: personalised contact and professional referrals. We sent invitation emails to a selected pool of software architects drawn from two sources: practitioners' profile database provided our research group's industry liaison personnel and industry contacts of the involved researchers.

2.5 Conducting the Focus Group Session

A focus group session should be conducted by carefully managing time and ensuring all the participants get equal opportunity to share their opinion on the topics of interest. During the session, moderator can apply various techniques describes in [17] to steer the discussion process. Session discussion can be recorded by a scribe and/or using audio and/or video instruments.

We held two focus group sessions, each of them lasting approximately two hours. Each session started with a brief introduction of the participants and researchers. The introduction included the name of the attendees, their organizations, current position, professional background and experience and application domain and the type of industry. The sessions were audio recorded with participants' consent. One of the researchers also acted as a scribe and took extensive notes.

2.6 Data Analysis

The data analysis step involves transcribing the recorded discussion using appropriate coding schemes. The transcribed data can be analysed using one or more of the qualitative data analysis techniques reported in [15] . The focus group sessions of this study resulted in approximately four hours of audio recording and extensive notes. This data needed to be transcribed and analysed. The audio recording of both sessions were transcribed by one of the researchers. However, in order to verify that there was no bias introduced during transcription, we performed an inter-rater reliability test by involving an independent person in the transcription process. The transcription of the primary researcher was time stamped and compared with the transcription of an independent researcher. The independent researcher (not any of the authors of this report) randomly listened to several transcribed parts of the focus group discussions. Both transcriptions were compared and no big differences were found. We did not perform a Kappa analysis for reliability of the transcribed content as there was no major disagreement between the transcriptions of two independent researchers. After this stage, content analysis and frequency analysis were used to examine the data

Analysis of the transcribed data followed the iterative content analysis technique to prepare qualitative data for qualitative or quantitative analysis. Content analysis applies certain procedures to make valid inferences from text-based qualitative data. Krippendorf [18] defines the content analysis techniques as follows: "content analysis is a research technique for making replicative and valid inferences from data to their context". A content analysis strategy is extensively used in focus group and interview-based empirical studies in software engineering (e.g. [19, 20].

During content analysis, the transcribed data was coded using Strauss and Corbin's [21] open coding method. Using the open coding technique, data are broken into discrete parts, and closely examined and compared for similarities and differences. Events, happenings, actions and interactions that are found to be conceptually similar in nature or related in meaning were grouped under more abstract categories. We analysed transcripts and identified the major emergent themes following the above procedure. For each participant's transcript we repeated the above procedure and identified the emerging themes. The coding process was independently carried out by two researchers for reliability purposes.

Self-reported qualitative data can be transformed by coding into qualitative data [15]. However, this transformation does not eliminate the subjectivity aspect of the data. The frequency analysis performed on the transformed data can help identify the relative importance of each factor's influence on organisational practice in software architecture evaluation. The presentation of data along with their frequencies is considered an effective mechanism for comparing and contrasting within, or across groups of variables. For frequency analysis, we counted the occurrences of each theme and placed each theme along with its respective frequency of occurrence under one of the higher level categories of factors influencing architecture evaluation practices. These higher level categories were organizational, technical, managerial, business, and socio-political.

3   Results and Discussion

In this section, we present the results of the data analysis and discussion on their implications for software architecture researchers and practitioners.

3.1 Demographics

Table 1 shows the profile of the participants of the focus group session. The participants were invited based on the participant selection criteria developed during the planning stage. All of the participants had several years of experience in software development and software architecture design and evaluation. The mean number of years of experience of software development possessed by each participant was 16.8 years, the minimum 9, the maximum 34, and the mode was 16 years. The mean number of years of experience of designing and evaluating software architectures was 8 years, the minimum 5, the maximum 15, and the mode was 7 years.

The participants' companies were of varying sizes in terms of number of employees (ranging from 50 to 6000 employees) and some of the companies were large multinationals (number of employees mentioned are for Australian operations only). The participants had backgrounds in different business domains (e.g., telecomms, finance, health, education) and had designed and/or evaluated software architectures for systems from multiple application domains. While the majority of the participants came from in-house software development units, there was representation from product

Table 1. Demographic information about the participants

ID	Experience in SD	Experience in SA	Company Size	Domain	Type of company
1	10	21	100	Telecom	Vendor
2	5	10	100	Business Intelligence	Vendor
3	7	12	50	Defence	Consultant
4	6	12	2000	Retail	In-house development
5	12	16	600	Finance	Consultant
6	6	16	2000	Govt	In-house development
7	7	20	6000	Finance	In-house development
8	8	34	2500	Finance	In-house development
9	5	9	800	Health	In-house development
10	15	18	1000	Telecom	In-house development

vendors and consultants. Moreover, the participants from in-house software development houses had extensive experiences of working and dealing with external consultants and vendors' representatives for software architecture evaluation.

The demographic information about the participants of our study gives us confidence that we have gathered data from practitioners who are experienced in software architecture design and evaluation. Many of them came from companies, which have processes and procedures in place for evaluating software architectures and had established architecture review boards in their organisation. Hence, despite not being able to apply systematic random sampling because of the abovementioned reasons, the results are representative of architects with similar characteristics.

3.2 Factors Influencing Software Architecture Evaluation Practices

The data analysis found 254 unique themes from the transcription of the focus group sessions. The mean number of themes identified by the participants was 42, the minimum number 18, the maximum number 70, and the mode was 47.

3.2.1 Organizational Factors
These factors can have organization wide influence on architecture evaluation practices. They include engagement models, funding models, governance frameworks, support structures, training, and formats and forms for documenting software architecture design decisions.

Engagement model – There were 39 themes related to this factor. Participants in the study considered that having a structured model of engagement for evaluating software architecture is vital. Participants described that an engagement model has significant influence on the dynamics of architecture evaluation process. They mentioned several issues caused by not having a well-defined engagement model; for example, project team evaluating architecture itself, resistance to engage people external to the project, evaluating architecture on an ad hoc basis to check the health of a system rather than evaluation tightly embedded in a project's development plan.

Table 2. Organisational factors that influence architecture evaluation practices

Factors	Brief definition	F
Engagement model	How does an engagement model affect architecture evaluation in an organisation? What are the different models being used?	39
Governance framework	Is there a governance framework to comply with during architecture evaluation?	32
Support structure	Having organisational structure and support system for rigorous architectural practices?	21
Design decision documentation	Documenting design decision/rationale to support communication and understanding.	19
Funding model	How is architecture evaluation funded? Is it Project-based, centralised, or hybrid?	17
Training	What kind of training is available? How the evaluation is used for staff training?	13

Several participants reported that their organisations had an Architecture Review Boards (ARB) based engagement model designed for using evaluators external to the project under evaluation. As noted by one of the participant: *"We have a fairly structured engagement model, which is designed to help business units to achieve their goals. Since the architecture team are fully engaged, businesses do not consider them outsiders. Because of having a structured engagement model, the old style of saying 'give me the documentation and I will tell you what is wrong' has disappeared as a work practice. Our CIO sits on the management committees of various business units and it forces the architecture team to align architectural decisions with the CIO's insights into the needs of different business units."*

Many large organisations have emphasised the need of having an architecture review board, which can be responsible for several aspects of getting architectures evaluated throughout an organisation [13]. Moreover, to assure impartiality, evaluators should be independent of the project being evaluated [22]. Participants also described various ways of engaging external evaluators such as having a pool of evaluators, architectural experts from sister or parent companies, or consultants.

Governance Framework – The study data suggested that an organisation needs to have a governance framework to comply with during architecture design and evaluation activities. Participants mentioned that without having a governance framework, various organisational units may be developing and applying different policies, procedures, templates and methods to support architecture evaluation. Participants were of the opinion that having a governance model helps achieve organisation wide consistent practices. One participant noted: *"It is vital to have a governance framework for architecture evaluation and this framework needs to have the backing of all the key players in an organisation. Since a large organisation may have different operations, cultures, and procedures in different business units, a governance framework can provide consistency for architectural practices."*

Support structure – Table 2 shows that there were 21 themes that mentioned the need for a suitable support structure. Participants suggested that non-existence of a suitable support structure is one of the reasons why architectural decisions may not comply with organisational standards or may be incommunicable to a wide range of stakeholders. Several participants thought that there should be a suitable organizational mechanism for bridging the gap between enterprise architecture and development teams to facilitate architecture evaluation and realization activities in accordance with the requirements of quality attributes and architectural decisions. The data also suggested the architecture group should have representation in the higher management to raise the visibility of critical architectural decisions.

Design decision documentation – Problems caused by insufficient documentation of design decisions and contextual information have been widely reported by architecture researchers and practitioners [23, 24]. There were 19 themes related to design decision documentation. Several participants emphasised the need for documenting design decisions along with rationale and justification. All the participants reported that architecture decisions are documented in their respective organisations. However, they found it quite challenging to understand the different format and forms of documenting architecture decisions as sometimes they find just a few PowerPoint slides; other times, there can be huge documentation describing architectural decisions and rationale. Participants thought that organisations should have standard procedures and templates for documenting and communicating architecture decisions and rationales to interested stakeholders. As in [23, 25], participants reported that the use of templates brings consistency in capturing the necessary information about a decision.

Funding model – There were 17 themes in the data mentioning the effects of a funding model on architecture evaluation practices. Participants described that cost related issues usually discouraged managers from carrying out rigorous evaluations of their systems' architectures. Many of the participants mentioned that if there are additional funds available to a project for architecture evaluation, it is likely that project managers will attempt to utilize those funds, otherwise they may not want to release resources from the project budgets for evaluating architectures. As noted by several of the participants: *"One way of encouraging a project manager to get their architecture evaluated regularly is to apply the 50-50 rule: 50% of the cost born by the project and 50% of the cost picked up by the organisation. If a portion of the cost comes from the ARB, it provides a justification for them to get their members embedded into the projects, which can improve the chances of compliance with the architectural policies and procedures. That is why in our organisation, 50% of the fund required for architecture evaluation comes from outside of the project's budget, which provides us an opportunity to work with a project team for ensuring that architecture design and process are governed by organisational policies."*

Training – There were 13 themes related to this factor. Participants reported that getting suitably trained staff is a challenge, which has considerable effects on the architecture evaluation process. Many participants suggested that evaluations be used as training mechanism to help staff gain skills in architecture evaluation. It was reported that in large organisations, where multiple teams work on a system, architecture is used for assigning work and project coordination. This use of architecture helps different teams to understand the contribution that each makes to the realization of architecture design and help them to understand ways of improving reusability at the architecture level. On the role of architecture evaluation in staff training, one participant noted: *"There are several issues related to keeping technical knowledge updated. At times, people engaged in architecture evaluation may not have enough training and skills in the tools and techniques used. Enterprise architects may also loose touch with reality, what developers are doing, what system architects are doing, what people in support are doing? They may make decisions without carefully thinking about the wider ramifications of those decisions. A suitable training program can help gain the required skills and visibility in the work of others."*

3.2.2 Technical Factors

These factors are related to the technological aspects of architecture evaluation. They include quality attributes being evaluated, challenges caused by integration issues, techniques and tools for representing and visualizing architectures, types of evaluation required, and methods and guidelines used.

Quality attributes: The data from this study carried 37 themes, which mentioned the affect of the quality attributes being evaluated on the selection of a certain technique. Researchers have reported that different types of quality attributes (such as performance, maintainability, and security) need to be evaluated by using different approaches [10, 26]. Participants were also of the opinion that having a good understanding of the types and levels of required quality attributes is a vital factor as the types of attributes to be evaluated usually have significant influence on the choice of methods and practices. As mentioned by several of the participants: *"The challenge is to clearly understand the quality requirements for evaluating architecture. Many stakeholders do not have a good understanding of what level of performance, security or usability is required to support their business processes. For example, some businesses may be able to live with cold standby for availability, while others may require site level failover. Moreover, a reference architecture may also need to be evaluated for extensibility and flexibility. Performance is the biggest area and it is very difficult to test performance in a simulated environment because it is different to the real environment where there would be so many factors to affect a system."*

Integration issues – Table 3 shows that 35 themes identified in the data were related to evaluation issues specific to integration projects. Participants mentioned that more than 80% of the projects evaluated by them had some types of integration aspects involved; either integrating existing systems or building new systems by integrating COTS components. Participants mentioned that evaluating for integration influences evaluation practices as integration projects involve several unique challenges such as lack of knowledge about suitable evaluation methods and techniques, insufficient architectural information, vendors' dubious claims, and no significant input from

Table 3. Technical factors that influence architecture evaluation practices

Factors	Main themes	F
Quality attributes being evaluated	How to decide about a suitable evaluation strategy for certain quality attributes?	37
Integration issues	How can the architectures of systems/components effectively and efficiently be evaluated for integration?	35
Representing and visualizing Architectures	How can architecture be represented or visualised to support architecture evaluation? Which description language?	32
Types of evaluation	What type of evaluation is usually carried out? e.g., Ad-hoc, formal, prototyping etc.	25
Methods and guidelines	Does an organisation have developed/adopted methods and/or guidelines for evaluating architectures?	17

technical people in major purchasing decisions. One participant summarised the issues in these words. *"The biggest problem is that people purchases large components without thinking about the integration issues and when it comes to quality requirements like performance, availability, and exception handling, acquisition decision makers are usually not aware of these issues. We have seen business people coming without having an integrated infrastructure layer and asking for a portal of integrated information with strict performance, security, and usability requirements. Evaluation for integration poses extra challenges because architectural information about the systems to be integrated is usually insufficient."*

Documenting and visualizing architectures – Software architecture documentation is one of the key inputs to architecture evaluation [1]. The data from this study included 32 themes related to documenting and visualizing architectures. Participants believed that the use of an appropriate notation and abstraction level is important for communicating an architecture. They also emphasised the role of views or any other pictorial representation for visual communication of architectural information. However, participants also mentioned that commonly used notations and tools suffer from several deficiencies. Many mentioned they have proprietary notations and tools to document and visualise architectures. One of the participants described the problems in these words. *"Describing architectures is a big challenge. We use UML for this purpose but UML tools have very poor integration with documentation packages like MS Word. Hence, we always face a huge problem. There is a real need for tools that enable architects to design an architecture and then put the design into a format that is comprehensible to business people. Lack of integration requires a lot of duplication. For example, drawing diagrams in UML based case tools and cutting/pasting into MS Word for presenting to business clients. Hence, there is a need for an integrated environment that incorporates modelling, text composition, and knowledge management features for supporting architectural practices."*

Types of evaluation – There were 25 themes that suggest architecture evaluation practices can be planned or ad hoc; qualitative or quantitative; prototyping or theoretical using mathematical models. Participants also suggested that the approach to evaluation also depends on the evaluation goals. One of the participants talked about evaluation approaches in these words: *"There can be different types and forms of architecture evaluation. For example, we do two evaluations: architecture evaluation and IT peers review. The first concentrates on the compliance side of architectural decisions. The second is more a financial review to find out the cost effectiveness of the proposed architectural solution. Architecture evaluation also depends on the types of quality attributes considered. It may be qualitative based on evaluators' experiences or quantitative using various models and prototypes. Rigor of evaluation also varies depending upon the cost of a project."*

The experiences of the participants of this study corroborate the literature that suggests several kinds of evaluation, including questioning, measurement, scenario-based and prototyping [5]. Each kind of evaluation may need different types of methods, techniques, and tools and hence influence the evaluation practice.

Methods and guidelines – The data in this study included 17 themes related to the importance of having organisational wide standardized methods and guidelines for architecture evaluation and their influence on evaluation practices. Participants mentioned the benefits and drawbacks of standardizing methods and guidelines across an organisation. Participants also discussed the ways their organizational methods and guidelines have evolved and the influence of those methods and guidelines on their evaluation practices. As noted by one participant: *"It is a challenging task to standardized methods and guidelines as a lot depends upon what someone is trying to do. That is why it is vital to have fluid processes but strict guidelines. There is definitely a need for standardizing in terms of publication of standards and methodologies being used. In the first instance, methods and processes can be derived from the experiences that usually exist in a large organization. External sources (such as TOGAF, IEEE 1471) can also be used to create templates and guidelines."*

Participants' emphasis on having standardized, albeit fluid, methods and guidelines for architecture evaluation is in line with contemporary architecture evaluation research, which is increasingly emphasizing the importance of having a defined process for evaluating architectures using suitable methods and guidelines [10, 11]. A method provides and organizes a set of techniques, guidelines, and rules that describe how to conduct the architecture evaluation. The guidelines state by whom, in what order, and in what way the techniques are used to accomplish the method's goals.

Table 4. Socio-political factors that influence architecture evaluation practices

Factors	Main themes	F
Soft skills	What kinds of soft skills required for making architecture evaluation valuable to all the involved stakeholders?	15
Organisational politics	What are organisational politics to have influence on architecture evaluation	13
Vendor involvement	Vendors' influence. Use of evaluation to thwart the purchase of unsuitable software/middleware.	8

3.2.3 Socio-Political Factors

These are related to the socio-political dimensions in an organisation such as soft skills, organisational politics, and vendor involvement to deal with socio-psychological aspects of architecture evaluation.

Soft skills – The data in this study suggests that architecture evaluation needs several kinds of soft skills including communication, leadership, team work, negotiation, and persuasion. There were 15 themes related to the influence of soft skills of the involved parties on architecture evaluation practices and outcomes in an organisation. Participants mentioned that architecture evaluation can be very socio-emotional exercise, which may be more influenced by the soft skills of the involved people than their technical understanding of architectural concepts and skills. Participants' experiences are similar to the ones reported in the literature [4, 13] about the importance of soft skills in software architecture evaluation.

Organisational politics – Participants mentioned 13 themes related to the influence of organizational politics on architecture evaluation practices.

Vendor involvement – There were 8 themes in the data related to the influence of vendor involvement in designing and evaluating software architectures. Many of the participants said vendors can oversell a particular technology, which may not be suitable to organisational needs. They mentioned that evaluation of software architectures based on such technologies may be influenced by vendor involvement. Since vendors get themselves involved in organisational processes through higher management, they also attempt to influence the choice of evaluation techniques and tools, which can produce favourable results for their technologies.

3.2.4 Managerial Factors

These influence managers' decisions about different aspects of software architecture evaluation practices.

Management support and commitment – Table 4 shows that there were 17 themes in the data related to the management support and commitment to software architecture evaluation practices in an organisation. Participants reported several experiences of not being able to successfully institutionalizing planned software architecture evaluation because of insufficient management support and commitment. Many of them thought that managerial support and commitment have significant influence on whether architecture evaluation is ad hoc or tightly integrated in the development process. Participants also described a cases in which the positive results from ad hoc evaluation convinced management to support evaluation on regular basis. As one of the participants noted: *"Our first evaluation was initiated by our CIO, who in a project's monthly review meeting advised that the architecture be evaluated by someone external to the project to see whether or not project could be put on the track. Hence, the influence came from the top and it put pressure on everyone involved that it needed to be done properly. Once that evaluation proved to be a success, it has become a norm in the organization to have an architecture evaluated before committing significant resources."*

Table 5. Managerial factors that influence architecture evaluation practices

Factors	Main themes	F
Management support and commitment	How much managerial support is provided for architecture evaluation? Does management appreciate the practice?	17
Objectives of evaluating architectures	What are the main objectives of evaluating architecture? Do stakeholders have the same understanding of the objectives?	17
Stakeholder-centric issues	How are stakeholders selected? How to get them fully involved?	11

Objectives of evaluating architectures – The data contains 17 themes related to the influence of an evaluation's objective on various practices. Participants were of the opinion that clarifying the objectives of evaluation is vital for selecting suitable techniques and tools. Some participants mentioned the challenges involved in evaluating from a quality attribute perspective when an organization's staff are trained and used to evaluate architecture only from a functional point of view. Previously, it has been reported that an evaluation's objective usually has a large influence on the method and techniques used [9, 10]. An architecture can be analysed for several objectives such as risk assessment, maintenance cost prediction, architecture comparison, and trade-off analysis. Several specialized methods have been proposed to evaluate architecture for different objectives such as ATAM for trade-off analysis [1], PASA for performance analysis [27], and ALMA for assessing maintenance cost [28]. Each of these applies different techniques for similar tasks; for example generating scenarios, ATAM gathers scenarios from stakeholders, PASA distils them from use cases, and ALMA gets them from architects and designers [29].

Stakeholder-centric issues – Table 4 shows that there were 11 themes related to stakeholder issues and their potential effects on architecture evaluation and outcomes. Participants mentioned that one of the main challenges of architecture evaluation is to identify, select, and involve suitable stakeholders. The decision made on different aspects of stakeholders involvement can have a significant effect on evaluation output. They emphasised the need for having effective strategies for getting stakeholder involvement in the process and subsequent approval of architecture design. As mentioned by a participant: *"I am convinced that the skill of getting stakeholder engagement is more important than anything else. It is hard to identify suitable stakeholders. There are common examples when project managers do not have any idea about the prospective stakeholders and how to get them involved."*

Software architecture researchers have also identified the influencing role that involvement of suitable stakeholders can have on architecture evaluation. Clements et al. [1] describe the active participation of stakeholders in the architecture evaluation process as absolutely essential for a high-quality evaluation. Parnas [30] regards the presence of wrong people in the design review sessions as the one of the major problems with the conventional design review approaches.

3.2.5 Business factors

These are aspects of architecture evaluation process that affect or are affected by external or internal business consideration.

Business needs and industry standards – Many of the participants mentioned that business needs and industry standards greatly influence architecture evaluation practices in their organisation. There were 25 themes related to the influence of business needs and industry standards on architecture evaluation practices.

Table 6. Business factors that influence architecture evaluation practices

Factors	Main themes	F
Business needs and Industry standards	How do business needs and industrial standards and competition influence architecture evaluation practices	25
Requirements of business case	What is required of the evaluation to perform a business case analysis?	8

Requirements of business case – It was also gathered from some participants' discussions that the output of software architecture evaluation is used for supporting a business case for or against a particular technology. Participants reported that if the output is required for business case, the requirements of the business case greatly influences an architecture evaluation exercise. However, there were only 8 themes related to this factor in the data.

4 Conclusion and Future Work

Recently, software architecture evaluation has emerged as an important area of research and practice. Researchers and practitioners have been active in developing methods, techniques, and tools to support architecture evaluation. Many studies have reported technical and non-technical factors that may influence organisational practices in this area. However, there remains a need for systematically accumulating and widely disseminating evidence about the factors that may influence the selection and use of different methods, techniques, and tools for architecture evaluation.

The overall goal of our research is to develop and empirically assess a taxonomic framework for studying and understanding factors that can influence architecture evaluation practices and identifying the various strategies to deal with the impact of those factors. To achieve that objective, this study was designed and executed with the aim of exploring practitioners' experiences and perceptions to understand the challenges of evaluating architectures. Furthermore, it was also intended to find out the strategies practitioners apply to deal with the challenges caused by the influence of those factors.

This research has gathered empirical evidence to advance the knowledge about the factors that influence industrial practices for evaluating software architectures. The findings also provide empirical evidence to confirm several factors considered influential in architecture evaluation by many researchers based on their experiences and anecdotal evidence (such as reported in [4, 12, 13]). Moreover, it has also reported new factors (such as funding models, governance frameworks, vendor involvement, integration issues, business needs, industry standards, and requirements of a business case), which are perceived to have significant influence on architecture evaluation practices by the participants of this study. The findings of this study have revealed that there are many similarities between the experiences and perceptions of experienced researchers and practitioners from mainly two domains (i.e., telecommunication and defence) and architects from a wide variety of domains (such as education, manufacturing, finance, health). Additionally, it has also identified many more factors than previously reported. One possible explanation may be the diversity of domains from where the participants originate and variation in sizes of the systems with which they have been working.

The research results provide information that can be useful for practitioners' understanding of several factors that can influence architecture evaluation practices. Practitioners can take into account each factor and its potential effect, and suitable approaches while considering the introduction of architecture evaluation in their organizations. To deal with the challenges caused by the identified factors, practitioners can make use of not only the approaches reported by the participants of this study, but can also benefit from adapting/tailoring methods, techniques, and tools developed by research community to support planned and disciplined architecture evaluation. Practitioners can derive architecture evaluation practices from the experiences of researchers and practitioners reported in [4, 12, 13] based on evaluating architectures of hundreds of systems.

The research results presented here can be used by researchers in several ways. For example, the results provide a framework for further research on the influence of various factors on developing and implementing architecture evaluation approaches, techniques, and tools in an organization. For factors found as important (based on high frequency) to architecture evaluation, studies should be conducted to ascertain aspects of causality, in particular, what independent variables impact aspects of the factors and should be considered while planning architecture evaluation. Moreover, studies should also be conducted to determine if significant peculiarities exist for architecture evaluation practices because of cultural differences caused by geographical location of staff within one company or among different companies. It is also hoped that the results of this study will stimulate researchers to discover the underlying model that leads to and/or influences the understanding and use of different architecture evaluation practices based on the factors within one category or interaction among factors of different categories.

We are further analysing the data for identifying the similarities and differences among the factors reported by participants based on the size and business domain of their organizations. We hope this work will help us to propose a taxonomy of the factors influencing software architecture evaluation practices in various sizes of organisations in different business domains. A framework for taxonomic analysis of architecture evaluation factors is expected to enable practitioners and researchers to gain an understanding of the architecture evaluation challenges caused by each of the identified factors and suitable approaches to dealing with the challenges.

Acknowledgement. We are thankful to the participants of our study. This research was carried out at the National ICT Australia.

References

[1] Clements, P., Kazman, R., Klein, M.: Evaluating Software Architectures: Methods and Case Studies. Addison-Wesley, Reading (2002)

[2] Lung, C.-H., Kalaichelvan, K.: An Approach to Quantitative Software Architecture Sensitivity Analysis. International Journal of Software Engineering and Knowledge Engineering 10(1), 97–114 (2000)

[3] Bass, L., Clements, P., Kazman, R.: Software Architecture in Practice, 2nd edn. Addison-Wesley, Reading (2003)

[4] Kazman, R., Bass, L.: Making Architecture Reviews Work in the Real World. IEEE Software 19(1), 67–73 (2002)

[5] Abowd, G., Bass, L., Clements, P., Kazman, R., Northrop, L., Zaremski, A.: Recommanded Best Industrial Practice for Software Architecture Evaluation, Tech Report CMU/SEI-96-TR-025, Software Engineering Institute, Carnegie Mellon University (1997)

[6] Kazman, R., Bass, L., Abowd, G., Webb, M.: SAAM: A Method for Analyzing the Properties of Software Architectures. In: Proceedings of the 16th International Conference on Software Engineering (1994)

[7] Kazman, R., Klein, M., Barbacci, M., Longstaff, T., Lipson, H., Carriere, J.: The Architecture Tradeoff Analysis Method. In: Proceedings of the International Conference on Engineering of Complex Computer Systems (1998)

[8] Bengtsson, P.: Architecture-Level Modifiability Analysis. Ph.D. Thesis. Blekinge Institute of Technology, Sweden (2002)

[9] Dobrica, L., Niemela, E.: A Survey on Software Architecture Analysis Methods. IEEE Transactions on Software Engineering 28(7), 638–653 (2002)

[10] Ali-Babar, M., Zhu, L., Jeffery, R.: A Framework for Classifying and Comparing Software Architecture Evaluation Methods. In: Proceedings of the 15th Australian Software Engineering Conference (2004)

[11] Kazman, R., Bass, L., Klein, M., Lattanze, T., Northrop, L.: A Basis for Analyzing Software Architecture Analysis Methods. Software Quality Journal 13, 329–355 (2005)

[12] Obbink, H., et al.: Software Architecture Review and Assessment (SARA) Report, Tech Report SARA W.G (2001)

[13] Maranzano, J.F., Rozsypal, S.A., Zimmerman, G.H., Warnken, G.W., Wirth, P.E., Weiss, D.M.: Architecture Reviews: Practice and Experience. IEEE Software 22(2), 34–43 (2005)

[14] Kontio, J., Lehtola, L., Bragge, J.: Using the Focus Group Method in Software Engineering: Obtaining Practitioner and User Experiences. In: Proceedings of the International Symposium on Empirical Software Engineering (2004)

[15] Seaman, C.B.: Qualitative methods in empirical studies of software engineering. Software Engineering, IEEE Transactions on 25(4), 557–572 (1999)

[16] Kitchenham, B., Pfleeger, S.L.: Principles of Survey Research, Parts 1 to 6, Software Engineering Notes (2001-2002)

[17] Templeton, J.F.: The Focus Group: A Strategic Guide to Organizing, Conducting, and Analyzing the Focus Group Interview. McGraw-Hill, New York (1996)

[18] Krippendorff, K.: Content Analysis: An Introduction to Its Methodology. Sage, Thousand Oaks (2004)

[19] Beecham, S., Hall, T., Rainer, A.: Software process improvement problems in twelve software companies: An empirical analysis. Empirical Software Engineering 8, 7–42 (2003)

[20] Niazi, M., Wilson, D., Zowghi, D.: A framework for assisting the design of effective software process improvement implementation strategies. Journal of Systems and Software 78(2), 204–222 (2005)

[21] Strauss, A.L., Corbin, J.M.: Basics of Qualitative Research: Grounded Theory Procedures and Techniques. Sage Publications, Thousand Oaks (1998)

[22] Fagan, M.E.: Design and Code Inspections to Reduce Errors in Program Development. IBM Systems Journal 15(3), 182–211 (1976)

[23] Tyree, J., Akerman, A.: Architecture Decisions: Demystifying Architecture. IEEE Software 22(2), 19–27 (2005)

[24] Bosch, J.: Software Architecture: The Next Step, European Workshop on Software Architecture (2004)

[25] Kazman, R., Bass, L., Klein, M.: The essential components of software architecture design and analysis. Journal of Systems and Software 79, 1207–1216 (2006)

[26] Bosch, J.: Design & Use of Software Architectures: Adopting and evolving a product-line approach. Addison-Wesley, Reading (2000)

[27] Williams, L.G., Smith, C.U.: PASA: An Architectural Approach to Fixing Software Performance Problems. In: Proceedings of the International Conference of the Computer Measurement Group (2002)

[28] Bengtsson, P., Lassing, N., Bosch, J., van Vliet, H.: Architecture-level modifiability analysis (ALMA). Journal of Systems and Software 69(1-2), 129–147 (2004)

[29] Ali-Babar, M., Gorton, I.: Comparison of Scenario-Based Software Architecture Evaluation Methods. In: Proceedings of the 1st Asia-Pacific Workshop on Software Architecture and Component Technologies (2004)

[30] Parnas, D.L., Weiss, D.M.: Active Design Reviews: Principles and Practices. In: Proceedings of the 8th International Conference on Software Engineering (August 1985)

A Bayesian Model for Predicting Reliability of Software Systems at the Architectural Level

Roshanak Roshandel[1], Nenad Medvidovic[2], and Leana Golubchik[2,3]

[1] Computer Science & Software Engineering Department
Seattle University, Seattle, WA 98122, USA
roshanak@seattleu.edu
[2] Computer Science Department, University of Southern California
Los Angeles, CA 90089, USA
{neno,leana}@usc.edu
[3] EE Systems Department, IMSC, University of Southern California
Los Angeles, CA 90089, USA

Abstract. Modern society relies heavily on complex software systems for everyday activities. Dependability of these systems thus has become a critical feature that determines which products are going to be successfully and widely adopted. In this paper, we present an approach to modeling reliability of software systems at the architectural level. Dynamic Bayesian Networks are used to build a stochastic reliability model that relies on standard models of software architecture, and does not require implementation-level artifacts. Reliability values obtained via this approach can aid the architect in evaluating design alternatives. The approach is evaluated using sensitivity and uncertainty analysis.

Keywords: Reliability, Software Architecture, Dynamic Bayesian Networks.

1 Introduction

Software systems are now an inseparable part of our life. From online banking, to power grids, and nuclear power plants, software controls various aspects of people's daily lives. It is inevitable that dependability of these software systems (Reliability, Safety, Security, Availability, and Performance) has become as critical as the functionality they provide. Ensuring the dependability of the system after the bulk of implementation is complete as an afterthought (e.g., via analysis done during testing, deployment, and maintenance) is no longer an acceptable or cost-effective approach to quality assurance. Dependability must be "built into" the software systems, and doing so requires models to represent and further analyze dependability throughout the software development life cycle (SDLC). Early dependability analysis is particularly challenging, because the exact context in which the system will be used may be unknown. Moreover, the operational profile of the system, in the early stages of the development process may not be known apriori. Our research focuses on modeling and analyzing dependability of software systems during the software architecture phase.

S. Overhage et al. (Eds.): QoSA 2007, LNCS 4880, pp. 108-126, 2007.

The architecture and design phases are in many ways the most critical stages of the development process. Software architectures provide high-level abstractions for representing the structure, behavior, and key properties of complex software systems. Important design decisions –from specific interactions among components and connectors in the system, to policies for exception and error handling, to anticipating extensions to the system in the future– are made at the architecture phase. Changes to these decisions and adopting alternative approaches late in the development process can cost millions of dollars. While existing architecture modeling approaches offer sophisticated *qualitative* analyses of the architecture, *quantitative* models sill lag behind. Quantitative models are essential in comparing and contrasting design choices and identifying cost-effective approaches to defect mitigation. In this paper, we present our approach to predicting reliability of systems based on their software architecture.

Software reliability is the probability that the system will perform its intended functionality under specified design limits. Software reliability techniques are aimed at reducing or eliminating failures in software systems. Existing approaches to reliability modeling largely rely on the availability of implementation-level artifacts. Even those approaches applicable at the architecture level, require information about the operational profile that can only be obtained from a running system. Our approach is novel as it leverages standard software architecture models, and quantifies the system reliability in terms of specific architectural defects that may result in a failure, once the system is operational[1]. We do so by first predicting reliability of individual components, as a function of analysis results performed on their structure and behavior [21]. We then incorporate these component reliability values into a system-level reliability model. Our approach is applicable to cases where no runtime information is available, and can handle uncertainties associated with early reliability prediction.

Our reliability technique leverages well-known architectural modeling approaches and uses Dynamic Bayesian Networks [13] to perform reliability analysis. We evaluate the approach using sensitivity and uncertainty analyses applied to several case studies with two major goals in mind: to demonstrate that our approach to reliability prediction is both *possible* (i.e., as a proof of concept) and *meaningful*.

The rest of this paper is organized as follows: In Section 2, we provide background information, discuss the related work, and introduce the basics of Dynamic Bayesian Networks. We also introduce a running example. In Section 3 we present our reliability model and offer its evaluation in Section 4. Section 5 offers a high-level discussion of uncertainties associated with early reliability prediction. We conclude in Section 6 and discuss future directions of this research.

2 Background and Related Work

Modeling, estimating, and analyzing software reliability –during testing– is a discipline with over 30 years of history. Many reliability models have been proposed:

---

[1] We define an *error* as a mental mistake made by the designer or programmer. A *fault* or a *defect* is the manifestation of that error in the system: it is a requirements, design, or implementation flaw or deviation from a desired or intended state [11]. Finally software *failure* is the occurrence of an incorrect output as a result of an input value that is received, with respect to specification [18].

Black-box models treat the software system as a monolithic entity and ignore the internal structure of the system. *White-box* approaches on the other hand, consider a system's internal structure in reliability estimation. Goseva-Popstojanova et al. further classify white-box techniques into *path-based* and *state-based* [7]: path-based models compute software reliability based on the system's possible execution paths, while state-based models use the control flow graph to represent the system's internal structure and estimate its reliability analytically.

A common theme across all of these approaches however, is their reliance on implementation-level artifacts. Even those approaches assumed to be applicable to other development phases rely on estimates of the code size [5]. When incorporating architectural information, most approaches consider only the structure of the system. Exceptions are [6,19,26,27]: Reussner et al. [19] build architectural reliability models based on both structural and behavioral specifications of a system, but assume the reliability of individual component services to be known. Wang et al. [27] leverage architectural configuration while focusing on architectural styles for building a prediction model that is mostly concerned with sequential control flow across components. Gokhale et al. [6] offer an analytical approach that leverages software architecture, but relies on testing data to characterize failure behavior. Finally, Yacoub et al. [26] use a scenario-based model of a system's behavior and build component dependency graphs.

However, none of these approaches offer a compositional model that predicts the reliability of both the components and the entire system using the software architecture. They simply assume that the component reliability, or the reliability of some of its elements is known. Additionally, with the exception of [6], they rely on the availability of a running system to obtain the frequency of component service invocations. Our approach is different in that both our component- and system-level reliability models only rely on architectural models to predict reliability. Our approach thus, can be used to provide analysis of design decisions and their ramification on system reliability.

When predicting software reliability in the early stages of development, some level of uncertainty is inevitable. A few approaches assess the uncertainties in reliability estimation: using heuristics, with variable operational profiles, and via techniques such as method of moments and simulation-based techniques such as Monte Carlo simulation [7]. Other techniques however, assume fixed (apriori known) operational profiles and varying component reliability, and apply traditional sensitivity analysis [3, 25]. We address uncertainties using a set of parameters representing components' reliabilities, system startup process, and human-system interactions, as discussed in Section 5.

In our prior work, we leveraged architectural models of software components, and given the result of standard analysis, provided a prediction of the component's architectural reliability [21]. This approach is different from the related techniques above in that it only relies on architecture-level artifacts, and does not require runtime data. It does so by directly leveraging results obtained from architectural analysis to model components' failure behavior. Our component-level reliability model in turn, allows us to explore system-level reliability in a compositional way. In this paper, we describe the details of our system-level reliability model.

2.1 Dynamic Bayesian Networks

A Bayesian Network or Belief Network (BN) is a probabilistic graphical model in the form of a directed acyclic graph (DAG). The nodes in a BN represent variables, and the links connecting these nodes denote the dependency relations among them. A Bayesian Network models a stochastic relationship among the nodes, in terms of the conditional probabilities of some nodes with respect to the others. Given the topology of a BN and the probability distribution values at some of the nodes, the probability distribution value at other nodes may be obtained. This is known as *inference*. A BN consists of two parts: *qualitative* and *quantitative*. The qualitative part is a DAG consisting of set of nodes and directed links connecting them. The links denote the dependency between probability distribution values at each node. The quantitative part embodies conditional probabilities among nodes and their parents.

Bayesian Networks have been extensively used in Artificial Intelligence, Machine Learning, Decision Making, Medical Diagnosis, and Bioinformatics. They have also been used to model reliability of software systems during testing, based on the operational profile obtained from system monitoring [2,12,16]. However, little work has been done on predicting reliability early in the development process.

Dynamic Bayesian Networks (DBNs) is an extension of the basic BN and incorporates the concept of time into the analysis. In DBNs, in addition to the basic links described above, *delay links* are used to associate *timing* with the model [13]. We leverage DBNs to model time-dependent cyclical relations among reliabilities at various states, resulting from interactions in the system. Inference and other analysis performed on a BN can also be performed on a DBN. To do this, a DBN is first expanded for a period of time resulting in a "regular" Bayesian Network.

2.2 SCRover Case Study

Throughout this paper, we use a simple example of a robotic rover to illustrate the introduced concepts. *SCRover* [24], is designed and developed under the HDCP Project in collaboration with NASA's Jet Propulsion Laboratory, and in accordance with their Mission Data System (MDS) methodology. To avoid unnecessary complexity, we discuss a simplified version of the application with a particular focus on SCRover's "wall following" behavior. The rover uses a laser rangefinder to determine the distance to the wall, drives forward while maintaining a fixed distance from that wall, and turns both inside and outside corners as needed. This scenario also involves sensing and controlled locomotion, including reducing speed when approaching obstacles.

As shown in Figure 1, the system contains five main components: *controller, estimator, sensor, actuator*, and a *database*. The sensor component gathers physical data (e.g., distance from the wall) from the environment. The estimator accesses the data and passes them to the controller for control decisions. The controller issues commands to the actuator to change the direction or speed of the rover. The database stores the "state" of the rover at certain intervals or when values change.

3 System Reliability Modeling

An architectural approach to system modeling considers the system's structure in terms of its constituent components and their configuration, as well as system's behavior in terms of the interaction among components. We use an approach to architectural modeling called *Quartet*, to comprehensively model the properties of a software system [22]. It offers four complementary views to model *interface, static* and *dynamic behavior* and the *interaction protocol* of each component in the system. These views can be analyzed to detect possible inconsistencies both within a component's models and across models of communicating components. The inconsistencies signify architectural defects, which may result in a failure at runtime, thus adversely affect the system's reliability.

Using Quartet, components exhibit an interaction protocol that determines their code of behavior in relation to other components. The overall behavior of a system is thus represented by a compositional model that combines interaction protocols of all components. A suitable model for reliability prediction at the architectural level must take the compositional nature of behavioral models into consideration. Architecture-level reliability analysis can be leveraged to perform trade-off analysis, aimed at evaluating design alternatives.

Our approach for predicting a system's reliability is compositional in nature: the system's reliability is estimated in terms of the reliabilities of its constituent component and their interactions. We extend our work on component-level reliability prediction [21], and combine individual components' reliabilities via a compositional model of their interactions, to estimate system reliability.

Dynamic Bayesian Networks (DBNs) are used to model components interactions in terms of the causal relationships among their reliabilities; when a change of state in a component causes a change of state in another component, the reliability of the second component depends on the reliability of the first. This DBN is then augmented with the

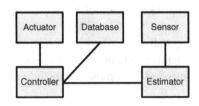

Fig. 1. SCRover's Software Architecture

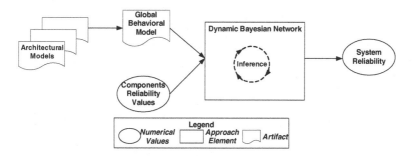

Fig. 2. Overview of the System Reliability Prediction Approach

notion of a failure state: any state in a component may result in a failure. Unreliability at each state can impact the probability of the system's failure (i.e., its unreliability).

Our approach involves two major steps: first we build a compositional model representing the overall behavior of the system in terms of interactions among its components. This model is then used for stochastic analysis of the system's reliability.

Since our approach is intended to be applied in the early stages of the software development life-cycle, lack of knowledge about the system's operational profile poses a major challenge in building a reliability model. In the absence of such data, we use an analytical approach that relies on domain knowledge as well as the system's architecture. In cases where an operational profile is available (e.g., when analyzing the reliability of a system that is a minor upgrade to an existing version), our reliability model can leverage existing data, and provide a more accurate reliability analysis.

Figure 2 shows a high-level overview of our approach. Architectural models of systems structure and behavior form the core of our model. A Global Behavioral Model (GBM) is constructed to represent the system's behavior in terms of the behavior of its components. A DBN then leverages the GBM as well as the individual components' reliabilities to predict system reliability. The rest of this section, presents our approach to modeling the global behavior of a system as well as the Bayesian reliability model.

3.1 Global Behavioral Modeling

The behavior of a software system is a function of the collective behavior of its constituent components. These components interact to achieve system-level goals. The interactions are often very complex, and capturing them requires sophisticated modeling techniques, capable of representing request-response relations, as well as related timing issues. These interactions are often described in terms of components' provided and required functionality, exhibited through their interfaces.

We model the collective behavior of components using a set of concurrent state machines [8]. Each state machine within this concurrent model represents the interaction protocol of a single component. Figure depicts the conceptual view of the interactions among the SCRover's components. The left hand side diagram is the view of the system's configuration. The right hand side shows a concurrent state machine

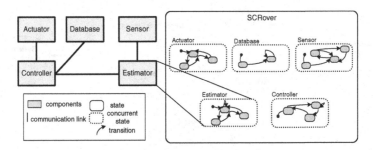

Fig. 3. View of SCRover System's Collective Behavior

containing interaction protocols of individual components. In the interests of clarity, labels on the transitions, events, actions, parameters, and conditions have been omitted.

In a concurrent state machine representing the system-level behavior of n communicating components, at any point in time, the active state of the system is represented using a set of component states $\{Sm_1.S_i., Sm_2.S_j..., Sm_n.S_k\}$, where n is the number of components in the system, and $Sm_k.S_i$ corresponds to the active state (S_i) in the state machine Sm_k corresponding to the kth component. The interactions among components are represented via *event/action* pairs. Each event/action pair acts as a synchronizer among the state machines and describes how invocation of a component's services affects another component. Figure 3 depicts the interaction protocols of the controller, estimator, and actuator components in the SCRover system. To avoid unnecessary complexity in this discussion, we discuss the SCRover's system model in terms of these three components. However, the approach and techniques presented here can be applied to a greater number of components.

The Statechart semantics [8,9] permit two types of interactions among concurrent state machines. The first type concerns concurrent events. Given the appropriate active state of components, *all of the transitions with the same event are activated at the same time*. For instance, in the case of the SCRover model (Figure 4), if the active state of the controller component is *controller.S_2* and the active state of the actuator component is *actuator.S_1*, then invocation of the *executeSpeedChange* interface results in generation of the corresponding event, which in turn causes a change of state in both components (to *controller.S_3*, and *actuator.S_2*, respectively). Note that the generation of this event has no effect on the state of the estimator component, regardless of its active state.

The second type of interaction concerns the event/action pair semantics. Given the appropriate state of components, *generation of an event in one component may result in the invocation of an action, which in turn may result in generation of another event in another component*. In SCRover, assuming that *{controller.S_2, estimator.S_1, actuator.S_1}* is the system's active state, invocation of the *executeSpeedChange* interface in the actuator component results in generation of the *executeSpeedChange* event. In turn, this results in the triggering of the corresponding transition in the controller component, causing the *notifyDistChange* action. The concurrent nature of

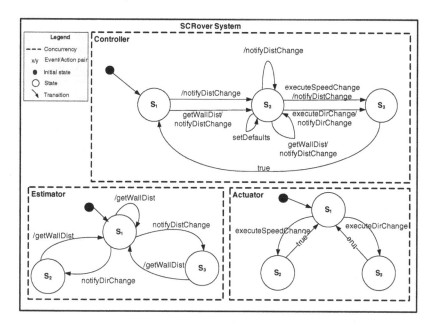

Fig. 4. SCRover's Global Behavioral View in terms of Interacting Components

the three state machines results in triggering of the *notifyDistChange* transition in the estimator component (event caused by the action in the controller component), as well as the *executeSpeedChange* transition in the actuator component (original event). The new active state of the system will then be *{controller.S₃, estimator.S₃, actuator.S₂}*. The above semantics summarized here and presented in [8,9] form the basis for the Global Behavioral Model. We use the GBM to construct our reliability model.

3.2 System Reliability Modeling

Our Bayesian reliability model uses the Global Behavioral Model as its core. This model represents the dependencies between reliability values at various system states, incorporates the notion of failure nodes, and offers reliability analysis of the system based on its architectural models. Our approach leverages a classification of architectural defects [23] to differentiate among different classes of failures. However, the model can be used to either differentiate among various types of failures, or a generic failure state can be used. When multiple failure types are modeled, the overall reliability is estimated in terms of the cumulative effect of different types of failures in the system.

3.2.1 Qualitative Representation of the Bayesian Network
In this section, we describe how to a build the graphical part of the dynamic bayesian network given the model of components' interactions. The DBN is described in terms of nodes and links, denoting the reliability dependency among the nodes.

Nodes. Each node in the Bayesian Network corresponds to a state in the GBM. Moreover, a "super" node (*init*) is added to represent the instantiation of the system. This node will be used to model the reliability of the system's startup process. In addition, for every component, a set of *failure nodes* are added to the Bayesian Network. Each failure node represents the occurrence of a specific type of failure in a component. A failure may be due to an internal fault in a component, or to its interaction with the rest of the system.

We also incorporate individual component reliability values (called *raw* reliability values) in the system reliability estimation. These values may be obtained from other methods such as [21], or in the case of off-the-shelf components could be advertised by the vendor. The raw component reliability values are represented as a node in the BN. For each component, this node serves as a root (a parent to the node corresponding to its initial state). Alternative approaches may be taken in this regard. We discuss the rationale for this decision in Section 5.

Links. Three types of links in the Bayesian model capture the dependencies between reliabilities at various nodes: *instantiation, failure,* and *dependency links.* Instantiation links are added from the init node to all nodes corresponding to initial states of components. They model the system's startup process and signify that the reliability of the system depends on the failure-free instantiation of all of its components.

Failure links represent the possibility of occurrence of various types of failures in the different states of the system. While in general, every type of failure may occur while the system is in any particular state, we employ the result of our architectural analysis to determine the relevance of specific failure types at each state. Particularly, if a specific defect of type d_1 associated with a component service is revealed as a result of some analysis, we designate a failure link between each state where an outgoing transition corresponding to that operation exists, and the failure node f_i (corresponding to defect d_i). Details of our technique may be found in [20].

Finally, dependency links depict the reliability relationship among various nodes in the system. There are two types of dependency links: *inter-component* and *intra-component* links. The intra-component links are directly derived from each component's protocol model. For every transition in the interaction protocol model of the component, there is a directed arc from the node corresponding to its origin state, to the node corresponding to its destination in the BN. These links indicate that reliability at each node depends on the reliability of its parent node. For example, in the SCRover's GBM, a transition from *controller.S1* to *controller.S2* signifies that the system's reliability at *controller.S2* depends on the reliability of the system at *controller.S1,* justifying a link in the Bayesian Network from the latter to the former.

The inter-component dependency links represent the relationship between reliabilities of the states among interacting components. The notion of event/action interactions described earlier serves as the logical core of these links. Recall that generation of an event in one component may *cause* a change of state in a different component. More specifically, for each e_i/a_o pair in a component's state machine Sm_j, we seek all transitions in all other components' state machines where an event matches the action a_o. A link is then added from the origin node of e_i / a_o in Sm_i to the destination nodes of all events a_o in the other state machines. The inter-component links denote that the reliability (probability of success) in the nodes of interacting components are influenced by the reliability at the node of the component initiating the interaction.

A final issue concerns *cycles* in a Bayesian Network. By definition, a Bayesian Network is a directed acyclic graph. Following the above approach may result in creation of cycles in the graph. However, it is important to note that these cycles are time sensitive: for example, while there are links in both directions between the *estimator.S_1* and *estimator.S_3* in Figure 4, the two links are not representing a dependency between the two nodes in the same time-step. That is, since the estimator component cannot be in both *estimator.S_1* and *estimator.S_3* states at the same time, the cycle introduced in the BN graph represents reliability dependencies at different points in time. To address the issue of cycles, before adding a link to our Bayesian model, we check for cycles that may be created once the link is added. If by adding the link a cycle is generated, that link is marked as a *Delay Link* (dashed lines in our graphs). Delay links are a standard concept in time-sensitive BNs and convert a simple Bayesian Network to a Dynamic Bayesian Network (DBN) [13]. Inference performed on a BN can also be performed on a DBN by expanding the model for a period of time. The result of this expansion is a "regular" Bayesian Network which depicts the reliability dependencies over time.

3.2.2 Quantitative Representation of the Bayesian Network

A major challenge of reliability prediction before the system's implementation phase is its unknown operational profile. If the operational profile of the system were available, the conditional probability values at various nodes could be obtained via statistical techniques. The problem of estimating reliability would be then transformed to performing standard inference methods on the available data. However, given the uncertainties associated with early reliability prediction, analytical methods must be employed. One such technique relies on the software architect, to derive formula that describe the conditional probability values at each node, given the reliability of the parent nodes. This is done by leveraging the known information about the system (its topology, components' interactions, and individual components' reliabilities).

In this section, we discuss a few basic relationships between the reliability of a node and its parents. This step of the reliability prediction process is application specific, and the software architect must define these relationships given the application. In particular we define two main relationships and offer insights into a few others.

A node and its parents are known to be in a *serial* relationship when the node's reliability directly depends on the reliability of *all* of its n parents. In other words, a low reliability of any of its parents, directly (negatively) affects the reliability of the node, regardless of the reliability of the other parents:

$$R_{node} = \prod_{i=1}^{n} R_i$$

where: R_{node}: Reliability of a give node

R_i = Reliability of the parent node i

A *parallel* relationship between a node and its parents represents the concept of redundancy. The node's reliability is at least equal to or greater than the reliability of its most reliable parent. In this case, the *unreliability* of a node with n statistically independent parallel parents is the product of the unreliability value of all parents. In other words, in a parallel setting, all n parents must have very low reliability for the node to be very unreliable, i.e., if any of the n parents is highly reliable, then the node will still be very reliable:

$$R_{node} = 1 - \prod_{i=1}^{n} (1 - R_i)$$

where: R_{node}: Reliability of a give node

R_i = Reliability of the parent node i

Other customized configurations may describe the relationship between parent and child nodes in a complex system. Examples include *min*, *max*, and partial parallel configuration known as *k-out-of-n parallel configuration*. In the latter type, k or more parents out of the total of n parents of a node must fail, in order for the node to fail. An example of a type of system when this configuration is relevant is in a four-engine airplane, where a minimum of two engines are required for it to be able to fly and still satisfy minimal reliability requirements *($k=2$ out of $n=4$)*.

3.2.3 System Reliability Analysis
Once the relationships among all the nodes have been devised by the architect, and given the *raw* component reliability values (e.g., obtained by component-level architectural reliability models [21]), the probability of various types of failures in the system can be estimated using standard Bayesian inference. Aggregation of probabilities of various failures represent the unreliability of the system. Determining the aggregation formula that combines probabilities of various failures is application specific. For the purpose of our evaluation, we use a generic approach using a Radar Chart (a.k.a. Polar Chart and Spider Chart) to calculate the cumulative effect of each component's failure probabilities on the system. The value of each failure probability (F_i) is plotted on an axis on the chart. The number of axes is equal to the number of failure nodes (*numF*), the maximum length of each axis is one, and the angles between all axes are equal $(\frac{2\pi}{numF})$. The area under the polygon formed by various failure probabilities can be calculated by a triangulation method as follows:

$$area = \frac{1}{2} \times \frac{1}{MaxArea} \times \sin(\frac{2\pi}{numF}) \times (F_1 \times F_2 + F_2 \times F_3 + ... + F_{numF} \times F_1)$$

where *MaxArea* is the maximum surface area of the polygon when all F_i values are at the maximum of one.

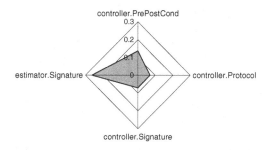

Fig. 5. Cumulative Effect of Different Failures in SCRover

Figure 5 depicts the instantiation of the Radar chart for the SCRover system. Four axes represent controller's *PrePostCondition, Protocol,* and *Signature* failures[2] as well as the estimator's *Signature* failure. A point closer to the center on any axis depicts a low value, while a point near the edge of the polygon depicts a high value for the corresponding failure probability. The cumulative effect of the failures can be obtained by calculating the surface area formed by all the axes. Using this technique, the overall system reliability for the SCRover is estimated as 0.982

$$area = \frac{1}{2} \times \frac{1}{2} \times sin(\frac{2\pi}{4})[0.136829*0.07093+0.07093*0.07093+$$
$$0.07093*0.262404+0.262404*0.136829]$$

$$Reliability = 1-area = 0.982686738$$

Other techniques, such as those incorporating costs into this aggregation may be employed [20] if analysis beyond a basic reliability prediction is desired.

4   Evaluation

Evaluation of our reliability model is presented in terms of sensitivity analyses aimed at demonstrating that architecture-level reliability modeling of software systems is both *possible* and *meaningful*. The results are demonstrated in the context of two case studies. The analyses demonstrate that the model reacts meaningfully to changes in its parameters. Moreover, they demonstrate that our approach can be used to identify critical components in a system whose mitigation has a greater impact on improving the system reliability. Furthermore, analysis can determine the effect of specific system configurations on the reliability, which can be used as a decision support tool for evaluating various design alternatives.

---

[2] Failure types discussed here are tied to an architectural defect classification [23]. Discussion of failure types is outside the scope of this paper. Other classifications may be used without impacting the approach.

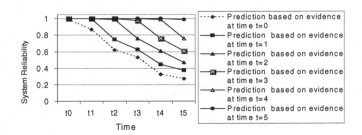

Fig. 6. Updated Prediction of Reliability over Time based on New Evidence

Figure 6 depicts reliability analysis of the SCRover system over a period of five time steps. Recall that system reliability at time t_i depends on the reliability of the system at previous time steps $t_1, t_2,..., t_{i-1}$. Lack of failure at time t_j can be treated as *evidence* for new inferences to obtain the reliability at time t_{j+1}. The y-axis depicts the system reliability while the x-axis shows the progression of time. Each curve depicts the system reliability over time, based on evidence (of lack of failure) in the previous time steps. For example the curve on the bottom depicts the reliability over 5 time steps. The next curve shows the changes to reliability once evidence of lack of failure at time t_0 is incorporated into the model used in the previous curve. The third curve incorporates evidence from t_0 and t_1, and so on.

Sensitivity analysis based on individual component reliabilities can help identify critical components in the system. Using our analysis, we found that changes in the reliability of the controller component have the most significant impact on the system reliability. The sensitivity of the model to the system's startup process was also studied. This *init* node in the DBN is specifically designated to model the uncertainties associated with the system's startup process. The architect must supply a value for this parameter, and such values may depend on the development process. Discussion of how to estimate this parameter is beyond the scope of this paper [20]. Sensitivity of the SCRover model to changes in the reliability of the startup process is depicted in Figure 7 (left), and the results are consistent with our intuition: as the reliability of the system's startup process decreases, the system's ability to perform its operations successfully decreases (regardless of the reliabilities of individual components).

Finally we analyzed the sensitivityf the model to the failure probabilities. These probabilities are estimated using Bayesian inference given the individual components' reliabilities, and their interactions. However, as discussed earlier, the inference can be updated using evidence that may be available. We model elimination of a particular failure by assigning it zero probability, and observing the effect on the system's reliability. This type of analysis could be used as a decision tool to devise cost-effective defect mitigation strategies, by prioritizing failures. Figure 7 (right) shows that ensuring that the estimator's signature failure does not occur has the largest impact on the system's reliability, improving it from the 90% (original prediction) to 97.7%.

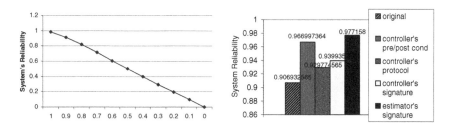

Fig. 7. System Reliability Given Different Startup Process Reliability (left), and the Effect of Elimination of Particular Failures on SCRover System's Reliability (right)

In summary, sensitivity analyses on the SCRover demonstrate that our reliability model is meaningful, and that the results are useful in making architectural decisions.

We also performed similar analysis in the context of other case studies, including NASA's Object Oriented Data Technology (OODT) system [15]. OODT is a methodology, a middleware, and a software architecture for development of distributed data-intensive systems. The middleware offers access to geographically distributed and heterogeneous data sources, by concealing the details of mediation at each data source, and offering an extensible and flexible data sharing and transporting methodology. An OODT system consists of a set of *Clients*, one or more *ProfileHandlers*, and a set of *ProfileServers*. *Clients* request a set of services that may be provided by different *ProfileServers*. The Client is oblivious to the number, type, and location of these servers. *ProfileHandlers* act as mediators, and route requests and responses between Clients and Servers. A high-level architecture and the corresponding DBN of such a system is depicted in Figure 8.

In our adaptation of OODT we assumed that multiple disparate databases provide data to clients via the web. In particular, two independent ProfileServers serve two independent datasets. In this scenario, since the two servers access independent and non-identical data sources, it is crucial for both servers to operate reliably, in order for the system to operate reliably. In other words, the reliability of the system depends on the reliable operation of all of its components, including the two servers. This is in contrast to cases where one server may be a backup for the other server, in which case reliable operation of at least one of the servers is sufficient for the reliable operation of the system. We first analyze the system when the two independent and different datasets are configured, and later demonstrate the result of modeling a different scenario, where the two servers are considered to act as back-ups for identical datasets.

Figure 9 (left) depicts the effect of changes to components' initial reliabilities on the system reliability. Since the two ProfileServer components are effectively identical in their functionality (although serving different datasets), as expected, changes to their reliabilities show very similar trends in the changes in the system's reliability. Additional analysis confirmed this results and may be found in [20].

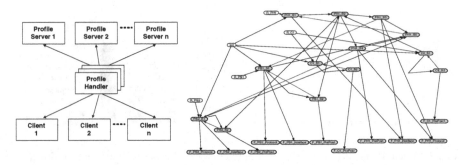

Fig. 8. OODT's (a) High-level Architecture (left) and Bayesian Network (Right)

Similar to the SCRover experiment, the overall system reliability decreases over time (unless evidence of failure free operations is incorporated). Moreover, as depicted in Figure 9 (left), it can also be seen that changes in the ProfileHandler and Client components result in a greater range of system reliability. For example, changes to the reliability of the Client component result in estimated system reliability values ranging from 18% to 91%, while changes to the reliability of the ProfileServer components result in system reliability variations between 52% and 91%.

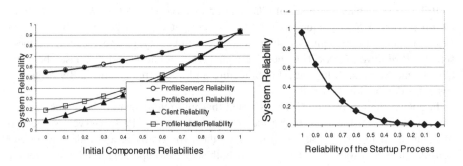

Fig. 9. OODT Model's Sensitivity to Different Initial Component Reliabilities (left) and Different Startup Process Reliabilities (Right)

Analysis of the model's sensitivity to the reliability of the startup process is shown in Figure 9 (right). Similar to other experiments, system's reliability has a direct relationship with the reliability of the startup process.

We have also performed analysis to evaluate the impact of system configuration and interaction semantics on systems's reliability. In the case of OODT, we model redundancy by designating the two ProfileServer components as backups for one another. The left diagram in Figure 10 demonstrates the system reliability (depicted via a line) as the reliability of ProfileServer 1 increases. The diagram on the right shows that while increasing the reliability of ProfileServer1, the system reliability remains unchanged (comparing to the left), if the reliability of ProfileServer2 decreases.

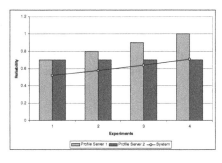 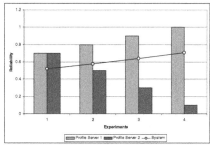

Fig. 10. Modeling Redundancy in OODT

We also studied the effect of changes to the system's structure, on the overall system's reliability. While a structural change is considered an addition or removal of components in a system, the impact on the interactions among components directly affects the system reliability. For example, in the case of the OODT system, the ProfileHandler component seems to act as a bottleneck for the system. As the number of clients increases, the load on the ProfileHandler increases. This may adversely affect the system reliability. To mitigate the problem, additional ProfileHandlers may be instantiated to balance the load.

Reliability results based on several configurations are shown in Figure 11. The x-axis represents various configurations while the y and z-axes represent time and system reliability, respectively. At each time step, an increase in the number of clients, adversely affects the reliability. However, once a new instance of the ProfileHandler is added to the system, the reliability improves. The new ProfileHandler component is set up such that it is responsible for handling communication to and from the fourth and fifth Clients. It can be seen that the reliability of the system with two ProfileHandlers is similar to the reliability of the system with three Clients and a single ProfileHandler, which can be rationalized, given the load balancing described above.

Analysis of the OODT system further confirms that the system-level reliability model produces meaningful and useful results. Our experience with a set of synthesized models, as well as other case studies confirm the conclusions presented here.

Remark. Traditionally, many of the analyses performed on Bayesian Networks are NP-hard [4]. In our approach, Bayesian Networks are only used in a simplified *predictive* context: given the probabilistic relations among the nodes (assigned by the domain expert), we predict the probability of failure nodes. Consequently, the complexity of our analysis is greatly reduced and can be described as a function of the number of *nodes* in the system, and the *time* period which the analysis is performed. Furthermore, by incorporating evidence of the system's reliability at time t_i when estimating the reliability at times $t_{i+1}, t_{i+2}, \ldots$ we can systematically control the number of nodes to disallow the model to grow arbitrarily complex.

On the other hand, the number of nodes in the DBN in turn, depends on the number of states in the Interaction Protocol models of the components that comprise the system. The complexity of the Interaction Protocol Models is bound by the number of externally visible interfaces of each component. The principles of component-based software engineering, and encapsulation in Object-Oriented design, typically prevent a component from having arbitrarily large number of interfaces. Consequently, following good software design practices directly helps in creating models with reasonable numbers of externally visible interfaces. In turn, this curbs the model's complexity.

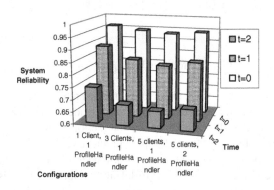

Fig. 11. Impact of Different Configurations on OODT System Reliability

5 Modeling Uncertainties

Modeling reliability of a software system in a compositional manner early during software development process, when implementation is not available and the operational profile is unknown, requires dealing with various sources of uncertainties. Accommodating these uncertainties results in a more realistic prediction of the reliability of the architecture. Our approach makes an effort to handle a variety of uncertainties: *uncertainty of components reliability values, uncertainty of system startup process,* and *uncertainties of human-system interactions.*

Component reliability estimation typically happens in isolation. A component, whether an "in-house" or an OTS one, is designed, built, and tested either in isolation, or in an environment that may not be typical of its intended use. Consequently, the reliability values associated with a component may not be accurate if the component is used in a different setting. While such reliability values are useful as an "estimate" of how component may perform in a system, it cannot be treated as an absolute number. Treating component reliability values as nodes in our DBN, facilitates evaluation of uncertainties. This is consistent with the stochastic nature of our approach.

Furthermore, building a system out of fully reliable components may not result in perfect reliability of the final system. This may be due to various sources of uncertainties introduced in the integration process. Starting up a system is a critical step in the integration, which could greatly impact its reliability. By introducing an *init* node in the DBN, we have allowed uncertainties to be associated with the startup process.

Finally, uncertainties of human interactions with a software system is an important and potentially serious problem when dealing with software systems. One way to eliminate such uncertainties is to design appropriate constraints in the system. Using the Quartet, such constraints can be implemented as pre/post conditions, guards, and other types of assertions in the functional specification. While some harmful interactions may be prevented this way, other measures may need to be blended into the reliability model to address this form of uncertainty. Modeling human-computer interactions, and associated uncertainties is beyond the scope of our approach.

6 Conclusion and Future Work

Despite the maturity of software reliability techniques, predicting the reliability of software systems before implementation has not received adequate attention in the past. Studies have shown that early discovery of defects in the software development life cycle results in a more cost effective mitigation process. Reliability prediction early during the software development life cycle is critical in building reliability into the software system. Given the uncertainties associated with software systems early in the development process, appropriate reliability models must be able to accommodate uncertainties and produce meaningful results. Our approach to reliability prediction leverages Dynamic Bayesian Networks and calculates system's overall reliability as a function of individual components' reliabilities, and their complex interactions. Our focus so far has been on building a basic architectural reliability model. In the future, we plan to continue this research in several promising directions including modeling reliability of software connectors, the effect of architectural styles or patterns on reliability, and trade-off analysis aimed at identifying design alternatives in software product families.

Acknowledgment

This work was supported by the NSF 0509539, 0312780, 0091474, 0417274, and 9985441 grants. This work also made use of Integrated Media Systems Center Shared Facilities supported by the NSF under Cooperative Agreement No. EEC-9529152. Any opinions, findings, conclusions or recommendations expressed in this material are those of the authors and do not necessarily reflect those of the National Science Foundations.

References

1   Allen, R., Garlan, D.: A Formal Basis for Architecture Connection. ACM Transactions on Software Engineering and Methodology 6(3), 213–249 (1997)
2   Amasaki, S., et al.: Bayesian Belief Network for Assessing the Likelihood of Fault Content. In: Proceedings of the 14th International Symposium on Software Reliability Engineering (2003)
3   Cheung, R.C.: A user-oriented software reliability model. IEEE Trans. on Software Eng. (1980)
4   Cooper, G.F.: The Computational Complexity of Probabilistic Inference Using Bayesian Belief Networks. Artificial Intelligence 42(2-3), 393–405 (1990)

5 Dalal, S.R.: Software Reliability Models: A Selective Survey and New Directions. In: Pham, H. (ed.) Handbook of Reliability Engineering, Springer, Heidelberg (2003)

6 Gokhale, S., Wong, W.E., Trivedi, K.S., Horgan, J.R.: An Analytical Approach to Architecture-Based Software Reliability Prediction. In: Proc. of Intl. Performability and Dependability Symposium (IPDS 1998), pp. 13–22, Durham, NC (September 1998)

7 Goseva-Popstojanova, K., Mathur, A.P., Trivedi, K.S.: Comparison of Architecture-Based Software Reliability Models. In: Proceedings of the 12th IEEE International Symposium on Software Reliability Engineering (ISSRE-2001), Hong Kong (November 2001)

8 Harel, D.: Statecharts: A visual formalism for complex systems. Science of Computer Programming 8(3) (June 1987)

9 Harel, D., Naamad, A.: The STATEMATE Semantics of Statecharts. ACM Transactions on Software Engineering Methodology 5(4), 293–333 (1996)

10 Jelinski, Z., Moranda, P.B.: Software Reliability Research. In: Freigerger, W. (ed.) Statistical Computer Performance Evaluation, Academic Press, London (1972)

11 Leveson, N.: Safeware: System Safety and Computers. Addison Wesley, Reading (1995)

12 Littlewood, B.A., Verrall, J.L.: A Bayesian Reliability Growth Model for Computer Software. Applied Statistics 22, 332–346 (1973)

13 Murphy, K.: A Brief Introduction to Graphical Models and Bayesian Networks (1998), http://www.cs.ubc.ca/ murphyk/bayes/.html

14 Musa, J.D., Okumoto, K.: Logarithmic Poisson Execution Time Model for Software Reliability Measurement. In: Proceedings of Compsac 1984, pp. 230–238 (1984)

15 NASA Object Oriented Data Technology (OODT), http://oodt.jpl.nasa.gov

16 Okamura, H., Furumura, H., Dohi, T.: Bayesian Approach to Estimate Software Reliability in Fault-removal Environment. In: Proceedings of the 15th IEEE International Symposium on Software Reliability Engineering (ISSRE 2004) (Fast Abstract), Saint-Malo, France (2004)

17 Pai, G.J., Dugan, J.B.: Enhancing Software Reliability Estimation Using Bayesian Networks and Fault Trees. In: Proc. of the 12th IEEE Int. Symp. on Software Reliability Engineering (2001)

18 Pham, H.: Software Reliability. Springer, Heidelberg (2002)

19 Reussner, R., Schmidt, H., Poernomo, I.: Reliability Prediction for Component-based Software Architectures. Journal of Systems and Software 66(3) (2003)

20 Roshandel, R.: Calculating Architectural Reliability via Modeling and Analysis, Ph.D. Dissertation, Computer Science Department, University of Southern California (2006)

21 Roshandel, R., Banerjee, S., Cheung, L., Medvidovic, N., Golubchik, L.: Estimating Software Component Reliability by Leveraging Architectural Models. In: Proceedings 28th International Conference on Software Engineering (ICSE 2006), Shanghai, China (May 2006)

22 Roshandel, R., Medvidovic, N.: Multi-View Software Component Modeling for Dependability. In: de Lemos, R., Gacek, C., Romanovsky, A. (eds.) Architecting Dependable Systems II. LNCS, vol. 3069, Springer, Heidelberg (2004)

23 Roshandel, R., Schmerl, B., Medvidovic, N., Garlan, D., Zhang, D.: Understanding Tradeoffs among Different Architectural Modeling Approaches. In: Proc. of the 4th Working IEEE/IFIP Conference on Software Architecture, WICSA 2004, Oslo, Norway (June 2004)

24 SCRover Project: http://cse.usc.edu/hdcp/iscr

25 Seigrist, K.: Reliability of systems with Markov transfer of control. IEEE Trans. on Software Engineering (1988)

26 Yacoub, S., Cukic, B., Ammar, H.: Scenario-Based Analysis of Component-based Software. In: Proceedings of the Tenth International Symp. on Software Reliability Engineering (1999)

27 Wang, W., Wu, Y., Chen, M.: An Architecture-based Software Reliability Model. In: Proceedings of Pacific Rim International Symposium on Dependable Computing (1999)

Performance Prediction of Web Service Workflows*

Moreno Marzolla[1] and Raffaela Mirandola[2]

[1] INFN Sezione di Padova, via Marzolo 8, 35131 Padova, Italy
`moreno.marzolla@pd.infn.it`
[2] Dip. di Elettronica e Informazione, Politecnico di Milano, via Ponzio 34/5, 20133
Milano, Italy
`mirandola@elet.polimi.it`

Abstract. Web Services play an important role in the Service-oriented Architecture paradigm, as they allow services to be selected on-the-fly to build applications out of existing components. In this scenario, the Business Process Execution Language notation can be used as an *orchestration language* which allows the user to describe interactions with Web Services in a standard way. The performance of a BPEL workflow is a very important factor for deciding which components must be selected, or to choose whether a given sequence of interactions can provide the requested quality of service. Due to its very dynamic nature, workflow performance evaluation can not be accomplished using traditional, heavy-weight techniques. In this paper we present a multi-view approach for the performance prediction of service-based applications encompassing both users and service provider(s) perspectives. As a first step towards the realization of this integrated framework we present an efficient approach for performance assessment of Web Service workflows described using the BPEL notation. Starting from annotated BPEL and WSDL specifications, we derive performance bounds on response time and throughput. In such a way users are able to assess the efficiency of a BPEL workflow, while service provider(s) can perform sizing studies or estimate performance gains of alternative upgrades to existing systems. To bring this approach to fruition we developed a prototype tool called `bpel2qnbound`, using which we analyze a simple case study.

1   Introduction

The Service-oriented Architecture (SOA) paradigm foresees the creation of business applications from independently developed services. In this vision, providers offer similar competing services corresponding to a functional description of a service; these offerings can differ significantly in some Quality of Service (QoS) attributes like performance [1]. On the other side, prospective users of services

---

* Work partially supported by EU FP7 STREP Project "PLASTIC" (IST 026955), and by Italian MUR-FIRB project "ART DECO".

S. Overhage et al. (Eds.): QoSA 2007, LNCS 4880, pp. 127–144, 2007.

dynamically choose the best offerings for their purposes. Using the SOA paradigm to build applications, services can be dynamically selected and integrated at run-time, so enabling system properties like flexibility, adaptiveness, and reusability.

In this context, the key point is to build applications through the composition of available services. The application can be specified as a process in Business Process Execution Language (BPEL) language in which the composed Web Services (WSs) are specified at an abstract level. The interfaces of individual services are specified using Web Service Description Language (WSDL), the W3C standard to model WSs interfaces, with documented quality properties. Specifically, the agreed performance attributes and levels can be specified by means of appropriate notations that augment the service specifications [2].

Applications built on services face different challenges: on one hand they should ensure that users experience the required performance, and on the other hand they have to maximize the resource utilization, so that provider incomes are maximize. Besides, due to the high dynamism of the applications, the quality assessment should be performed both at development and at run time. In fact the quality of the application depend not only on the selected services but also on the underlying support systems and on the network resources.

All these aspects pose a mix of new and old problems whose solution give rise to a multi-view approach employing different techniques to performance analysis/prediction. Specifically we envisage a new approach called Multi-views Approach for Performance analysis of web Services (MAPS) that encompasses users and providers viewpoints. One of the goal of MAPS is to validate the provided performance of an application keeping the aspects strictly pertaining to the observed system separated from the aspects that depend on the underlying platform.

To this end we distinguish two different levels: the first one, called MAPS-U(sers), is concerned with the description of the application level behavior, described as a BPEL workflow. The second level, called MAPS-P(roviders), describes the physical resources where the provided services are deployed. Those levels are combined, and we show how to derive performance bounds based on the well-known operational laws of Queueing Network (QN) analysis [3]. The bounds can be used to analyse bottlenecks at the system specification level, without requiring the explicit derivation of the performance model. This makes the approach well suited for efficiently answering many performance-related questions without the need for providing too many details.

The advantage of the proposed approach is that performance bounds can be obtained with little computational effort, allowing the client to quickly answer a set of common performance-related questions arising during the application development cycle. If necessary, more accurate bounds can be derived by simply applying different techniques (e.g., the one described in [4]). Our approach can be applied: (1) at design time, to select services based on their expected performance, or to estimate the expected overall system performance; (2) at run time to reconfigure the system, e.g., to deal with changes of users requirements or with modification of the underlying environment. On the other hand, a more complex, detailed and precise approach can be applied off-line at the resource level, to update the performance information published with the services.

To implement part of the proposed approach, we developed a prototype tool called **bpel2qnbound**, using which it is possible to parse of the annotated BPEL (and associated WSDL) specifications and obtain as outputs the performance bounds, as will be shown in more details in the following sections.

This paper is organized as follows. Section 2 briefly surveys related work. In Section 3 we present the proposed multi-view approach, while in Section 4 we give the details of the approach for early performance assessment of workflows described using a combination of annotated BPEL and WSDL descriptions. In Section 5 we show how the proposed approach can be applied to a case study. Finally, conclusions and future work are described in Section 6.

2 Related Work

Recently, QoS issues in WSs selection and composition have obtained great interest in the Web Service research community. Different approaches have been followed so far, spanning the use of QoS ontologies [5], the definition of ad-hoc methods in QoS-aware framework [6,7], and the application of optimization algorithms [8,9,10].

One of the first works in this area is proposed in [1] where a framework for composed services modeling and QoS evaluation is presented. A composite service is modeled as a directed weighted graph where each node corresponds to a WS and edge weights represent the transition probabilities of two subsequent tasks. The author shows how to evaluate quality of service of a composed service from basic services characteristics and graph topology.

Some recent proposals face the problem of composition of WSs by implementing genetic algorithms [10]. In Canfora et al. [10] the reduction formulas presented in [11] are adopted, and the problem is also periodically re-optimized in order to take into account WS performance variability. However, only suboptimal solutions are identified since WSs specified inside execution loops are always assigned to the same Web service implementation.

Proposals of QoS-aware frameworks can be found in [6,12,7]. Yu and Lin [7] present a broker-based framework for the dynamic integration of Web services with end-to-end QoS constraints. The main functions of the proposed QoS broker include: service tracking, dynamic service composition model, dynamic service selection, and dynamic service adaptation. WebQ [6] is a QoS-based WS framework where the service selection is based on the parallel execution and monitoring of the candidate target services. Serhani et al. [12] propose a broker-based architecture which adopts QoS verification and certification in the service selection process. Zeng et al. [8] present a global planning approach to select an optimal execution plan by means of integer programming. Yu and Lin [13] discuss selection algorithms for multiple QoS attributes defining the problem as a multi-dimension multi-choice 0-1 knapsack problem as well as a multi-constraint optimal path problem. Ardagna and Pernici [9] model the service composition as a mixed integer linear problem where both local and global constraints are taken into account. Their approach is formulated as an optimization problem handling the whole application instead of each execution path separately. Claro et al. [14] propose the use of multi-objective optimization techniques to find a set of optimal Pareto solutions from which a requestor can choose.

The works closest to ours concern methods to derive performance related measures of workflow processes [15,16]. Cardoso [15] proposes two different metrics to evaluate the control-flow complexity of BPEL web processes before their actual implementation. In [16] a mathematical model based on operations research techniques is proposed to estimate the influence of the execution of orchestrated processes on utilization and throughput of the system. Being based on QN analysis, our approach has the advantage that the bounding technique used in this paper is one of the many possible solution algorithms of the performance model. It if hence possible to compute more precise results by simply applying more sophisticated QN solution techniques [17].

3   Overview of the Proposed Approach

In this section we illustrate the main steps of our methodology for the performance evaluation of WS applications, while the description of the realized tool is deferred to section 5.

We generically consider WS-based applications, built up from software services glued together by means of some integration mechanism. In this context, the services provide the application-specific functionalities (and are considered as black boxes), and the glue defines the workflow that integrates these functionalities to deliver the functionalities required from the application.

We envisage a two layers approach to derive performance indices of the WS application. At the service providers level we can analyze the set of resources devoted to provide a service (including, if necessary, network resources) by means of a QN. The QN analysis results are then used as performance annotation characterizing the service. The users, at the upper level, use this information without concerning with the characteristics of the underlying platform.

In Fig. 1 we show a UML Activity Diagram with the main steps of MAPS. Boxes show who is responsible for executing each action.

Users side The Users-side of our approach starts from the application workflow specifications and derive performance bounds on the application response time and throughput, as follows:

Identify application requirements. At this step the user describes the application (s)he intends to realize and details its functional and non-functional requirements.

Discover and compose services. The user sees only the services with their performance annotations and builds its application based on the service

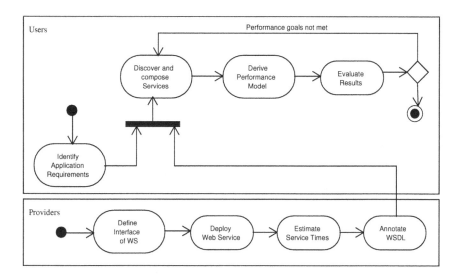

Fig. 1. Activity diagram for the proposed methodology

description using tools like BPEL and performing service discovery and composition using methods like [18]; the details of this step are beyond the scope of the paper.

Derive Performance model. The annotated BPEL specifications are used to implicitly derive a QN model. The activities in BPEL describe the sequence of requests which customers perform on service centers. The QN model is used to compute performance bounds on throughput and response time. Such information correspond to bounds on throughput and response times of the resources on the software system under evaluation. A detailed description of this step is given in Section 4.

Evaluate Results. The user exploits the computed performance bounds to choose among the services available those that better fulfill the performance requirements; performance results can also be used to answer "what-if" questions about the system. Based on the analysis results, the client can reach a more informed decision about the system design. If the performance requirements are fulfilled, (s)he can proceed with the acquisition of the pre-selected WSs; otherwise (s)he has to iterate the process by repeating the steps described, or lastly admit the unfeasibility of the performance requirements with the acquisition of publicly offered services.

Providers-side. At this side, the service providers must deploy the set of WS on suitable physical resources, exposing a well-defined WSDL interface annotated with QoS-oriented information. Service providers will execute the following steps:

Define interface of WS. At this step, the service providers must define the interface of the services they offer. In the WS scenario this is done by defining an appropriate WSDL which clearly describes the interfaces, including the operations provided, the input parameters and the type of the returned results.

Deploy WS. At this step, the service providers must define the physical deployment of the services they offer. This means that the services must be implemented and installed on the appropriate hardware resources. Further resources (disk space, additional CPUs, dedicated network connections and so on) must be allocated, depending on the nature of the functionalities provided by the WS.

Estimate Service times. At this step, the service providers must estimate, for each individual operation they provide through their WSs, the average service time on each of their resource. Thus, the service providers not only have to compute the mean response time of each operation, but also break down this response time to identify the fractions of it spent on each resource. Service times can be estimated by the providers by using synthetic workloads and monitoring the response times of the physical resources. It is possible to constantly improve the estimate of the response times by continuously profiling the resource usage under real workloads: that is, providers monitor the resources utilization as client applications access them, and dynamically adjust the advertised average service times as better estimates are computed.

Annotate WSDL. The information collected during the previous step are inserted as performance annotations in the WSDL of the services. Those information, combined with the structure of the BPEL workflows which are executed on the system, are used to compute the performance bounds as will be shown in Section 4.

4   Performance Modeling of BPEL Workflows

In this section we present the main contribution of this paper. Specifically, we provide an algorithm for efficient computation of performance bounds for WSs driven by BPEL workflows. We compute optimistic and pessimistic bounds for system throughput and response time, where the "system" is the set of all physical resources (CPUs, disks, network connections) where all the WSs referenced by a BPEL are deployed.

Bounding techniques are interesting for several reasons [19]. First, they quantify the critical effect of bottleneck devices on system performance; it is also easy to analyze the performance improvements which are gained by replacing the bottlenecks. Moreover, bounds can be computed quickly and efficiently: they can be used during early planning stages to answer many performance-related questions, and eliminate inadequate design alternatives at early design phases, and at run-time assisting reconfiguration operations.

BPEL allows users to describe interactions with WSs; each interaction (request, response, one-way remote method invocation) is described by an appropriate BPEL action; moreover, elements are provided to model loops and branches.

The WS-BPEL version 2.0 [20] specifies, among others, the following types of activity:

⟨**receive**⟩ The executing process waits for a specific incoming message to be received;

⟨**reply**⟩ Sends a message in reply to a message which was received through a ⟨**receive**⟩ tag;

⟨**invoke**⟩ Invokes a one-way or request-response operation on a partner;

⟨**wait**⟩ Waits for a given time period, or until a certain time has passed;

⟨**sequence**⟩ Denotes a set of activities which should be executed sequentially; for each activity it is possible to specify additional dependencies, that is, other activities which must complete before executing the current one.

⟨**if**⟩ Selects one activity from a set of choices;

⟨**while**⟩ Repeats an activity until a certain predicate is no longer true;

⟨**repeatUntil**⟩ Repeats an activity until a condition becomes true;

⟨**forEach**⟩ This activity repeats its child activity for a number N of times; the child activity instances can be executed sequentially, or in parallel;

⟨**pick**⟩ The process blocks until a certain message is received, or a timeout goes off. When one of these events occurs, the associated activity is executed and the pick completes;

⟨**flow**⟩ Denotes a set of concurrent activities;

⟨**switch**⟩ Allows the process to choose exactly one branch of an activity with multiple choices.

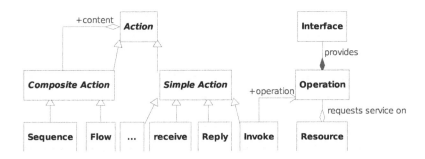

Fig. 2. Class diagram of a portion of the BPEL performance metamodel

We illustrate in Fig. 2 a portion of the BPEL metamodel as a UML class diagram. There are two kinds of BPEL actions: *composite* actions (such as Sequence and Flow), which act as containers, and *simple* actions (such as Invoke and Reply) which represent atomic actions. In particular, the Invoke action is used to perform a two-way (request-response) WS operation, which is described in an appropriate WSDL. Each WS operation requests service on a set of resources. For example, a WS operation may require CPU time, disk I/O operations, or in general use other (physical) resources on the executing host.

From a performance point of view, a BPEL workflow applies a *workload* on the resources. The workload may be *open* (if there is an infinite stream of instances of the BPEL which are executed at a given rate λ), or *closed* (if there is a finite population of N BPEL instances, each spending Z time units outside the system before being executed again).

We see in Fig. 3 the mapping between the BPEL model and the QN performance model. Resources in the BPEL model correspond to service centers, and BPEL actions represent requests which arrive to the service centers.

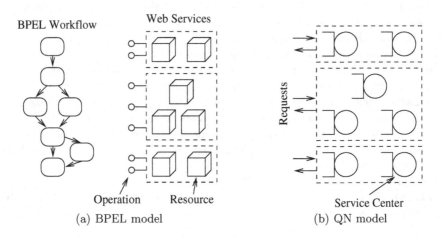

(a) BPEL model   (b) QN model

Fig. 3. BPEL model and QN performance model

We consider the system made of all resources where WSs are deployed. Our approach computes bounds on the system response time and throughput, from which bounds on individual resources utilization, throughput and response times can be obtained. We now briefly recall the main results related to QN bound analysis, which will be used later in this section; more details on bound analysis can be found in [3,19].

Let us consider a BPEL specification $\mathbf{A} = \{A_1, A_2, \ldots A_N\}$, with actions $A_1, A_2, \ldots A_N$. Let X be the system throughput (i.e., the rate of completion of BPEL $\mathbf{A}$). Let $\mathbf{R} = \{R_1, R_2, \ldots R_K\}$ be the set of all the K resources available in the system, that is, all the resources used by WS operations. Then, according to the *utilization law*, the utilization of resource $R_i \in \mathbf{R}$ can be expressed as:

$$U[R_i] = X[R_i] S_i = XD[R_i] \tag{1}$$

where $U[R_i]$ is the utilization of device R_i, X is the whole system throughput, $D[R_i]$, $X[R_i]$ and S_i are resource R_i service demand, throughput and mean service time, respectively. The utilization law states that the utilization of resource R_i is proportional to its service demand. Thus, the device R_{max} with the highest resource demand (and hence utilization) is the *bottleneck device*. Note that bottleneck identification should be one of the first steps in any performance study; any system upgrade which does not remove the bottleneck(s) will have no impact on the system performance at high loads.

The first step in the bound derivation process is to compute the service demand $D\,[R]$ for each resource $R \in \mathbf{R}$. In this paper we analyze the scenario in which a single kind of BPEL workflow is executed in the system; from the QN model perspective, this results in considering a QN performance model with a single customer class. Extension of the proposed approach to the scenario of multiple kinds of workflows being executed on the system would result in the computation of bounds for multiclass QN models. The same approach described in [21] applies to BPEL workflows as it did for UML Activity diagrams. However, bounding techniques are seldom used in multiclass QN analysis: the reason is that bounds are mainly used to study bottleneck centers for which single class models suffice.

Let Service $[A, R]$ be the average service time on resource R for a single invocation of action A; let Visits $[A]$ be the *visit count* to action A. The visit count is defined as the ratio of the number of visits to action A and the number of completions of the whole BPEL $\mathbf{A}$. The total *service demand* $D\,[R]$ for resource R is given by:

$$D\,[R] = \sum_{A \in \mathbf{A}} \text{Visits}\,[A] \times \text{Service}\,[A, R] \qquad (2)$$

Let us denote with $D = \sum_{i=1}^{K} D\,[R_i]$ the sum of all service demands; let D_{max} and D_{ave} denote the maximum and average of the service demands at the centers of the model, respectively.

Different kind of bounds can be computed, depending whether the BPEL represents a closed or open workload. Let us consider the two cases separately.

Bounds for Open Workloads. Let λ be the rate at which the BPEL $\mathbf{A}$ is executed; let $X(\lambda)$ and $R(\lambda)$ respectively denote the system throughput and response time with respect to parameter λ. Then the following equations hold [19]:

$$X(\lambda) \leq 1/D_{max} \qquad (3)$$

$$\frac{D}{1 - \lambda D_{ave}} \leq R(\lambda) \leq \frac{D}{1 - \lambda D_{max}} \qquad (4)$$

Bounds for Closed Workloads. Let N the total number of instances of BPEL $\mathbf{A}$ which are executed; let Z be the time spent by each BPEL instance outside the system before being executed again. If we denote with $X(N)$ and $R(N)$ the system throughput and response time as a function of the request population N, then the following equations hold [19]:

$$\frac{N}{D + Z + \frac{(N-1)D_{max}}{1 + Z/(ND)}} \leq X(N) \leq \min\left(\frac{1}{D_{max}}, \frac{N}{D + Z + \frac{(N-1)D_{ave}}{1 + Z/D}}\right) \qquad (5)$$

$$\max\left(ND_{max} - Z, D + \frac{(N-1)D_{ave}}{1 + Z/D}\right) \leq R(N) \leq D + \frac{(N-1)D_{max}}{1 + Z/(ND)} \qquad (6)$$

Note that Equations 3–6 provide bounds for the whole system throughput and response time. These quantities are very important for customers executing BPEL workflows on a system. From the system provider point of view, individual resource utilization $U[R_i]$ are an equally important parameter. Note that according to the utilization law (Eq. 1), bounds on $U[R_i]$ can be directly derived from bounds on X, by multiplying the latter by $D[R_i]$ (we will show shortly how to compute $D[R_i]$).

The modeler can specify whether the BPEL represents an open or closed workload by putting a suitable annotation in the BPEL specification. For example, a closed workload can be modeled with this code fragment (note that the `workload` element is in a different namespace with respect to the other standard BPEL elements):

```
<bpws:process>
  <perf:workload type="closed" thinktime=Z />
  ...
</bpws:process>
```

Similarly, an open workload can be modeled as follows:

```
<bpws:process>
  <perf:workload type="open" arrivalrate=λ />
  ...
</bpws:process>
```

In order to be able to compute the bounds, we need to know the service demand $D[R_i]$ for each resource (see Eq. 2). The service demand can be computed if we know the visit count $\mathsf{Visits}[A]$ for each action $A \in \mathbf{A}$, and the average service time on resource R for each execution of action A. Let us address these two issues separately.

Definition of the Service Time

In order to compute the mean service time $\mathsf{Service}[A_i, R]$ from Eq. 2, the system modeler is requested to annotate each method of the the WSs with which the workflow interacts with their average service time. This can be done using suitable XML elements in the WSDL specifications of the WS. Performance-oriented extensions of WSDL have been proposed in the literature (see [22,2] for one of these proposals). As we are only interested in representing service time for WSDL operations, we adopt here a stripped down notation for the sake of simplicity. Of course, our performance modeling approach is completely independent from the notation actually used to enrich BPEL and WSDL specifications with performance-oriented information.

Consider the following (simplified) WSDL describing an interface for an electronic flight booking application. Only the `checkAvailability` and `bookFlight` operations are shown; we also omit all details related to the input and output data types of such methods.

```
<wsdl:definitions name="BookingApp">
  <wsdl:portType name="BookingAppType">
    <wsdl:operation name="checkAvailability">
       ...
       <perf:PAdemand resource="disk" value="5"/>  <!-- (1) -->
       <perf:PAdemand resource="CPU" value="1"/>   <!-- (2) -->
    </wsdl:operation>
    <wsdl:operation name="bookFlight">
       ...
       <perf:PAdemand resource="disk" value="2"/>
       <perf:PAdemand resource="CPU" value="15"/>
    </wsdl:operation>
  </wsdl:portType>
</wsdl:definition>
```

In this code we added the child elements ⟨perf:PAdemand⟩ of ⟨wsdl:operation⟩ which are used to specify the mean service time of the operation on various resources; the PAdemand name has been chosen for similarity with the notation adopted in the UML Profile for Schedulability, Performance and Time Specification (UML-SPT profile [23]). The line labelled (1) denotes a mean service time of 5 on a resource named "disk", while line (2) denotes a service demand of 1 on a resource named "CPU". Both service times are related to the *checkAvailability* operation.

We use the **perf** prefix to denote the namespace where performance-oriented annotations are defined; this is to distinguish the new elements from the standard WSDL ones. The value of the **resource** attribute is a string denoting the name of a resource; the name is used for identification purposes only. The **value** attribute is a real number denoting the service time required by the specific resource. The WSDL should be annotated by the service provider, who of course is in the position of knowing how the operations are implemented, and can measure or estimate their service time.

Now we show how to compute the value of $\mathsf{Service}\,[A, R]$, for each $A \in \mathbf{A}$, $R \in \mathbf{R}$. If A is not an ⟨invoke⟩ action, then $\mathsf{Service}\,[A, R] = 0$ for every $R \in \mathbf{R}$. If A is an ⟨invoke⟩ action, defined as:

$$
A \equiv \boxed{\begin{array}{l} \texttt{} \end{array}}
$$

and the operation Op is defined and annotated in a WSDL as follows:

$$
Op \equiv \boxed{\begin{array}{l} \texttt{<wsdl:operation name=}Op\texttt{>} \\ \quad \ldots \\ \texttt{<perf:PAdemand resource=}R_1 \texttt{ value=}v_1\texttt{/>} \\ \texttt{<perf:PAdemand resource=}R_2 \texttt{ value=}v_2\texttt{/>} \\ \quad \vdots \\ \texttt{<perf:PAdemand resource=}R_K \texttt{ value=}v_K\texttt{/>} \\ \texttt{</wsdl:operation>} \end{array}}
$$

then, for each $i \in \{1, \ldots K\}$ we let $\mathsf{Service}[A, R_i] = v_i$. We assume $\mathsf{Service}[A, R_i] = 0$ if the $\langle \mathtt{perf:PAdemand} \rangle$ tag is omitted for resource R_i.

Computation of Visit Counts

We recall that the visit count $\mathsf{Visits}[A_i]$ represents the ratio of the number of visits to BPEL activity A_i versus the number of completions of the whole BPEL **A**. Visit counts can be computed by solving a system of linear equations; the equations are derived by structural analysis of the BPEL activity, as follows. Given a BPEL fragment A_i, we denote with $\mathcal{E}[A_i]$ a set of linear equations. The function is defined by structural induction on A_i, according to the rules shown in Table 1.

5   Case Study

In this section we illustrate how the technique described in Sec. 4 can be applied to a case study. As a motivating example, we consider a set of WSs which can be used to execute jobs in a computational Grid [24]; in fact, the Basic Execution Service (BES) [25] and Open Grid Services Architecture Data Access and Integration (OGSA-DAI) [26] are WS interfaces for job submission and data transfer respectively, which are being standardized in an effort to allow interoperability between Grid components provided by different projects.

Let us consider a system where the following WSs are available: a *Storage Element*, which is responsible for storing (possibly large amount of) data; a *Computing Element*, which is a WS which can accept and execute computational jobs; an *Analysis Element*, which is a service for analyzing the output data produced by running some application on the Computing Element. The annotated WSDL interfaces of these services are reported in a simplified form in Appendix A.2. Each operation is annotated with the (estimated) average service time on the resources they require.

We consider the BPEL sketched in Appendix A.1. The BPEL represents a closed workload, where each workflow spends 120 time units outside the system (*think time*) before being executed again. The workflow executes the following sequence of actions:

– The user authenticates on the system.
– The executable application and the files it needs to operate (called *Input SandBox*) are transferred in parallel with the input data that must be processed by the application.
– The executable is started a number of times, possibly with different parameters (this latter detail is not shown in the BPEL); this is done by iterating the $\mathtt{JobStart}$ operation inside a $\langle \mathtt{while} \rangle$ statement until a certain condition (not shown in the BPEL) is false. The probability of the condition being true is set to be 0.7.
– The output produced by the executable (called the *Output SandBox*) is transferred to another WS to be analyzed.
– The output data are finally analyzed.

Table 1. Computation of the visit count

$A_i \equiv$	```
	<sequence|flow>
	    A_{j_1}
	    $\vdots$
	    A_{j_k}
	</sequence|flow>
	``
		$\mathcal{E}[A_i] = \begin{cases} \text{Visits}[A_{j_1}] = \text{Visits}[A_i] \\ \quad\quad \vdots \\ \text{Visits}[A_{j_k}] = \text{Visits}[A_i] \\ \quad \mathcal{E}[A_{j_1}] \\ \quad\quad \vdots \\ \quad \mathcal{E}[A_{j_k}] \end{cases}$

$A_i \equiv$	```
	<if>
	    <condition perf:prob=p_{j_1}>
	      C_1 </condition>
	      A_{j_1}
	    <elseif>
	      <condition perf:prob=p_{j_2}>
	        C_2 </condition>
	        A_{j_2}
	    </elseif>
	    $\vdots$
	    <else>A_{j_k}</else>
	</if>
	``
		$\mathcal{E}[A_i] = \begin{cases} \text{Visits}[A_{j_1}] = p_{j_1}\text{Visits}[A_i] \\ \quad\quad \vdots \\ \text{Visits}[A_{j_{k-1}}] = p_{j_{k-1}}\text{Visits}[A_i] \\ \text{Visits}[A_{j_k}] = \left(1 - \sum_{t=1}^{k-1} p_{j_t}\right) \\ \quad\quad\quad\quad \times\text{Visits}[A_i] \\ \quad \mathcal{E}[A_{j_1}] \\ \quad\quad \vdots \\ \quad \mathcal{E}[A_{j_k}] \end{cases}$

$A_i \equiv$	```
	<pick>
	    <onMessage perf:prob=p_{j_1} ...>
	      A_{j_1} </onMessage>
	    $\vdots$
	    <onMessage perf:prob=p_{j_k} ...>
	      A_{j_k} </onMessage>
	</pick>
	``
		$\mathcal{E}[A_i] = \begin{cases} \text{Visits}[A_{j_1}] = p_{j_1}\text{Visits}[A_i] \\ \quad\quad \vdots \\ \text{Visits}[A_{j_k}] = p_{j_k}\text{Visits}[A_i] \\ \quad \mathcal{E}[A_{j_1}] \\ \quad\quad \vdots \\ \quad \mathcal{E}[A_{j_k}] \end{cases}$

$A_i \equiv$	``` <repeatUntil> A_j <condition perf:prob=p> C </condition> </repeatUntil> ```	$\mathcal{E}[A_i] = \begin{cases} \text{Visits}[A_j] = \frac{1}{p}\text{Visits}[A_i] \\ \quad \mathcal{E}[A_j] \end{cases}$

$A_i \equiv$	```
	<while>
	    <condition perf:prob=p>
	      C </condition>
	    A_j
	</while>
	``
		$\mathcal{E}[A_i] = \begin{cases} \text{Visits}[A_j] = \frac{p}{1-p}\text{Visits}[A_i] \\ \quad \mathcal{E}[A_j] \end{cases}$

$A_i \equiv$	```
	<forEach>
	    <startCounterValue>
	      S </startCounterValue>
	    <finalCounterValue>
	      T </finalCounterValue>
	    <scope>A_j</scope>
	</forEach>
	``
		$\mathcal{E}[A_i] = \begin{cases} \text{Visits}[A_j] = (T - S + 1)\text{Visits}[A_i] \\ \quad \mathcal{E}[A_j] \end{cases}$

We developed a command-line tool written in C++ which is able to parse the annotated BPEL (and associated WSDL) specifications and outputs the

Table 2. Service demands for the case study

Resource	Visit count	Service Demand
CE:CPU	5.33	22.33
CE:Disk	2.0	150.00
DA:CPU	1.0	100.00
DA:Disk	1.0	30.00
DF:CPU	1.0	1.00
DF:Disk	1.0	120.00
Network	3.0	170.00

performance bounds computed using Eq. 3–6. The tool, called `bpel2qnbound`, builds a BPEL performance model based on the metamodel shown in Fig. 2. The tool, then, computes the visit counts and the service demands using the approach described in Section 4, and produces the appropriate bound equations as output.

By using the `bpel2qnbound` tool, we get the visit counts and service demands shown in Table 2. As can be seen, the bottleneck device is the network. This means that system performance, at heavy load, will not improve unless that bottleneck is removed.

Given that the BPEL of the case study represents a closed workload, the bounds from Eq. 5 and 6 apply. Fig. 4 shows the upper and lower bounds for the Response Time and Throughput, as a function of the request population size N.

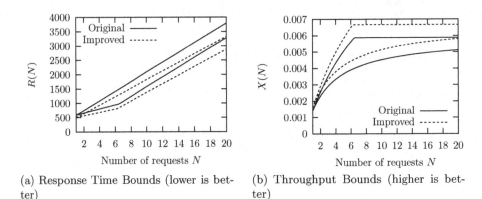

(a) Response Time Bounds (lower is better)

(b) Throughput Bounds (higher is better)

Fig. 4. Performance Bounds for the Case Study, original system vs. an improved one where the bottleneck is removed

One of the most important questions a system modeler may ask is: "What should be done in order to improve the system throughput/response time?". This question is easily answered by looking at the service demands on Table 2: better performance can be obtained if the system bottleneck (the network, in this case) is removed. According to Eq. 2, the service demand decreases if either (1) fewer visits are made to the bottleneck device, or (2) the average service time is shortened. Solution (1) implies that the BPEL workflow (and possibly the system as well) is restructured so that fewer network communications are required. On the other hand, solution (2) requires moving to a faster network. If we consider an improved system where the service demand on the network is exactly half of that on the original system, we obtain the new bounds shown with the dashed lines in Fig. 4. The service demand on the network for the improved system is 85, so that the bottleneck device becomes the disk on the Computing Element. From the figure, the improved system offers definitely better performance (both throughput and response time) than the original one, as the request population size N increases.

6   Conclusions

In this paper we described a multi-view approach for the performance prediction of service-based applications encompassing both users and service provider(s) perspectives. As a first step towards the realization of this integrated framework we described an algorithm for efficient computation of performance bounds for BPEL workflows. Our approach applies QN analysis techniques directly on the BPEL specification of the workflow and the WSDL associated with the Web Services it references. We showed how to compute bounds for the system throughput and response time using QN bounds. The approach can be fully automated: we developed a prototype tool, called `bpel2qnbound`, which automatically derives the appropriate bounds from the annotated workflow specification. Our technique does not require the derivation (and solution) of the underlying QN model; nevertheless, bounding techniques are useful to identify and quantify the effect of system bottlenecks, and to perform quick analysis and discard inappropriate (performance-wise) alternatives at an early stage of a study. The results of the `bpel2bound` tool can be interpreted both from a customer perspective, to select among the available WSs those providing the best performance, and also from a system provider perspective, to identify bottlenecks and estimate the performance gains obtained by upgrading different parts of the system.

The research described in this paper can be extended in several directions. A technique very similar to that described in [27] can be applied to explicitly derive a multiclass QN model from annotated BPEL specifications; while the resulting model would be more difficult to analyze, it would provide more accurate performance measures. The long term goal is to integrate different performance analysis techniques for BPEL into a single tool, where the system modeler can choose the most appropriate type of analysis depending on speed/accuracy tradeoff.

References

1. Menasce, D.A.: QoS Issues in Web Services. IEEE Internet Computing 6(6), 72–75 (2002)
2. D'Ambrogio, A.: A model-driven WSDL extension for describing the qos of web services. In: 2006 IEEE International Conference on Web Services (ICWS 2006), Chicago, Illinois, pp. 789–796. IEEE Computer Society Press, Los Alamitos (2006)

3. Denning, P.J., Buzen, J.P.: The operational analysis of queueing network models. ACM Comput. Surv. 10(3), 225–261 (1978)
4. Balbo, G., Serazzi, G.: Asymptotic analysis of multiclass closed queueing networks: Multiple bottlenecks. Performance Evaluation 30, 115–152 (1997)
5. Maximilien, E.M., Singh, M.P.: A Framework and Ontology for Dynamic Web Services Selection. IEEE Internet Computing 8(5), 84–93 (2004)
6. Patel, C., Supekar, K., Lee, Y.: A QoS Oriented Framework for Adaptive Management of Web Service Based Workflows. In: Mařík, V., Štěpánková, O., Retschitzegger, W. (eds.) DEXA 2003. LNCS, vol. 2736, pp. 826–835. Springer, Heidelberg (2003)
7. Yu, T., Lin, K.J.: A Broker-Based Framework for QoS-Aware Web Service Composition. In: Proc. of 2005 IEEE Int'l Conf. on e-Technology, e-Commerce and e-Service, Hong Kong, China (March 2005)
8. Zeng, L., Benatallah, B., Ngu, A.H.H., Dumas, M., Kalagnanam, J., Chang, H.: QoS-Aware Middleware for Web Services Composition. IEEE Trans. Softw. Eng. 30(5), 311–327 (2004)
9. Ardagna, D., Pernici, B.: Global and Local QoS Guarantee in Web Service Selection. In: Proc. of Business Process Management Workshops, pp. 32–46 (2005)
10. Canfora, G., Penta, M.D., Esposito, R., Villani, M.L.: An Approach for QoS-aware Service Composition Based on Genetic Algorithms. In: Proc. of Genetic and Computation Conf., Washington, DC (June 2005)
11. Cardoso, J., Sheth, A.P., Miller, J.A., Arnold, J., Kochut, K.: Quality of service for workflows and web service processes. J. Web Sem. 1(3), 281–308 (2004)
12. Serhani, M.A., Dssouli, R., Hafid, A., Sahraoui, H.: A QoS Broker Based Architecture for Efficient Web Services Selection. In: Proc. of 2005 Int'l Conf. on Web Services, Orlando, pp. 113–120 (July 2005)
13. Yu, T., Lin, K.J.: Service Selection Algorithms for Composing Complex Services with Multiple QoS Constraints. In: Proc. of 3rd Int'l Conf. on Service Oriented Computing, Amsterdam, The Netherlands, pp. 130–143 (December 2005)
14. Claro, D.B., Albers, P., Hao, J.-K.: Selecting Web Services for Optimal Composition. In: Proc. of ICWS 2005 2nd Int'l Workshop on Semantic and Dynamic Web Processes, Orlando (July 2005)
15. Cardoso, J.: Complexity analysis of BPEL web processes. Software Process: Improvement and Practice 12(1), 35–49 (2007)
16. Rud, D., Schmietendorf, A., Dumke, R.: Performance modeling of ws-bpel-based web service compositions. In: Services computing workshops, SCW 2006, pp. 140–147. IEEE Computer Society Press, Los Alamitos (2006)
17. Bolch, G., Greiner, S., de Meer, H., Trivedi, K.S.: Queueing Networks and Markov Chains. J. Wiley, Chichester (1998)
18. Cardellini, V., Casalicchio, E., Grassi, V., Mirandola, R.: A framework for optimal service selection in broker-based architectures with multiple QoS classes. In: Services computing workshops, SCW 2006, pp. 105–112. IEEE Computer Society Press, Los Alamitos (2006)
19. Lazowska, E.D., Zahorjan, J., Graham, G.S., Sevcik, K.C.: Quantitative System Performance: Computer System Analysis Using Queueig Network Models. Prentice-Hall, Englewood Cliffs (1984)
20. Alves, A., et al.: Web service business process execution language version 2.0 Committee Draft (May 17, 2006)
21. Balsamo, S., Marzolla, M., Mirandola, R.: Efficient performance models in component-based software engineering. In: EUROMICRO 2006: Proceedings of the 32nd EUROMICRO Conference on Software Engineering and Advanced Applications, pp. 64–71. IEEE Computer Society Press, Los Alamitos (2006)

22. D'Ambrogio, A.: A WSDL extension for performance-enabled description of web services. In: Yolum, p., Güngör, T., Gürgen, F., Özturan, C. (eds.) ISCIS 2005. LNCS, vol. 3733, pp. 371–381. Springer, Heidelberg (2005)
23. Object Management Group (OMG): UML profile for schedulability, performance and time specification. Final Adopted Specification ptc/02-03-02, OMG (March 2002)
24. Foster, I., Kesselman, C.: The Grid 2: Blueprint for a New Computing Infrastructure. Morgan Kaufmann Publishers, San Francisco (2003)
25. OGSA Basic Execution Service Working Group:
http://forge.gridforum.org/projects/ogsa-bes-wg
26. Antonioletti, M., Krause, A., Paton, N.W., Eisenberg, A., Laws, S., Malaika, S., Melton, J., Pearson, D.: The WS-DAI family of specifications for web service data access and integration. SIGMOD Record 35(1), 48–55 (2006)
27. Balsamo, S., Marzolla, M.: Performance evaluation of UML software architectures with multiclass queueing network models. In: Proc. of the Fifth International Workshop on Software and Performance (WOSP 2005), pp. 37–42. ACM Press, New York (2005)

A   Appendix

A.1   BPEL for the Case Study

```
<bpws:process>
  <perf:workload type="closed" thinktime="120"/>
  <bpws:import importType="http://schemas.xmlsoap.org/wsdl/"
    location="CaseStudy.wsdl">
  <bpws:sequence>
    <bpws:invoke operation="Authenticate"/>
    <bpws:flow>
      <bpws:invoke operation="TransferISB"/>
      <bpws:invoke operation="TransferData"/>
    </bpws:flow>
    <bpws:while>
      <bpws:condition prob="0.7"/>
      <bpws:invoke operation="JobStart"/>
    </bpws:while>
    <bpws:invoke operation="TransferOSB"/>
    <bpws:invoke operation="Analyze"/>
  </bpws:sequence>
</bpws:process>
```

A.2   WSDL for the Case Study

```
<!-- Interface for Storage Element -->
<definitions>
  <portType name="DataFactory">
    <operation name="TransferData">
```

```
      <perf:PAdemand resource="DF:CPU" value="1"/>
      <perf:PAdemand resource="DF:Disk" value="120"/>
      <perf:PAdemand resource="Network" value="80"/>
    </operation>
  </portType>
</definitions>

<!-- Interface for Computing Element -->
<definitions>
  <portType name="JobFactory">
    <operation name="Authenticate">
      <perf:PAdemand resource="CE:CPU" value="10"/>
    </operation>
    <operation name="TransferISB">
      <perf:PAdemand resource="CE:CPU" value="2"/>
      <perf:PAdemand resource="Network" value="10"/>
      <perf:PAdemand resource="CE:Disk" value="120"/>
    </operation>
    <operation name="JobStart">
      <perf:PAdemand resource="CE:CPU" value="4"/>
    </operation>
    <operation name="TransferOSB">
      <perf:PAdemand resource="CE:CPU" value="1"/>
      <perf:PAdemand resource="Network" value="80"/>
      <perf:PAdemand resource="CE:Disk" value="30"/>
    </operation>
  </portType>

<!-- Interface for Analysis Element -->
<definitions>
  <portType name="DataAnalysis">
    <operation name="Analyze">
      <PAdemand resource="DA:CPU" value="100"/>
      <PAdemand resource="DA:Disk" value="30"/>
    </operation>
  </portType>
</definitions>
```

Predicting the Performance
of Component-Based Software Architectures
with Different Usage Profiles

Heiko Koziolek, Steffen Becker, and Jens Happe

Graduate School Trustsoft[*]
University of Oldenburg, Germany and
Chair for Software Design and Quality
University of Karlsruhe, Germany
{koziolek,sbecker,happe}@ipd.uka.de

Abstract. Performance predictions aim at increasing the quality of software architectures during design time. To enable such predictions, specifications of the performance properties of individual components within the architecture are required. However, the response times of a component might depend on its configuration in a specific setting and the data send to or retrieved from it. Many existing prediction approaches for component-based systems neglect these influences. This paper introduces extensions to a performance specification language for components, the Palladio Component Model, to model these influences. The model enables to predict response times of different architectural alternatives. A case study on a component-based architecture for a web portal validates the approach and shows that it is capable of supporting a design decision in this scenario.

1   Introduction

Performance problems in large distributed software systems, such as high response times and low throughput, often result from poor architectural decisions during early development stages [25,20]. When they are discovered in a running system, they might require a costly redesign of the architecture and often cannot be fixed by simply revising small parts of the code. To avoid redesigns, software architectures should be analysed for their performance properties as early as possible.

As large software architectures are composed of (possibly third-party) components [27], architects need performance specifications of each individual component to conduct performance predictions for the planned architecture. However, specifying the performance of a software component is difficult, as component developers cannot make any assumptions on the context (i.e., underlying hardware, operating system, usage profile, performance of required services, etc.) of their components and thus need to specify the performance independently of the context. Many existing approaches for component-based performance prediction [3,6,12,13,9,7,29] neglect one or more context dependencies in their component specifications. Especially the context-dependent

---

[*] This work is supported by the German Research Foundation (DFG), grants GRK 1076/1 and RE 1674/1-2.

S. Overhage et al. (Eds.): QoSA 2007, LNCS 4880, pp. 145–163, 2007.

configuration of components as well as the input and output parameters of component services as part of the usage profile are usually disregarded.

This paper extends our existing component specification language, the Palladio Component Model (PCM) [5], with constructs to model the performance influences by configuration parameters of a component as well as input and output parameters. Component developers may characterise a set of configuration parameters for their components (called component parameters), which can be adopted by software architects to a specific usage profile. For example, a performance-relevant component parameter might be the size of data the component uses for computation or a compression rate for a component compressing files.

We have implemented a transformation of an architectural model composed out of such component specifications into a formal analysis model, which can be used to predict response times for use cases of the architecture as probability distributions. Our approach aims at evaluating the architectures of large distributed systems. It does not try to make accurate predictions for real-time systems, but to guide design decisions for distributed systems at early development stages, where some performance-relevant details might still be unknown.

The contributions of this paper are i) extensions to an existing component performance specification language (PCM) for modelling component parameters as well as input and output parameters, ii) the implementation of a model transformation algorithm to automatically map component performance specifications to an analytical model, and iii) a proof-of-concept case study on a component-based architecture. We validate the applicability of our approach by comparing our predictions for different usage profiles of the same architecture with measurements from an implementation. Our results show that the approach is capable of validating a service level agreement in our scenario.

The paper is organised as follows: Section 2 introduces extensions to the Palladio Component Model, our specification language for component and architecture performance, and includes an example of the newly introduced concepts. Section 3 details the analytical model's syntax and solution. After listing assumptions and limitations of the approach, Section 4 contains a case study of performance predictions with our method for a larger component-based software architecture. Section 5 surveys related work in the area of model-based performance prediction for software architectures. Section 6 concludes the paper and points out future work.

2   Design Model

Our approach for performance prediction follows the established separation between a design-oriented and an analytical model [3]. Developers create the design model during early development stages of a software system with an UML-like modelling language assisted by tools. It is then transformed via tools into a restricted stochastic process algebra, which is solved mathematically to reveal bottlenecks or violated performance requirements in the architecture. This approach hides the complexity and analytical concepts of the underlying algebra from the developers, thereby possibly enabling even non-performance specialists to manage a performance prediction.

2.1 Palladio Component Model

The design model used in our approach is the Palladio Component Model (PCM) [5]. It is a meta-model specified as an instance of MOF (Meta-Object Facility) [21] (similar to the UML meta-model) and can been seen as a domain-specific modelling language for QoS (Quality-of-Service) predictions, which has been aligned to different developer roles in CBSE.

Using the PCM, *component developers* specify their components' performance properties with so-called service effect specifications (cf. Section 2.2). *Software architects* compose these component specifications from repositories to build an application specification. *Deployers* model the middleware and hardware resources of the targeted application environment and allocate component specifications to these resource models. Finally, *business domain experts*, who are familiar with expected user behaviour, model the usage profile of the application.

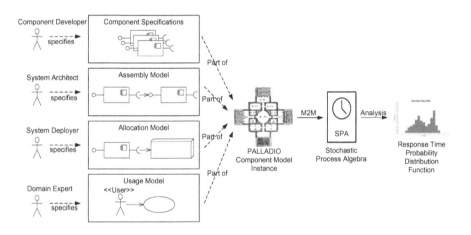

Fig. 1. Process Model: Performance Prediction with the PCM

The PCM provides a modelling language for each of these roles (Figure 1), and each language only includes concepts familiar to this role. This approach enables the division of work targeted by CBSE, and reduces the model's complexity for each role. Once all models are specified, they can be combined and then be transformed into the analytical model (cf. Section 2.4). More details about the PCM's process model are available in [16].

In the following, the paper will focus on the component specification language of the PCM, which has been specified with the Eclipse Modeling Framework (EMF) in Ecore [8]. A description of the other specification languages (e.g., component assembly model, resource model) can be found in [22]. Software components are black box entities with contractually specified interfaces [27]. In the PCM, components are either composite components, which are assembled out of inner components, or basic components, which cannot be further decomposed. Interfaces are first-class entities in the

PCM and can be associated to a component in a providing or requiring role. An interface consists of a number of service signatures, which contain a list of parameters, a return type, and a list of exceptions.

2.2 Service Effect Specification

To specify the performance properties of a component's service, our approach uses service effect specifications (SEFF) [5,23], which describe how a provided service calls required services and how it uses system resources. Such a specification makes the dependencies between resource usage and input parameters explicit, because component developers cannot know in advance how the component will be used by third parties. The SEFF is a strong abstraction from the service's source code including only performance-relevant information and thus does not violate the black box principle.

The SEFF-metamodel in the PCM is shown in Fig. 2-4. A `BasicComponent` may contain a number of `ServiceEffectSpecifications` (Fig. 2), which each reference a signature of an associated provided interface. For performance predictions, our approach uses `ResourceDemandingSEFFs`, which contain a number of `AbstractActions`.

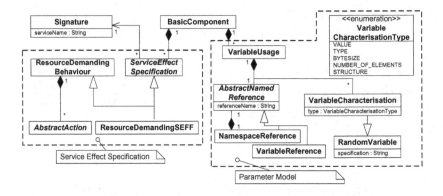

Fig. 2. Basic Component, Service Effect Specification, and Component Parameters

Component Parameters. As components are often implemented with object-oriented techniques, they can have an internal state at runtime, which can be the result of former service calls, constructor calls, or other forms of configuring the component (e.g., via deployment descriptors). In this paper, the elements of this state are called *component parameters*, as they can be accessed from any service of the component and are not local to a specific service. Essentially, component parameters extend the input space of the component's services. If they influence the performance of a component significantly, a characterisation of their values should be included in the performance specification.

Following the suggestions in [13] component parameters are treated as additional input parameters of a service. To avoid a state-space explosion in our model, we consider these values as unchangeable during service execution, which is a simplification but nevertheless covers a number of practical situations and is often sufficient to analyse single use cases. Furthermore, we assume that each client of the component's services accesses the same values in a specific use case, i.e., there are no client-specific component parameters.

Therefore, a `BasicComponent` may contain a number of `VariableUsages` (Fig. 2) to model component parameters, which in turn contain a name for the variable (`AbstractNamedReference`) and a description of its actual values (`Variable-Characterisation`). Variables can be characterised for their value, type, or size in bytes in the PCM, as all these properties may influence performance. Additionally, the number of elements and structure of collections can be characterised (see [17]). Variable characterisations are constant or discrete `RandomVariables` enabling the use of probability distributions, which is useful for characterising larger user groups with different habits. A variable may have multiple characterisations of different types (e.g., VALUE and TYPE at the same time). Composite data structures can be characterised by using multiple `VariableUsages` with the same `NamespaceReference` and different inner `VariableReferences` (e.g., "customer.name" and "customer.cash"). Only parameters influencing performance properties need to be included into SEFFs, all other parameters can be abstracted.

As an example of a component parameter, a component compressing files could contain a parameter compressionRatio, whose value domain ('high', 'medium', 'low') is characterised with a probability mass function (PMF) assigning a probability to each of the values (e.g., 10% 'high', 20% 'medium', 70% 'low'). Depending on the configured compression ratio and assuming fixed-size data, the response time of calling the component's services would change, as a high ratio would result in slow calls, whereas a low ratio would lead to faster executions. The component developer can specify this parameter in the component description and possibly also provide a default value (e.g., 100% medium). Upon including the component in an architecture, the value can be changed by domain experts or software architects.

Actions, Input- and Output-Parameters. Fig. 3 shows the different specialisations of `AbstractAction` from Fig. 2. Actions in SEFFs can either be `ExternalCall-Actions` referencing required services or `AbstractResourceDemandingActions` describing internal executions, which use the resources the component is deployed on. Actions are arranged in a chain, as each action references a predecessor and successor. The chain starts with a `StartAction`, then might contain internal executions, branches, loops, or forks (described later), and ends with a `StopAction`. `AcquireAction` and `ReleaseAction` allow the acquisition of passive resources, such as threads or semaphores.

`ExternalCallActions` contain variable usages to characterise the input parameters when calling a required service. Also, they allow to assign characterisations of output parameters from required service calls to local variables. Afterwards, the local variables can be referenced by following actions. The characterisations of input and output parameters are `VariableCharacterisations`, the same modelling entity as for component parameters. They might themselves depend on the input parameters of the specified service, for example if a parameter is processed internally and then passed to an external service (e.g., `extCallInput.VALUE = SEFFInput.VALUE`). To

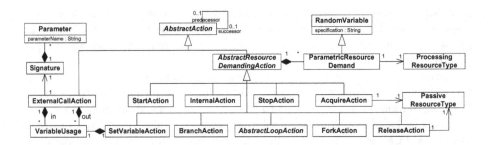

Fig. 3. Actions in Service Effect Specifications

express changes on the characterisation made by the service, our framework for stochastical expressions allows arithmetic operations on the corresponding random variables such as additions, subtractions, multiplication etc. For example, a service may add
some information to a file and then pass it to another service (e.g., extCallInput.-
BYTESIZE = SEFFInput.BYTESIZE + 100, where the byte sizes are specified
as random variables.).

We introduce a new action (SetVariableAction) to abstractly characterise the
return values of a service in a SEFF. It references a VariableUsage, which in turn
can include the name of a return value or of an output parameter. The characterisation
of these VariableUsages might again use input parameters of the SEFF. If multiple
SetVariableActions are specified in different branches of the SEFFs, the characterisation of the corresponding output parameter is weighted according to the (possibly
nested) branching probabilities. Using a SetVariableAction within a loop results
in a characterisation of the output parameter weighted with the probabilities for the
number of loop iterations.

To consume the resources the service is deployed on, all actions other than Ex-
ternalCallActions can contain a ParametricResourceDemand. As component developers can and should not know the concrete resources the component will
be deployed on by third parties, resource demands are specified for Processing-
ResourceTypes. These types can be for instance CPU, hard disk, network device,
etc. for which component developers specify the demand in terms of CPU cycles needed,
bytes read from hard disk, bytes sent over the network, etc. as random variables. Once
deployers specify the processing rates of concrete resources of these types, timing values can be derived from the resource demands. Resource demands may depend on input
parameters, and this dependency can be specified using the same stochastical expressions as decribed above.

Control Flow. Fig. 4 illustrates the control flow operations in the SEFF-metamodel.
The behaviour of a SEFF may include branches, loops, and forks. BranchActions
split the control flow with an OR-semantic, only one of the following branch transitions
is executed, while ForkActions split the control flow with an AND-semantic, i.e.,
each of its inner behaviours is executed concurrently.

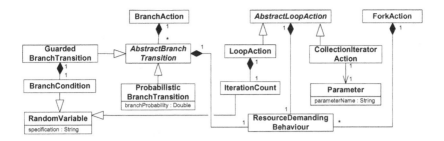

Fig. 4. Control Flow in Service Effect Specifications

Branch transitions can be guarded or probabilistic. In the former case, the component developer specifies a boolean random variable (`BranchCondition`) in relation to an input parameter of the SEFF. As our framework for stochastical expressions allows compare-operations such as equals, less, greater, etc. and also AND/OR combinations complex constraints on the input parameters for executing a branch can be expressed. The constraints shall always span the whole value domain of a parameter (e.g. $X < 10$ and $X >= 10$), and shall not intersect.

In the case of `ProbabilisticBranchTransitions`, the component developer specifies a probability for executing a specific branch. Though the behaviour of component services is usually not probabilistic, it might occur in complex services that a constraint on the input parameters for executing a branch cannot be specified easily. In this case, the component developer can specify just a probability.

`AbstractLoopActions` can either be `LoopActions`, which include an integer random variable for the number of loop iterations (`IterationCount`), or `CollectionIteratorActions`, which iterate over the elements of a collection provided as an input parameter to the service. In that case, the number of iterations is the same as the number of elements in the collection, which might have been specified as a probability distribution.

`LoopActions` assume the stochastical independence of parameters used in the loop body to reduce the necessary computations. Opposed to this, `CollectionIteratorActions` assume a stochastical dependency between the characterisations of the inner elements of the collections used in the loop body. If a characterisation of an inner element of the collection is used a second time within the loop body, its characterisation is stochastical dependent to its first use. For example, an integer variable might adopt the values 1 and 2 with a certain probability. If the random variable was evaluated to 1 on the first use of the variable, it also has to evaluate to 1 on the second occurrence. Including this stochastical dependency increases the computational complexity, but leads to more accurate predictions.

2.3 Example

Fig. 5 shows an example instance of the SEFF including most of the concepts introduced above. The concrete syntax is an UML activity and stereotype actions and annotations with the classes from our metamodel. Component1 provides Interface1, which

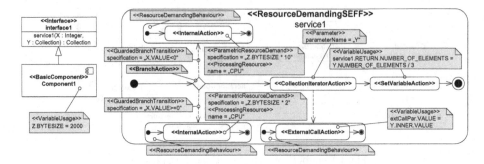

Fig. 5. Service Effect Specification

includes the signature of **service1** with two input variables **X,Y** as well as the return type **Collection**. Furthermore, a component parameter **Z** is specified for the component, and its bytesize is characterised with a constant (2000).

After the start action, the SEFF contains a branch, which includes two `Guarded-BranchTransitions` defining a constraint on the value of input parameter **X**. Once the value distribution for **X** is specified by the domain expert, the probability for the guards to become true can be determined. Both branched `ResourceDemanding-Behaviours` include an `InternalAction`, whose resource demand is specified in dependency to the bytesize of component parameter **Z**. After the branch, the service iterates over the elements of input collection **Y** with the `CollectionIterator-Action`. Within the `ResourceDemaningBehaviour` of this loop, an external service is called, and its input parameter **extCallPar** is characterised in dependency to the inner elements of input collection parameter **Y**. Finally, the SEFF characterises the number of elements of **service1's** return value in dependency of input collection **Y**.

Note, that the SEFF only contains performance-relevant information, such as resource demands, abstract control flow, and calls to external services. The actual code of the component can contain an additional amount of internal computations, which are not performance-relevant, and thus have been abstracted.

2.4 Transformation

In addition to the SEFFs by the component developers, the other three roles need to specify their model instances (i.e., usage model, resource environment model, assembly model, allocation model, etc.) in order to create a full PCM instance. Once all models are specified and combined, they can be transformed into our analytical model. For the specification of the model instances, we have implemented graphical editors using Eclipse GEF/GMF.

The transformation (implemented in Java) consists of two steps: First, the parametric dependencies in the SEFFs are resolved. This includes, for example, computing transition probabilities for guarded branch transitions and execution times for parametric resource demands. As an example, Fig. 6 shows a set of variable characterisations on the left side and the SEFF from the former section with solved parametric dependencies on the right side.

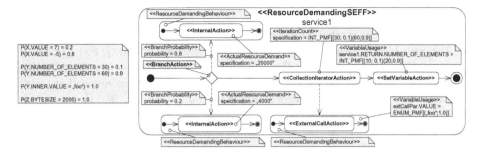

Fig. 6. Service Effect Specification with Solved Dependencies

Second, the the PCM instance is converted into an instance of our stochastic process algebra. This transformation merges a usage scenario with the participating SEFFs, and transforms the n-ary tree of actions in the PCM into the binary tree of the algebra, which will be explained in the next section.

3   Analytical Model

The computation of a service's execution time uses a stochastic process algebra (SPA) based on regular expressions. Its grammar is defined by the following BNF:

$$P := a \mid P \cdot Q \mid P +_\pi Q \mid P^{*(l)}$$

For the scope of this paper, we use the common semantics of regular expressions enriching it with a semantic for timed behaviour. Opposed to process algebras in general, recursive behaviour is forbidden here, instead our SPA uses the less expressive construct of loops. This allows us to perform a relatively straightforward analysis of the described systems. The complete version of the process algebra also supports parallel processes and synchronisation (preliminary version can be found in [14]). In the following, the time semantics of the rules above will be explained. Symbols will be denoted by small letters (a, b) and processes by large letters (P, Q).

3.1   Computations

The execution time of a **symbol** a is a random variable X_a characterised by its PDF $f_a(t)$. In our model, arbitrary distribution functions are allowed, which are assumed to be independent and identically distributed (iid, see Section 3.2). X_a specifies the time passed while processing a. If X_t is the time when $a \cdot P$ starts, the processing time of a is added to X_t when it finishes, so $X'_t := X_t + X_a$, and $a \cdot P$ then behaves like process P at time X'_t.

As for symbols, the execution time of process P is denoted by an iid random variable X_P characterised by PDF $f_P(t)$. The execution time of a **sequence** of two processes P and Q, $P \cdot Q$ is the sum of their execution times $X_{P \cdot Q} = X_p + X_q$. Since X_P and X_Q are assumed to be iid, their characterising PDFs can be convoluted

$$f_{P.Q}(t) = (f_p \circledast f_q)(t),$$

where $\circledast$ denotes the symbol for convolution.

The probabilistic choice or **alternative** of two processes P and Q, $P +_\pi Q$, either has the execution time of process P with probability π or of process Q with probability $(1 - \pi)$. To define this behaviour, the uniform distribution between zero and one $u(x)$ is used, where $u(\cdot)$ denotes drawing a sample from $u(x)$. Let $u = u(\cdot)$ be one sample of PDF $u(x)$, then

$$X_{P+_\pi Q} = \begin{cases} X_P, & \text{if } 0 \leq u < \pi \\ X_Q, & \text{if } \pi \leq u \leq 1 \end{cases}.$$

The PDF of the alternative is the weighted sum of the single PDFs

$$f_{P+_\pi Q}(t) = \pi f_P(t) + (1 - \pi)f_Q(t)$$

If process P is executed in a **loop**, $P^{*(l)}$, the number of loop iterations is specified by a probability mass function (PMF) $p_l(i) = P_l(X = i)$ denoting the probability that process P is executed i times in a row. Then, if $u = u(\cdot)$ is a sample of the uniform distribution $u(x)$ and $F_l(x)$ is the cumulative distribution function of $p_l(i)$, the execution time of a loop is

$$X_{P^{*(l)}} = \begin{cases} 0 & 0 \leq u < F_l(0) \\ X_{P,1} & F_l(0) \leq u < F_l(1) \\ X_{P,1} + X_{P,2} & F_l(1) \leq u < F_l(2) \\ \quad \vdots & \\ X_{P,1} + X_{P,2} + \ldots + X_{P,N} & F_l(N-1) \leq u < F_l(N) \end{cases}$$

where $N \in \mathbb{N}_+$ is last value with $p_l(N) > 0$ and $p_l(i) = 0 \quad \forall i \in \mathbb{N}_+, i > N$. $X_{P,i}$ is the ith instance of random variable X_P. The PDF of a loop can be computed by

$$f_{P^{*(l)}}(t) = \sum_{i=0}^{N} p_l(i) \left(\overset{i}{\underset{j=1}{\circledast}} f_P \right)(t)$$

Tools and techniques from signal processing efficiently compute the execution time of a process. We approximate continuous PDFs with discrete PMFs using a predefined sampling rate as described in [10].

3.2 Assumptions and Limitations

The following section briefly describes assumptions and limitations underlying our approach. More detail can be found in [17,5].

Independent and identically distributed random variables: Random variables characterising resource demand are assumed to be stochastically independent. This might not hold in some realistic cases, for example, if a resource is overloaded and all resource demands for this resource will lead to slow execution times. Furthermore, PDFs for resource demands are assumed to not change over time (e.g., to model a warm-up phase and a normal operation phase of the system).

Markov property on branches: As our SPA is based on Markov chains, our approach inherits their usual assumptions. For loops, the Markov property (the probability of going from one state to another is independent of the former execution path) has been weakened, as our SPA allows the specification of PMFs for the number of loop iterations and is not bound to a geometrical distribution. For branches, the Markov property is still present, but the SEFF-model contains branch conditions in dependency to input parameters.

Single-user analysis: As a first step, the analysis model assumes that only one user executes a scenario at a time. However, the results from our approach can be fed into existing tools for queueing networks to obtain predictions in a multi-user setting. Additionally, in [5] we have introduced a simulation tool for the PCM capable of simulating multiple concurrent users.

Availability of models: SEFFs for each component in the architecture must exist to apply our method. If new components are designed, it is possible to derive the SEFF specifications from the design documents and publish them in a component repository. For already existing components, we are working on code analysis tools for component developers, to derive SEFFs semi-automatically out of source code, so that legacy components can be integrated into our approach.

Static architecture: The PCM does not support dynamic component architectures, where new components can be created or the links between components can change at runtime. It is assumed that the set of components and their connection in the architecture are fixed for our performance prediction.

4 Case Study

We have conducted a proof-of-concept case study on a component-based architecture comparing response time predictions based on our models with response time measurements made with an implementation of the architecture. As the newly introduced component specifications allow evaluating an architecture under different usage profiles, we examined the architecture with two different usage profiles.

Specifically, the questions before the case study were: Can our method predict correctly, whether this component-based architecture can meet a service level agreement (SLA) under two different usage profiles? How large is the prediction error of our method in the measured usage scenarios?

4.1 Architecture, Scenario and Usage Profiles

The case study analyses the `MediaStore` architecture, a web shop for music and video files modelled according to the functionality of the iTunes Music Store. It is a three-tier architecture (Fig. 7) with a client tier, an application server hosting components implementing the business logic, and a database tier with two MySQL databases connected to the application server via Gigabit Ethernet. For the application server tier, we chose the open-source variant of Sun's Glassfish application server [11] which is fully EJB3 compliant.

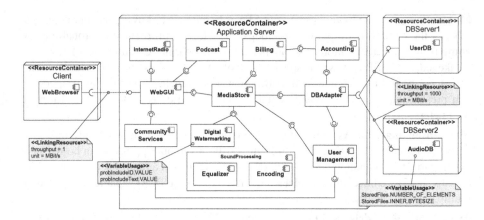

Fig. 7. Media Store: Static/Allocation View

In the usage scenario of our case study, a user downloads a set of files (e.g., a music album) from the store. Therefore, the user provides the `WebGUI`-component with a query resulting in a set of music titles, which is forwarded to the `MediaStore`-component. The database `AudioDB` is searched for the files, which afterwards get transferred from the database server via the network connection to the application server. Finally, the client can download the files. The `UserDB` database is not used in this scenario.

The filling degree of the `AudioDB` is a performance-influencing factor (e.g., when executing queries over the contained tables) and has been exposed with a collection component parameter (`StoredFiles.NUMBER_OF_ELEMENTS`). The actual value of this parameter depends on the context the component is used in. Furthermore, the size of the files stored on the database server influences the transmission delay between database server and application server, and is also modelled as a component parameter (`StoredFiles.INNER.BYTESIZE`).

As a measure for copy protection, we incorporate a component `DigitalWatermarking` into the architecture. It is able to unrecognisably watermark individual media files with additional information. This component can be configured to watermark media files with the current user ID, so that the user could be tracked down, should the file appear somewhere on the Internet. This configuration option has been modelled as a component parameter `probIncludeID`, which specifies the probability of including the ID. Additionally, the component can be configured to include additional texts like lyrics or subtitles into the files, which has been modelled with the component parameter `probIncludeText`.

Our performance prediction method shall check, whether the time between issuing the download request and starting the download is sufficiently short. From the requirements, there is a service level agreement (SLA) of at least 90% of calls returning in under 8 seconds, which has to be met even after watermarking is introduced.

The performance influencing information of the component services involved in the case study has been modelled using SEFFs illustrated in Fig. 8. The parametric

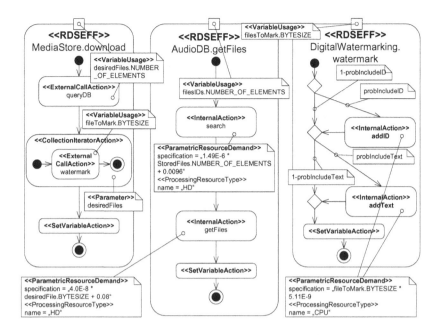

Fig. 8. MediaStore: Service Effect Specifications

dependencies within the SEFFs have been derived by monitoring the components and analysing the results using statistical regression techniques. This step has to be performed once for each component by its developer. Using such annotated SEFFs, different software architects can assemble the components to individual architectures and predict the performance under their individual usage profiles.

As an example, Fig. 9 illustrates the series of measurements and the linear regression for searching the database, if the number of files stored within changes. We used the derived values to specify the parameteric dependency for the `InternalAction` "search" of the service AudioDB.getfiles in Fig. 8.

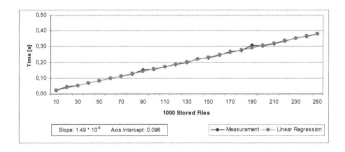

Fig. 9. Time for Searching the Database

Note, that this step of deriving parametric dependencies also has to be done parameterised by the hardware and middleware layer, on which the components are deployed on. However, this is out of the scope of this paper.

The case study considers two different settings. In Setting1, the components and the MediaStore architecture are used to build a music store, in which users usually request 10-14 files (a music album, number of files uniformly distributed) with their filesizes distributed as given in Fig 10. The database is filled with 250.000 entries of different music titles (i.e., AudioDB.StoredFiles.NUMBER_OF_ELEMENTS = 250000). Only the user ID branding from the watermarking component is used in this setting (i.e., probIncludeID=1.0, probIncludeText=0.0).

Size (MB)	0.0	1.0	2.0	3.0	4.0	5.0	6.0	7.0	8.0	9.0	10.0	11.0	12.0
Probability	0.0060	0.0223	0.0466	0.1038	0.1606	0.2038	0.1882	0.1137	0.0685	0.0293	0.0173	0.0093	0.0300

Fig. 10. File size distribution

In Setting2, the components and the architecture are used to build a video store, where users usually only request a single file (a movie), whose size is uniformly distributed between 95 and 105 MB. The database is filled with 10.000 entries of different movies (AudioDB.StoredFiles.NUMBER_OF_ELEMENTS = 10000). The software architect has configured the watermarking component to include the user ID and also subtitles for the movies (i.e., probIncludeID=1.0, probIncludeText=1.0).

For the implementation of the MediaStore, we exploit the architectural model we have used for the predictions. We have implemented a Model-2-Text transformation on the PCM model instance, which generates code skeletons implementing the components as EJB3. The code skeletons already contain the control flow parts of the SEFFs (i.e., loops, branches, etc.), only the logic of internal actions is missing and has been implemented manually. Additionally, build scripts, deployment descriptors, configuration files, and a test client for performing the response time measurements are generated. We introduce measurement probes into the implementation using aspects, which we weave into the code using AspectJ [1]. Finally, we have ensured in a pre-test run that the measurement probes do not distort the measured response times significantly. We have measured the response time in both settings approx. 500 times to get distribution functions.

4.2 Results

The predictions and measurements for the two settings of our case study can be found in Fig. 11- 12. The figures illustrate both predictions (dark grey) and measurements (light grey) as histograms and cumulative distribution functions (CDF), which are placed on top of each other to enable comparing them visually. Matching areas of both functions are shown in medium grey.

For Setting1, the probability functions widely overlap (Fig. 11(a)). The most probable predictions for the response time is at around 6 seconds, which matches the

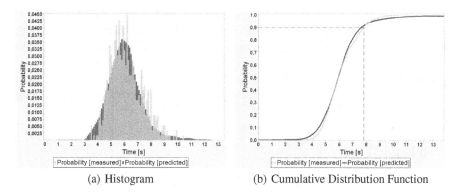

(a) Histogram   (b) Cumulative Distribution Function

Fig. 11. Response Times Setting1

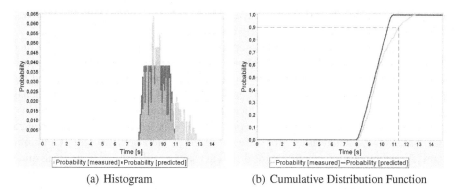

(a) Histogram   (b) Cumulative Distribution Function

Fig. 12. Response Times Setting2

measurements quite accurately. To test for goodness of fit, we used a Kolmogorov-Smirnov-Test [19] (KS-test), which was not able to reject our null hypothesis of prediction and measurement having the same underlying probability distribution at a significance level of $\alpha = 0.01$. From the CDF it can be derived that it was predicted that the SLA of 90% of the calls returning in less than 8 seconds could be met (Fig. 11(b)). This prediction also matched the measured values, where actually 92% of the calls returned in less than 8 seconds. The deviation between prediction and measurement at the 90% mark (7.7 seconds vs. 7.8 seconds) is approx. 0.1 seconds, i.e., a difference of 1.3 percent.

In Setting2, the probability functions overlap to a large extent, but the measured response times spread further than the predicted ones (Fig. 12(a)). This is due to the higher network load because of the larger file sizes, which leads to a higher distortion of the measurements [28]. However, the most probable predicted and measured values are both around 9.5 seconds. As in setting1, the KS-test was not able to reject our null hypothesis. In this case, it was predicted that 90% of the calls returned in 10.4 seconds, which would violate the required SLA of 8 seconds (Fig. 12(b)). The measurements confirmed that under Setting2 the SLA would indeed be violated, as the 90% of the calls returned in only 11.3 seconds. The error between prediction and measurement was 0.9 seconds or 8.0 percent.

Concludingly, our approach correctly predicted the compliance or violation of the required SLA in both studied cases. In these cases the pointwise error between prediction and measurement was below 10 percent.

5   Related Work

Model-based performance prediction methods for software architectures originate from the SPE (Software Performance Engineering) approach by Smith et al. [26]. They have been surveyed by Balsamo et al. [3] and, specifically for component-based systems, by Becker et al. [4]. We will briefly review usage profile modelling in other performance prediction approaches for component-based systems, before comparing our analytical model with established performance formalisms.

Bondarev et al. [7] proposed a similar approach to ours, but aim at components in an embedded system environment. Dependencies between input parameters and resource usage of a component are modelled explicitly in this approach, but it is assumed that input parameters can be characterised as constant values. Our approach allows stochastical characterisations of parameters, which is more accurate for the targeted domain of large distributed systems. The CB-SPE approach [6] is based on component specifications, which are parameterisable for different resource environments (e.g., CPU time, bandwidth, memory buffer), but not for different usage profiles. It furthermore assumes that it is known which required services are invoked in a component upon calling a provided services. This dependency is modelled explicitly in our approach. KLAPER [12] is an intermediate specification language for component performance and reliability aiming at reducing the effort for model transformations. It allows the specifications of input parameters, but does not contain component configuration parameters or output parameters. Hamlet et al. [13] aim at components resembling mathematical functions. They divide the input space of a component into several subdomains. The execution time for each subdomain is provided by the component developer, and the software architect needs to execute the component for each subdomain to deduce which other components are called.

Our approach uses a restricted stochastic process algebra (SPA) with generally distributed execution times (survey in [15]) as analytical model. Similar, even more expressive SPAs have been proposed, but due to their complexity they are usually only solvable via time-consuming and less precise simulations, whereas our restricted SPA can be efficiently solved analytically without simulation. Other analytical models for performance prediction include queueing networks [18] and stochastic Petri nets [2]. Analytical solutions to queueing networks with generally distributed service times are known only for very restricted cases. Layered queueing networks [24] only support mean-value analysis, while our approach results in a more expressive probability distribution function.

6   Conclusions and Future Work

This paper has introduced extensions to an existing component specifications language to model characterisations of component parameters as well as service input and output parameters. Such parameters can influence the resource usage or control flow of a component service significantly and should thus be included into QoS-predictions. We have described the fully automated model transformation, which maps an architectural model of our component specifications to a stochastic process algebra. Solving the algebra analytically has yielded response times for use cases of the system as distribution functions.

Component developers as well as software architects may benefit from this approach. Component developers can specify the performance properties of their components without exposing intellectual properties, and thereby increase their re-usability as users can quickly check the actual performance of the component in their environment. With the performance specifications, software architects can quickly evaluate different design decisions regarding the components used in their systems. By adjusting the parameters of the introduced models, they can check if performance requirements can be met under different system configurations.

Future work is directed at lowering the limiting assumptions of our approach. We are currently implementing code-analyses tools to semi-automatically derive SEFFs from existing legacy software components. This might reduce the effort for manually creating the models needed for the performance prediction. The concurrency modelling of our process algebra is still limited and needs to be extended and evaluated on multi-processor systems. We plan to better include characteristics and configuration settings of the middleware into our approach. In the long term, we will extend our approach for dynamic component architectures, where the bindings between components can change at runtime.

References

1. The AspectJ Homepage, http://www.eclipse.org/aspectj/
2. Baccelli, F., Balbo, G., Boucherie, R.J., Campos, J., Chiola, G.: Annotated bibliography on stochastic petri nets. Performance Evaluation of Parallel and Distributed Systems Solution Methods 105, 1–24 (1994)
3. Balsamo, S., Marco, A.D., Inverardi, P., Simeoni, M.: Model-Based Performance Prediction in Software Development: A Survey. IEEE Transactions on Software Engineering 30(5), 295–310 (2004)
4. Becker, S., Grunske, L., Mirandola, R., Overhage, S.: Performance Prediction of Component-Based Systems: A Survey from an Engineering Perspective. In: Reussner, R., Stafford, J., Szyperski, C. (eds.) Architecting Systems with Trustworthy Components. LNCS, vol. 3938, pp. 169–192. Springer, Heidelberg (2006)
5. Becker, S., Koziolek, H., Reussner, R.: Model-based Performance Prediction with the Palladio Component Model. In: Proceedings of the 6th International Workshop on Software and Performance (WOSP 2007), ACM Press, New York (2007)
6. Bertolino, A., Mirandola, R.: CB-SPE Tool: Putting Component-Based Performance Engineering into Practice. In: Crnković, I., Stafford, J.A., Schmidt, H.W., Wallnau, K. (eds.) CBSE 2004. LNCS, vol. 3054, pp. 233–248. Springer, Heidelberg (2004)

7. Bondarev, E., With, P.d., Chaudron, M., Musken, J.: Modelling of Input-Parameter Dependency for Performance Predictions of Component-Based Embedded Systems. In: Proceedings of the 31th EUROMICRO Conference (EUROMICRO 2005) (2005)

8. Budinsky, F., Steinberg, D., Merks, E., Ellersick, R., Grose, T.J.: Eclipse Modeling Framework. Eclipse Series. Prentice-Hall, Englewood Cliffs (2003)

9. Eskenazi, E., Fioukov, A., Hammer, D.: Performance prediction for component compositions. In: Proceedings of the 7th International Symposium on Component-based Software Engineering (CBSE7) (2004)

10. Firus, V., Becker, S., Happe, J.: Parametric Performance Contracts for QML-specified Software Components. In: Formal Foundations of Embedded Software and Component-based Software Architectures (FESCA). ETAPS 2005. Electronic Notes in Theoretical Computer Science, vol. 141, pp. 73–90 (2005)

11. GlassFish Open Source Java EE 5 Application Server,
https://glassfish.dev.java.net/

12. Grassi, V., Mirandola, R., Sabetta, A.: From Design to Analysis Models: a Kernel Language for Performance and Reliability Analysis of Component-based Systems. In: WOSP 2005: Proceedings of the 5th international workshop on Software and performance, pp. 25–36. ACM Press, New York (2005)

13. Hamlet, D., Mason, D., Woit, D.: Component-Based Software Development: Case Studies. In: Properties of Software Systems Synthesized from Components. Series on Component-Based Software Development, vol. 1, pp. 129–159. World Scientific Publishing Company (March 2004)

14. Happe, J., Koziolek, H., Reussner, R.: Parametric Performance Contracts for Software Components with Concurrent Behaviour. In: de Boer, F.S., Mencl, V. (eds.) Proceedings of the 3rd International Workshop on Formal Aspects of Component Software (FACS 2006), Prague, Czech Republic. Electronical Notes in Computer Science (September 2006)

15. Katoen, J.-P., D'Argenio, P.R.: General Distributions in Process Algebra. In: Lectures on Formal Methods and Performance Analysis: First EEF/Euro Summer School on Trends in Computer Science Berg en Dal, The Netherlands, July 3-7, 2000, vol. 2090, p. 375. Springer, Heidelberg (2001), (Revised Lectures)

16. Koziolek, H., Happe, J.: A Quality of Service Driven Development Process Model for Component-based Software Systems. In: Gorton, I., Heineman, G.T., Crnkovic, I., Schmidt, H.W., Stafford, J.A., Szyperski, C.A., Wallnau, K. (eds.) CBSE 2006. LNCS, vol. 4063, Springer, Heidelberg (2006)

17. Koziolek, H., Happe, J., Becker, S.: Parameter dependent performance specification of software components. In: Hofmeister, C., Crnkovic, I., Reussner, R. (eds.) QoSA 2006. LNCS, vol. 4214, pp. 163–179. Springer, Heidelberg (2006)

18. Lazowska, E.D., Zahorjan, J., Graham, G.S., Sevcik, K.C.: Quantitative System Performance - Computer System Analysis Using Queueing Network Models. Prentice-Hall, Englewood Cliffs (1984)

19. Massey Jr., F.J.: The Kolmogorov-Smirnov Test for Goodness of Fit. Journal of the American Statistical Association 46(253), 68–78 (1951)

20. Menasce, D.A., Almeida, V.A.F., Dowdy, L.W.: Performance by Design. Prentice-Hall, Englewood Cliffs (2004)

21. Object Management Group (OMG). Mof 2.0 core specification (formal/2006-01-01) (2006)

22. Reussner, R.H., Becker, S., Happe, J., Koziolek, H., Krogmann, K., Kuperberg, M.: The Palladio Component Model. Technical report, Universitaet Karlsruhe (TH) (2006)

23. Reussner, R.H., Schmidt, H.W., Poernomo, I.: Reliability prediction for component-based software architectures. Journal of Systems and Software – Special Issue of Software Architecture – Engineering Quality Attributes 66(3), 241–252 (2003)

24. Rolia, J.A., Sevcik, K.C.: The method of layers. IEEE Transactions on Software Engineering 21(8), 689–700 (1995)
25. Smith, C.U., Williams, L.G.: Performance Solutions: A Practical Guide to Creating Responsive, Scalable Software. Addison-Wesley, Reading (2002)
26. Smith, C.U.: Performance Engineering of Software Systems. Addison-Wesley, Reading (1990)
27. Szyperski, C., Gruntz, D., Murer, S.: Component Software: Beyond Object-Oriented Programming, 2nd edn. ACM Press and Addison-Wesley, New York (2002)
28. Verdickt, T., Dhoedt, B., Turck, F.D., Demeester, P.: Hybrid Performance Modeling Approach for Network Intensive Distributed Software. In: Proceedings of the 6th International Workshop on Software and Performance (WOSP 2007). ACM Sigsoft Notes, pp. 189–200 (February 2007)
29. Wu, X., Woodside, M.: Performance modeling from software components. SIGSOFT Softw. Eng. Notes 29(1), 290–301 (2004)

Pre-emptive Adaptation Through Classical Control Theory

Nurzhan Duzbayev and Iman Poernomo

King's College London
Strand, London, UK, WC2R2LS
{nurzhan.duzbayev,iman.poernomo}@kcl.ac.uk

Abstract. Self-adaptive systems are capable of changing their behaviour at runtime to meet target constraints. An important research question is how quality of service models can inform runtime adaptation.

This paper presents a solution to the problem by application of control theory to improve performance of queued systems by means of architectural adaptation.

In a paper presented at the previous year's QoSA conference, we showed how Auto-Regressive Integrated Moving Average techniques can be utilized to forecast how Quality of Service (QoS) characteristics are likely to evolve in the near future. This is particularly important in cases where systems can be adapted to counter QoS constraint violations. In this paper, we show how, given a similar type of QoS characteristic forecasts, strategies of architectural adaptation can be implemented that pre-emptively avoid QoS violations. The novelty of our approach is that we use classical control theory to ensure that our adaptation strategies are stable, in the sense that they do not oscillate between choices. We provide a description of how our control theoretic model can be implemented using context-based interception in .NET via model driven engineering.

1 Introduction

Self-adaptive systems are capable of changing their behaviour at runtime to meet target behavioural constraints. An important research question is how quality of service models can inform runtime adaptation. This paper presents a step towards solving this problem by application of classical control theory.

In a paper presented at the previous QoSA conference [7], we showed how Auto-Regressive Integrated Moving Average (ARIMA) techniques can be utilized to forecast how QoS characteristics are likely to evolve in the near future. This result allows us to detect warning signs that a system is tending towards violation of desired QoS levels. A warning can be given to a human administrator, who might then decide to reconfigure the system in such a way as to pre-empt the violation occurring.

However, clearly there is benefit from an automated means of controlling system parameters to provide such reconfiguration. The theory of dependability

S. Overhage et al. (Eds.): QoSA 2007, LNCS 4880, pp. 164–181, 2007.

offers a range of possible solutions for automated control for load balancing and fault tolerance. In this paper, we show how, given Auto-Regressive Moving Average (ARMA) predictions of likely future QoS characteristics, pre-emptive controllers can be developed by application of classical control theory. Our approach determines a control strategy that is optimal with respect to resource cost.

We focus on the problem of queued stability and utilization. The idea is that, if our system detects a dangerous trend towards a communication queue becoming unmanageably long, then a controller component should adapt the architecture of the system to improve influencing factors, such as service rate and the average number of calls entering the queue. For example, if the queue is becoming too long, the controller could create an alternative server and divert some calls to it, halving the service rate. In a world of limitless resources, the controller could solve the problem of QoS violation by creating a thousand such servers and, when the queue becomes shorter, the thousand servers may be replaced by one again. The problem is that each server has a cost, as does the adaptation action. The controller should adapt the architecture to provide the best QoS and yet be optimal with respect to cost.

A common approach is to perform adaptation by means of some form of a policy-based controller. Determining the optimal control strategy is difficult. A bad strategy yields a oscillating feedback problem: if the utilization improves significantly, so (to minimize cost) influencing parameters are changed again (by removing some servers for instance), and, consequently, the utilization worsens significantly, resulting in influencing parameters needing to be changed again, the utilization improving signficantly again, and so on. The best controller is one that provides an appropriate adaptation as quickly as possible but do not result in radical oscillations.

We develop the controller using root locus techniques to determine optimal non-oscillating control strategies. We also provide a description of how our control theoretic model can be implemented using context-based interception in .NET via model driven engineering.

The paper proceeds as follows:

- Section 2 summarizes relevant notions from queuing theory.
- Section 3 shows how to apply classical control theory to develop a controller providing optimal adaptation.
- Section 4 provides overview of how we employ model driven techniques to implement our control systems.
- An illustrate example is provided in section 5.
- Conclusions and related work are discussed in the final section.

2 Background

2.1 Queued Communication

Queuing theory enables the mathematical analysis of queued communication between clients and a server (or a set of servers) (see, for example, [13,5]). Such communication is commonplace in large-scale distributed systems, where there is a dependence on loosely coupled messaging and messages can potentially be sent from different sources to the same component. Performance evaluation of such systems is essential.

We understand queued communication as depicted in Fig. 1. A number of calls enter a queue per unit time. We write $X_i \geq 0$ for the random variable denoting the number of calls entering at unit time $i = 1, 2, \ldots$. Each call is numbered and served in some order. As soon as the server finishes servicing a call, it immediately starts to serve the next call (if there are calls remaining in the queue) and the served call leaves the system. If repeated processing is necessary, a call joins the queue right from the beginning. The server is called *idle* when there are no calls remaining in the queue.

There is a range of different *models* of queued communication, each with well understood QoS benefits and disadvantages. Factors effecting the values of QoS characteristics for a particular model include the distribution of incoming requests, the servicing discipline (for example, randomly selected, incoming order or some priority discipline) and serving rate distribution.

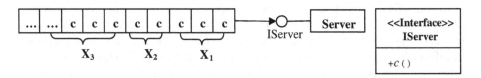

Fig. 1. A queued service. Invocations of the service's methods are queued, where each X_i is the number of invocations at unit time i .

For queued systems, a central QoS characteristic is stability. A system is defined to be *stable* when each queued call is served. It is *unstable* if there is a possibility that calls will not be served.

We compute stability via the notion of system utilization, defined as follows.

We assume each X_i is independent and equally distributed and with an average $\lambda = E[X_i]$, defining the average number of calls joining the queue per unit time. We assume that all calls have an average serving time $b > 0$ – this is the average unit time to process a single request. We consequently define the average service rate, the average number of requests that are served per unit time, to be $\mu = 1/b$.

Definition 1 (System utilization). *The utilization of a system, ρ is defined*

$$\rho = \lambda/\mu = \lambda b$$

where λ is average number of calls joining the queue per unit time and b is the average serving time. The system is stable *if, and only if, $\rho < 1$ and unstable if, and only if, $\rho > 1$. In case when $\rho = 1$, the system is stable only when $X_i = X_j$ for all i, j.*

Thus, if system works stable we have a finite queue length.

2.2 Forecasting Queue QoS

Given a system in which there are no trends in the number of calls made to a server or in the service time for a call, then the definition of ρ above provides the best means of predicting stability and QoS dependent characteristics.

While such situations are common, there are many contexts where trends in queue usage occur. For instance, if we are running a Google-like web service search engine, then, depending on various factors that influence the popularity of the service (our business plan, advertising strategies, the novelty and use of the service itself, etc), it is possible that there will be a genuine trend in the number of calls over time. In such a case, using an overall average to determine ρ will not provide the best immediate prediction of stability. It would be preferable to factor out earlier measures of calls (when the service was unpopular) and to emphasize the newer values, to predict if the system is likely to become unstable soon.

In our previous paper at QoSA [7], we considered the application of the ARIMA method for the purpose of predicting QoS characteristics for queued systems and presented some promising experimental results. Here, with the motive of applying control theory to the pre-emptive adaptation problem, we utilize a basic version of this average, the Auto-Regressive Moving Average (ARMA).

ARMA Forecasting Strategies. ARMA was developed to treat trends in a more sophisticated way than simple averages.

One of the simplest strategies for time series prediction based on trends is to take an average of recent values of the time series, ignoring earlier values. This is the *simple moving average* technique. Here, the average is computed as

$$SMA(X_n, r) = \sum_{i=n-r+1}^{n} \frac{X_i}{r}$$

where r is cycle length and n is the total number of observations. This is essentially an arithmetic mean, but over a shorter cycle length than the total number of observations.

ARMA extends the simple moving average and is widely used in financial domains for forecasting time series. It consists of two components

- A moving average component, associating weights with previous values in the time series, so that the forecasted next value depends more on the most recent value and less on the earliest value in the time series.
- An autoregressive component, factoring in errors of previous predicted values against actual values in order to minimize error in the predicted value.

The equation for ARMA is

$$y[k] = \sum_{q=0}^{m} x[k-q]\beta_q - \sum_{p=1}^{n} y[k-p]\alpha_p \tag{1}$$

where $x[i]$ is a time series of input values and $y[j]$ is a time series of forecasted values of x, β_i and α_j are weights for the moving average and autoregressive components and m and n define how much of the time series the prediction method should consider. Given a particular time series $x[i]$ we can use least squares regression to determine optimal values of these coefficients. There is a way of obtaining the confidence interval for an ARMA forecast – see [7] for details.

So, the ARMA prediction for the k-th arrival rate $\hat{X}_n$ will be

$$\hat{X}_k = \sum_{q=0}^{m} X_{k-q}\beta_q - \sum_{p=1}^{n} \hat{X}_{k-p}\alpha_p \tag{2}$$

Prediction of Utilization. Given the ARMA prediction of call arrivals, it is possible to forecast M/M/1 QoS characteristics by substitution of predicted values of X into the formula for utilization. Confidence intervals are calculated similarly.

We define the predicted utilization to be

$$\hat{\rho}_k = \hat{X}_k b$$

We can determine the confidence interval for predicted utilisation in terms of predicted arrival rate's error, using the fact that the error of $\hat{\rho}_k$ will be $\hat{X}_n b - X_n b = R_n^X b$:

$$[\rho_{n,k}^{min}, \rho_{n,k}^{max}] = \hat{\rho}_{n,k} \mp \frac{\xi}{\sqrt{k}} \sqrt{Var\left\{\sum_{m=1}^{k} R_{n,m}^X b\right\}}$$

Utilization prediction is useful in two cases:

- When there is a genuine trend towards instability. This is a serious problem for a queued system and pre-emptive notification can be very useful if an adaptation solution exists. For example, if a webservice has a predicted instability, administration could refuse any more requests until the queue normalizes.
- When there is a "local" trend towards instability. A time series might have a globally stable utilization, but with locally unstable segments. That is, a queued system might be able to respond to all requests eventually, but at certain times, might have an unacceptably high number of requests compared to service time. This situation can also benefit from pre-emptive notification to inform an adaptation strategy.

The previous confidence intervals for a prediction are helpful for determining the certainty we have of a current predicted trend in utilization.

See [7] for an explanation of how a number of related QoS characteristics can be forecast based on these calculations.

3   Control System Model

We now outline how classical control theory can be applied to develop a controller for changing a queue service rate pre-emptively in response to trends in utilization toward instability.

Specifically, we treat pre-emptive control of service rate in order to maintain a desired level of utilization. If the predicted utilization diverges above or below the desired level, we require our controller to apply a positive or negative *gain* to offset the divergence.

The idea is as follows. At any point in time, the utilization for the service can be computed in terms of the current average number of calls and average service rate. A predicted utilization model can also be determined, following the ARMA technique of the previous section, to give a picture of how we expect the utilization to continue, given known trends. Consider a constraint that the utilization should not exceed a certain amount. The *control error* of the service is the difference between the predicted utilization and a desired utilization. The controller is constructed to manipulate the average service rate in such a way that this error is minimized. The controller is characterised by a function over the error and a constant *gain* parameter. Each adaptation is associated with a cost, so the controller must also ensure that cost is minimal. We construct a closed-loop transfer function model for the system. This is a complex valued function. Root locus analysis is a technique whereby the poles of the transfer function are identified in order to determine the optimal gain for the controller function.

3.1   Automatic Control Systems

Control systems to consist of a series of interconnected 'plants'. The term 'component' is often used in place of 'plant' by control engineers, but to avoid confusion, we shall only use the term 'component' in the software engineering sense. However, a plant does have some similarities to a software component, that we expound upon in the next section. A plant is considered as a functional module, taking an input signal and returning an output signal.

Transfer Functions. The relationship between input and output relationship for a plant is often characterised by a transfer function. In the case of continuous relationships, where input and output are related via time-invariant, differential equations, the transfer function is given as the Laplace transform of the output over the Laplace transform of the input. The analogous situation for discrete relationships uses a Z-transform instead of a Laplace transform:

$$\text{Transfer function} = G(z) = \frac{\mathcal{Z}\{output\}}{\mathcal{Z}\{input\}}$$

The Z-transform $\mathcal{Z}$ is essentially a Fourier transform generalised over the complex plane [12]. Given a signal $x[n]$, the Z-transform is defined as

$$X(z) = \mathcal{Z}\{x[n]\} = \sum_{n=0}^{\infty} x[n]z^{-n}$$

where z is some complex number $z = Ae^{j\phi}$.

Transfer functions are used because they allow us to represent system dynamics by algebraic complex equations. If the highest power of z in the denominator of the transfer function is equal to n, the plant is called nth-order.

The transfer function for a plant enables us to understand its output for various forms of input. Transfer functions can be experimentally derived by studying how a plant reacts to a range of sample input values.

Automatic Control Systems and Block Diagrams. A block diagram of a system represents how signals flow from one plant to another. Each plant is represented by a square block, with the name of its transfer function drawn inside. Arrows connecting plants define the way in which the output of one plant is passed on as the input for another plant. Two signals can be added or subtracted from one another at what is called a *summing point*. A signal can split and be fed concurrently into several other blocks or summing points – the point of such a split is called a *branch point*.

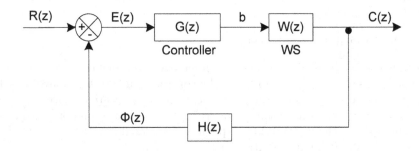

Fig. 2. Control flow for a single component architecture

A simple *automatic control system* is a system with the block diagram of Fig. 2. It consists of three plants with transfer functions $G(z)$, $W(z)$ and $H(z)$, with input and output signals being sent as depicted by the arrows. The output signal of $W(z)$ branches out of the system and also is fed into a summation point (depicted by the circle), where it is subtracted from a reference input R (summation of the two signals would be depicted by two positive symbols in the circle).

The entire system forms a plant, with an input R and an output C. It can therefore be associated with a transfer function of the form

$$\frac{C(z)}{R(z)} = \frac{G(z)W(z)}{1 + G(z)W(z)H(z)} \qquad (3)$$

This is called *the closed-loop transfer function* for the system. The term

$$G(z)W(z)H(z)$$

relates the signal $\phi(z)$ to the error signal $E(z)$, and is called the open-loop transfer function.

3.2 Control System for a Queued Service

Our intention is to define a control system of the form given in Fig. 2, where

- The reference input R is the desired level of utilization to be maintained for the service.
- The service is modelled by the plant W. We are not concerned with modelling the actual functionality of the service here. Rather, we are only interested in its current utilization. Therefore, in the control system, it is modelled as a function that takes in a controlled service rate b from the controller G and outputs a current utilization rate $c = Xb$, where X is the current number of calls joining the queue. The transfer function for the service is

$$G(s) = \frac{\mathcal{Z}\{output\}}{\mathcal{Z}\{input\}} = \frac{X(z)b(z)}{b(z)} = X(z)$$

Thus, the transfer function is parametrised over the model for the service's arrival process. For example, if we consider a service with a $M/M/1$ queue, we assume the service is characterized by a Poisson arrival process and a FIFO queue ordering discipline. In this case, the transfer function for G will be the Z-transform of a Poisson distribution for arrivals X.

- The current utilization is fed into an prediction plant H that forecasts the likely future utilization of the service, using an ARMA function of the form (1), with coefficients optimised according to the service's queuing model. There is a well-known result in discrete control theory that relates ARMA to a Z-transform, which tells us the Z-transform for (1) is

$$H(z) = \frac{\Phi(z)}{C(z)} = \frac{\displaystyle\sum_{q=0}^{m} z^{-q}\beta_q}{1 + \displaystyle\sum_{p=1}^{n} z^{-p}\alpha_p}$$

Control Laws. Our control system, following Fig. 2, should also include a controller plant. We then identify the controller plant defined by a function over the error signal, taken as the difference between the desired utilization and the predicted utilization

$$e = R - \phi$$

The controller plant G takes this error as input and will return a service time b that will attempt to offset any trends away from the desired utilization. This service time is taken as the input for the plant that models the queued service, W.

Control theory offers a range of possible equations that can define the controller's actions. Our approach works equally well with any of these strategies. For the purposes of illustration, we employ the integral control action strategy, in which the controller output value, the controlled service time, $b(t)$ is changed at a rate proportional to the error signal $e(t)$,

$$\frac{db(t)}{dt} = K_i e(t)$$

where K_i is a constant parameter, called the *gain* of the controller. Because we consider only discrete time, this becomes

$$b(t) = K_i \sum_{t=0}^{t} e(t)$$

The Z-transform for an integral controller is

$$G = \frac{K_i}{z}$$

Note that the strategy is a simplification: in practice, the control strategy will be implemented by discrete actions (for instance, increasing the service time by diverting calls to replicated servers) offering generally coarser shifts in b. The relation between the controller plant *model* and its implementation is addressed in the next section.

Clearly a higher value of K_i will lead to a faster correction to predicted divergence from a desired utilization. However, at some point, higher values of K_i will "overshoot", leading to a large predicted divergence in the opposite direction that will then require another large correction. When this occurs, the value of K_i results in feedback through the control system and oscillations in control actions. In terms of implementation, this is undesirable as oscillations will effect performance, as each control action will be associated with a cost.

So, we require the highest value of K_i that does *not* overshoot in this fashion. This can be determined through root locus analysis of the closed-loop transfer function for the control system.

The root locus method involves finding the roots of the characteristic equation for the closed-loop transfer function are plotted for all values of the gain parameter K_i. The characteristic equation for the closed-loop system is obtained by setting the denominator of (3) to zero. This occurs when the open loop transfer function GWH is equal to -1,

$$G(z)W(z)H(z) = -1$$

The method enables the analyist to determine the effects variations on K_i will have on the location of closed-loop poles. While theoretically quite complex, the solution for systems of our form can be easily determined automatically by MATLAB.

The *damping* ratio for a root locus plot determines the speed at which we would like the controller to converge to a desired value after a predicted divergence, assuming no further external perturbations to the utilization arising from changes to the arrival rate X. A lower damping ratio is desirable, but should be balanced with as high a value of K_i as possible. A given damping ratio r can be used to determine the value of K_i from the root locus plot: the value is found from the point on the plot that makes an angle $cos^{-1}r$ with the negative real axis. Because the ratio should be between 0 and 1, with a ratio above 1 leading to oscillations, all non-oscillating values of K_i are to be found in the upper left hand side of the complex plane for the the root locus plot.

4   Model Driven Development of Controlled Architectures

The method of the previous section developed a controller function that determines how the service rate should be changed in order to avoid undesirable trends in utilization. This function is a model of how control should work for a particular queued service. The this section sketches how we implement such models over an architecture through model driven engineering techniques.

4.1   Contexts and .NET

We use MDA to develop controlled service-based architectures built in .NET. Services are web services managed via the .NET UDDI infrastructure.

Our approach maintains encapsulation of functionality from instrumentation by means of *context-based interception*. A *context* in the .NET Framework is used as an objects execution scope and to intercept calls going to and from the object.

For the purposes of this paper consider the following conceptual semantics of a simple context, as illustrated in Fig. 3. We can consider a context as a type of container for .NET class objects. Contexts are associated with two kinds of method, a pre-call process and a post-call process. When clients, external to the context, invoke a contained class object, the context will execute the pre-call process. Immediately after the class object returns a value, and prior to returning control to the calling client, the context executes the post-call process. Calls to any components contained within the context will be treated in the same way, while calls within the context are not intercepted. In this way, a range of functions can be implemented as pre- and post-call processes that "cut across" the methods of all contained objects. The principle is therefore similar to aspect oriented programming.

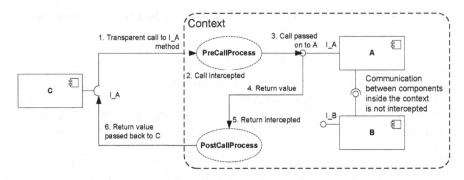

Fig. 3. Simplified semantics of context-based interception

For our purposes, context-based interception will be used to separate the service logic from control plumbing, by utilizing pre- and post-calls to provide information about a class object's behaviour without having to directly add instrumentation code to the class definition.

Our semantics is a simplified abstraction of how context-based interception is implemented in .NET with the `System.Runtime.Remoting` namespace. In .NET, contexts are implemented as custom attribute classes, providing the `IContextProperty` and `IContributeServerContextSink` interfaces. Interception code is associated with a context via *message sinks*, classes which implement the `IMessageSink` interface. Interception of sychronous method invocations is achieved by refining the `SyncProcessMessage` method of the following abstract sink class, `GenericSick`:

```
public class GenericSink : IMessageSink {      //This calls the object:
  IMessageSink m_NextSink;                     IMessagereturnedMessage =
  public GenericSink(IMessageSink nextSink)    m_NextSink.SyncProcessMessage(msg);
    { m_NextSink = nextSink; }                 //Post-call interception
  public IMessageSink NextSink                 PostCallProcessing(returnedMessage);
    { get { return m_NextSink; } }             return returnedMessage; }
  public SyncProcessMessage(IMessage msg) {    void PreCallProcessing(IMessage msg) {
    //Pre-call interception                      /* Do some pre call processing */ }
    PreCallProcessing(msg);                    void PostCallProcessing(IMessage msg) {
                                                 /* Do some pre call processing */ } }
```

We implement diversions to pre-call processing and post-call processing within the `SyncProcessMessage` method, by calling the class's `PreCallProcessing` and `PostCallProcessing` methods, respectively prior to, and immediately after invoking the requested class. It is possible to build a context that has a chain of such sinks, to combine sets of cross-cutting functions. Contexts can then be associated with classes using .NET's declarative custom attribute syntax.

4.2   Model Transformations

We now sketch our approach to controller generation. We first develop control systems for each constrained component of our extended version of the UML2

UML2 extension

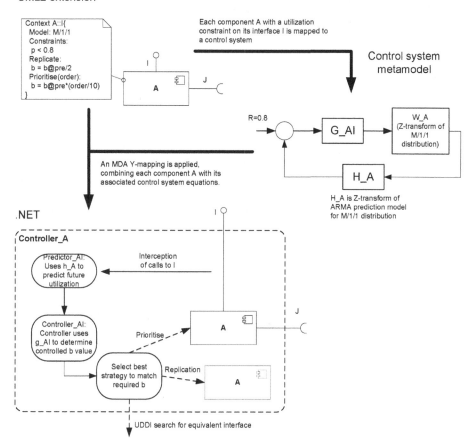

Fig. 4. Model driven development of the controlled system

superstructure. Then we apply a so called Y model-transformation, mapping UML components and their associated control systems to .NET based implementations.

We have implemented a beta version of our translations using the INRIA Triskell group's Kermeta transformation language. In this language, model transformations are defined as meta-operations of M2 metaclasses, whose input types are Platform Independent metaclasses and whose output types are Platform Specific metaclasses. This has the advantage of providing a unifying MOF-style framework for understanding both metamodels and model transformations.

We omit the full description of the transformations and instead describe their behaviour informally. As a motivating example for our transformations, we define a simple application of model transformation, involving a constraint over utilization imposed over method calls to a component.

Three models are given given in Fig. 4. We use the UML2 superstructure extended with QoS constraints, as defined in [3]. Our transformations map this to a control system model, that defines an adaptation strategy.

5   Example

To illustrate our predictive methods, we describe a simulated B2B webservice based system. The queued server *WSDistributor* is a computer component distributor selling for example chips or monitors. There are 30 Client web services *WSAssembler*$_1$, ..., *WSAssembler*$_{30}$ that act as communication points to businesses that use the distributor for purchasing components which they then assemble into computers. Clients could make one of the following three types of call: makeOrder, cancelOrder or makeQuery. For the sake of simplicity, we do not differentiate between the different calls, so that the arrivals per time unit X may consist of any number of these method invocations. The architecture of the system is shown in Fig. 5.

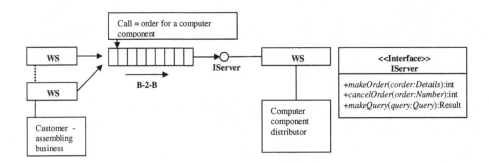

Fig. 5. Our B2B example

In order to obtain an initial working dataset of arrivals per time unit, we implemented the distributor webservice as an ASP.NET webservice, running on a Xeon 1,7GHz server running Windows Server 2003 and IIS 6. We ran the Microsoft Web Application Stress tool on a Pentium M laptop to simulate various demand profiles, both random and noisy trends.

We then ran least squares regression over the dataset to obtain an optimal set of 10 α_i and β_j parameters for an ARMA model of the form (1) with $n = m = 9$.

The model transformations of the previous section generate a context for the server, mapping this ARMA model to prediction pre-call code in the context. We assume each call type has the same processing time b.

The architecture of the system assumes an $M/M/1$ queuing model, with a Poisson arrival distribution. This information is used in the UML to Control theory transformation, generating a control system model with the following description:

$$\phi(n) = ARMA(c(n))$$

$$H(z) = \frac{\Phi(z)}{C(z)} = \frac{\sum_{q=0}^{9} z^{-q}\beta_q}{1 + \sum_{p=1}^{9} z^{-p}\alpha_p}$$

$$GWH = \left(\frac{K}{s}\right) HX = \left(\frac{K}{s}\right) H \left(\frac{2.55s - 2.023}{s + 1.3}\right)$$

$$GWH = \frac{2K\left(\beta_0 z^{10} + (\beta_1 - \beta_0)z^9 + (\beta_2 - \beta_1)z^8 + ... + (\beta_9 - \beta_8)z - \beta_9\right)}{z^{11} + (\alpha_1 + 1)z^{10} + (\alpha_2 + \alpha_1)z^9 + (\alpha_3 + \alpha_2)z^8 + ... + (\alpha_9 + \alpha_8)z^2 + \alpha_9 z}$$

We then apply root-locus analysis over this equation to determine the optimal value of K. We plot the roots of the characteristic equation against all values of K. This can be done easily in MATLAB, producing Fig. 6. The poles are denoted by an x and the zeros by a o. We can use this to determine the value of the gain that will make the damping ratio of the dominant closed-loop poles as prescribed. For example, valid, non-oscillating values for K_i are .1 with damping ratio .2, .5 with damping ratio .193 and 1 with damping ratio .63.

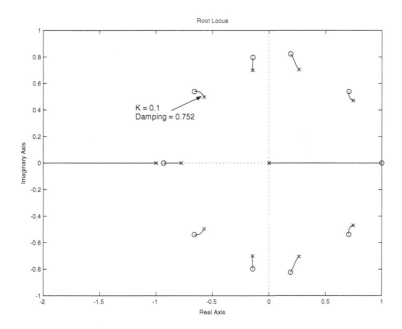

Fig. 6. Root loci for our example

Fig. 7 shows controlled utilization with valid, non-oscillating gain values (0.1 and 1) against uncontrolled utilization. As can be seen, higher gain results in faster response to trends away from the desired utilization level of 0.7. Because there is always random arrival rates, the controlled utilization will never be exactly at the desired level, but it maintains a satisfactory level of stability. Most

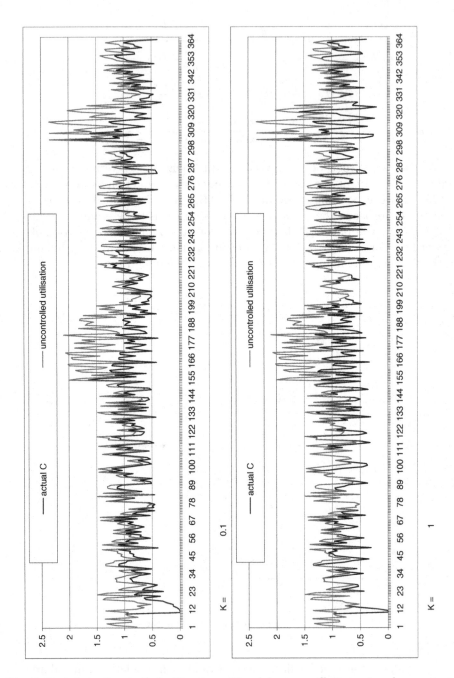

Fig. 7. Two plots of controlled utilization with valid, non-oscillating gain values against uncontrolled utilization)

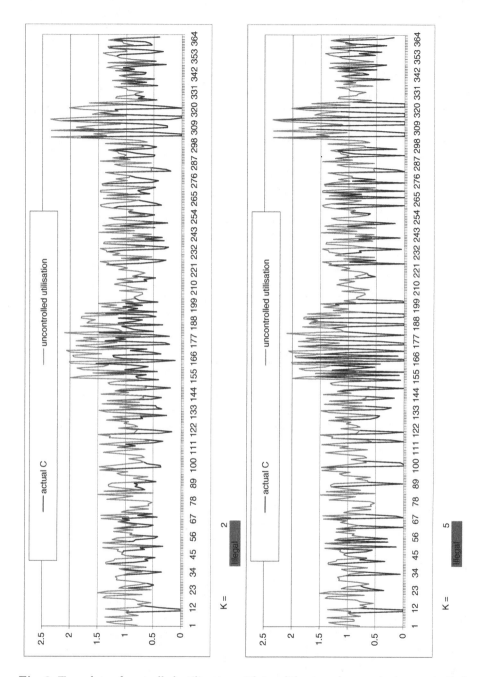

Fig. 8. Two plots of controlled utilization with invalid gain values against uncontrolled utilization)

notably, when the uncontrolled utilization moves into instability between time units 144-199 and 298-331, both graphs show the controlled utilization maintains a much better level of stability. Fig. 8 shows controlled utilization for oscillating gain values with a damping ratio of greater than 1. Clearly the controlled utilization here "overshoots" the correction to deviation from required utilization. In particular, the controller leads to undesirable oscillations between a near zero utilization (corresponding to, for instance, a very high number of replicated servers) and very unstable utilization (corresponding to a single overloaded server) at the points where uncontrolled utilization exhibits prolonged instability. This makes the controlled utilization worse than retaining ordinary utilization.

In the implementation, the service rate is changed by means of several adaptation strategies. 1) The server can be replicated n times, with yielding a new processing time equal to bn. 2) There are equivalent versions of the server available to access via UDDI, each with a variable serving time. If calls are diverted equally to one of these servers with service time b', then the new overall processing time is $b + b'$. These strategies are mapped to server selection code that forms the final part of the pre-call in the context generated by the transformation. Given a desired service level b, the selection code chooses the best strategy to meet the target. Provided the service rate change strategies are sufficiently fine grained enough, the selector can follow the controller's requests closely.

6 Related Work and Conclusions

There are many systems that permit dynamic adaptation of architectures based on real time QoS information [2,1,15,4,11]. The work of [15] is most similar to ours, as they use UDDI and QoS information to assemble web service architectures of optimal performance. Adaptation has also been proven to be useful in a range of other contexts. For example, [1] defines a language of QoS policies for grid services that are enforced by means of adaptation mechanisms. A different approach to QoS adaptation is considered in [14] for the case of embedded systems. These systems do not involve control theoretic notions or forecasting of values as part of their adaptation strategies. The ARMA methods need not only be applied to compute QoS queue characteristics. These strategies have the potential to be combined with such (non-queued) QoS-based runtime adaptation technologies.

Similar forecasting methods are used by Dinda for host load prediction [6] of CORBA based systems and the performance prediction methods of [2] and [8]. The difference with that works is that we adapt ARIMA methods to queued models, instead of load time estimation models. The intention behind our system is analogous to that of the Running Time Advisor of [6], but applied to widely distributed webservice component architecture.

Further work on stability for more complicated queuing strategies is given in [9]. These results could be adapted to our context, to enable us to predict stability for systems involving multiple servers.[10] presents the most completed overview of different stochastic methods to examine queued system to stability.

There are about ten methods. Each of them represents particular interest of investigation, study and especially applying. Most of these methods have been contrived to be applied in different parts of science, but never was applied to predict behaviour of complicated computer systems.

References

1. Al-Ali, R., Hafid, A., Rana, O., Walker, D.: An approach for quality of service adaptation in service-oriented grids. Concurrency and Computation: Practice and Experience 16(5), 401–412
2. Balsamo, S., Marco, A.D., Inverardi, P., Simeoni, M.: Model-based performance prediction in software development: A survey. IEEE Transactions On Software Engineering 30(5), 295–310 (2004)
3. Chan, K., Poernomo, I.: Qos-aware model driven architecture through the uml and cim. In: The 10th IEEE International Enterprise Distributed Object Conference (EDOC 2006), Hong Kong, 16-23 October 2006, pp. 345–355. IEEE Computer Society Press, Los Alamitos (2006)
4. Cysneiros, L.M., do Prado Leite, J.C.S.: Nonfunctional requirements: From elicitation to conceptual models. IEEE Transactions On Software Engineering 30(5), 328–350 (2004)
5. Bunday, B.D.: An introduction to queueing theory. Halsted Press, New York (1996)
6. Dinda, P.A.: Online prediction of the running time of tasks. Joint International Conference on Measurement and Modeling of Computer Systems, 336–337 (2001)
7. Duzbayev, N., Poernomo, I.: Runtime prediction of queued behaviour. In: Hofmeister, C., Crnkovic, I., Reussner, R. (eds.) QoSA 2006. LNCS, vol. 4214, Springer, Heidelberg (2006)
8. Fortier, P.J., Michel, H.E.: Computer Systems Perfomance Evaluation and Prediction. Digital Press (2003)
9. Foss, S., Chernova, N.: On stability of a partially accessible multi-station queue with state-dependent routing. Queueing Systems 1(29), 55–73 (1998)
10. Foss, S., Konstantopoulos, T.: An overview of some stochastic stability methods. Journal of the Operations Research Society of Japan 47(4), 275–303 (2003)
11. Heineman, G.T., Loyall, J.P., Schantz, R.E.: Component technology and qos management. In: International Symposium on Component-based Software Engineering (CBSE7), Edinburgh, Scotland (May 24-25, 2004)
12. Jury, E.I.: Theory and Application of the z-Transform Method. John Wiley and Sons, Chichester (1964)
13. Kleinrock, L.: Queueing Systems, vol. 1. J. Wiley, New York (1975)
14. Sharma, P.K., Loyall, J.P., Heineman, G.T., Schantz, R.E., Shapiro, R., Duzan, G.: Component-based dynamic qos adaptations in distributed real-time and embedded systems. In: International Symposium on Distributed Objects and Applications (DOA), Agia Napa, Cyprus, pp. 1208–1224 (October 25-29, 2004)
15. Zeng, L., Benatallah, B., Ngu, A.H.H., Dumas, M., Kalagnanam, J., Chang, H.: Qos-aware middleware for web services composition. IEEE Transactions On Software Engineering 30(5), 311–327 (2004)

Extending the Capabilities of Component Models for Embedded Systems

Ihor Kuz and Yan Liu

National ICT Australia
ihor.kuz@nicta.com.au, jenny.liu@nicta.com.au

Abstract. Component-based development helps to improve the modularity and reusability of embedded systems. Component models devised for embedded systems are typically restricted due to the limited computing, storage and power resources of the target systems. Most existing component models for embedded systems therefore only support a static component architecture and provide a simple and lightweight core. With the increasing demand for more feature-rich embedded systems these component architectures must be extended. In order to remain useful for the development of resource-restricted embedded systems, however, the extensions must be optional. Creating such extensions requires a cost-effective development process that can produce reusable, rather than application-specific, extensions. This necessitates a systematic approach to seamlessly integrate application specific requirements of the extension, the existing component model and the constraints of the computing environment. In this paper we propose a scenario-based architectural approach to extending the capabilities of the CAmkES component model. This approach is used to distil application specific requirements and computing constraints, summarise generic scenarios, drive the extension to the core CAmkES architecture. We illustrate our approach with a case study involving the addition of dynamic capabilities to CAmkES.

Keywords: embedded system, component, extension, scenario, architecture design.

1 Introduction

Component-based development helps to improve the modularity and reusability of software and is increasingly being applied to embedded and real-time systems. Component architectures for embedded systems have major differences from those for enterprise systems mainly due to the resource restrictions of embedded systems. Deployment, cost, and size concerns lead to significant restrictions in processing power, memory size, and energy resources. Developers of software for embedded systems must, therefore, ensure that their software can perform sufficiently on slower processors, can fit into reduced memory, and can run efficiently in order to conserve energy. Since component-based implementation of applications often demands extra computing resources, component architectures and models for embedded systems are devised to be simple and lightweight. They typically allow only static architectures that do no change

S. Overhage et al. (Eds.): QoSA 2007, LNCS 4880, pp. 182–196, 2007.

at runtime, limit the ways that components can be connected and do not provide for memory protection between components. This means that, for example, components cannot be created or destroyed at runtime, nor can new connections be created or existing connections be broken.

With increasing demand for more feature-rich embedded systems (including mobile phones, cars, multi-media systems, etc.) that require dynamic features such as downloading and updating of system software, dynamically changing configurations, etc. component models for embedded systems need to be extensible and flexible in order to support such features when they are required. The domain-specific nature of embedded systems means that features required by different types of devices (for example, mobile phones and cars) will be very different. This makes it impractical to devise a comprehensive component model that provides all the possible features.

One solution is to develop a component model that supports core features and also embeds services for developing extra features in a monolithic design. This is similar to the component models implemented for enterprise applications, such as J2EE and CORBA Component Model (CCM). In these approaches a container hosts the application components and also provides services such as transaction and security management. Such a solution leads to a heavy component model and has the disadvantage that restricted resources can prevent its practical use.

Another solution is to extend the static component models with only required features and develop a flexible architecture for incorporating newly added features. This solution imposes challenges for the design of the component architecture at two levels: first, the core model of the component architecture needs to be extended to incorporate new application specific requirements; second, in order to achieve cost-effective development, extensions to the core component model should be reusable by other applications with similar requirements. Furthermore, any resource restrictions that apply to the design and implementation of the component architecture will also apply to extensions.

This necessitates a systematic approach to the development of feature extensions for embedded systems that seamlessly integrates application specific requirements that originally led to the need for extensions, the existing component model, and the constraints of the computing environment. In this paper we propose a scenario-based approach to extending the capabilities of our CAmkES component model. Our approach distils the requirements of the target embedded application and integrates them with CAmkES components and relevant architectural patterns. We demonstrate our approach with an illustrative case study that involves adding dynamic capabilities to CAmkES.

2 Overview of CAmkES

CAmkES (Component Architecture for microkernel-based Embedded Systems) is an architecture that we have developed to enable the component-based development of embedded systems. Specifically, CAmkES targets embedded systems based on the L4 microkernel [10]. Since microkernels are light on resource requirements, provide good protection between applications and OS components, and make for a suitably small trusted computing base, they are a highly suitable base upon which to build reliable and trustworthy embedded systems [6]. In this paper we provide only a very brief introduction to the CAmkES architecture and development process, more details about the architecture can be found in [8].

Similar to standard component architectures, the CAmkES architecture provides components, interfaces, and connectors. However, CAmkES is targeted at potentially resource restricted embedded systems, which leads to three key features of the architecture (and its associated component model).

First, connectors are first class concepts and can be defined by users whenever specific communication functionality is required. This means that CAmkES allows developers to place components in the same address space, place components in separate address spaces, or even place the components on separate machines. CAmkES also provides the flexibility to tailor communication between components to application-specific needs.

Second, the core CAmkES component model makes it possible to reduce the overhead introduced by component-based computing by limiting built-in features. In particular, it only allows for static architectures that do not change at runtime. This means that components cannot be created or destroyed at runtime, nor can new connections be created or existing connections be broken. Since not all applications will require this kind of dynamic capability they should not have to pay for it.

Finally, the core CAmkES component model and architecture can be extended by adding components that act as *extensions*. These components implement functionality that extends the architecture's capabilities. For example, in order to allow the creation and destruction of components at runtime appropriate extension components must be added.

With regards to the development process, at design time a system architect defines components and their interface in an architecture description language (ADL). The full system application is also specified in ADL, including specification of all the components and connectors involved, and all the connections between components. The component functionality is implemented separately in a regular programming language such as C.

The ADL files are compiled to produce loading and initialisation code, communication stubs, and any other required runtime support code, all of which is compiled together with the component code, and combined with the L4 kernel to produce a loadable system image. At system boot time the system image is loaded into memory, the kernel starts up and invokes the CAmkES loader to load all the components. The loader creates and initialises all components and their connections, and after everything is ready starts the system running.

3   The Approach

Initially the need for an extension is driven by application specific requirements, such as being able to dynamically create a device driver instance at runtime, or being able to update components on-the-fly without bringing the system down. If the component model being used does not provide features required to do these things, the developer needs to extend the model with the appropriate capability. While a developer could work out application-specific solutions, such solutions are rarely reusable. As such, when later development requests for similar features arise, new implementations must be redeveloped. Moreover, the maintenance overhead also increases since the solutions are tangled within the different applications. Obviously this is time consuming and not a cost effective development process.

Rather than developing ad-hoc and non-reusable solutions, we envision a systematic approach that enables the development of generic extensions to a core component architecture. The extensions are implemented as components and services that support generic scenarios and are not specific to a particular application.

There is currently a gap in this process between the application-specific requirements and the generic extension components. We consider adopting a scenario-based software architecture analysis approach [13] to solve this problem. In scenario-based analysis of software architecture, scenarios (i.e., detailed requirement descriptions in specific contexts) are used as a tool to analyse quality attributes and the primary utilisation of these quality attributes. Kazman et al. use scenarios to express the particular instances of each quality attribute that are important to the customer of a system. In this paper the scenarios we refer to are consistent with the meaning as described in [13], which is *a brief description of an anticipated or desired use of a system.* The scenarios are usually described by a sentence, for example, "a PCI bus driver creates a device driver component instance at runtime."

Key application-specific scenarios can be derived from the application-specific requirements. By identifying these key application scenarios, we can better understand what is required of the component model and how components can be applied in the design and development of the application.

Our scenario-based approach to designing generalised and reusable extensions is summarised in Fig. 1. On the right-hand side we show the desired application and its requirements, while the left-hand side shows the four main steps of our approach. These steps are outlined below.

The first step is to derive key scenarios that cover the application-specific requirements. Many techniques for developing scenarios have been devised in scenario-based software architecture evaluation methods [2][4]. These techniques can be applied here to derive these key scenarios. For example, scenario brainstorming can be exercised with the goal of identifying the type of activities that the system must support.

The second step involves generalising the key scenarios. The challenge here is to capture all the major components and connections that are involved in the key scenarios and redesign them to be generic. An example of a general scenario is that CAmkES is able to identify a component type, find loaded code for the given component type and create a component instance.

Normally the scenario-based software architecture evaluation method starts with general and preliminary scenarios that have been gathered, classified and prioritised. During walk-through meetings, the architecture is evaluated according to these scenarios. Detail is added to the general scenarios and they evolve into application and context-specific concrete key scenarios.

In our approach we start with application specific requirements and come up with concrete key scenarios. Since our aim is to develop reusable extensions these key scenarios are further generalised into scenarios covering the common requirements of extensions that cover a broad range of applications. This demands expertise from the software architects and engineers who are responsible for designing the extension scenario and making decisions with regards to the selected scenarios. A practical approach is to start with the key scenarios and gather feedback from possible stakeholders and other software architects, then to revise the key scenarios toward more generic scenarios.

The third step requires extension of the component model to support these general scenarios. An important requirement is that the extension be generic and reusable. One approach to extension is to change the core component model to incorporate the new requirements. This has potential maintenance and integration issues since the changes may cause compatibility issues with legacy code developed for the original core component model. It is also possible that the core component model implementation is not available, or it is impractical to make changes to it. A better approach then is that the implementation of these extensions should utilise existing components to the maximum extent through a flexible architecture. In the case of CAmkES, an extension to allow the dynamic creation of a component instance can be implemented as a factory component. This factory could be implemented as a static CAmkES component and loaded into the system memory from the boot image at boot time. A concrete example is illustrated later in Section 4.

Finally, the resulting generic solutions are used in the design and development of the specific application. At this stage, patterns as best practices can be applied as part of the application architecture. The context in which a pattern is applicable must match the context of the application scenarios and the component model must support an appropriate programming paradigm for implementing the pattern.

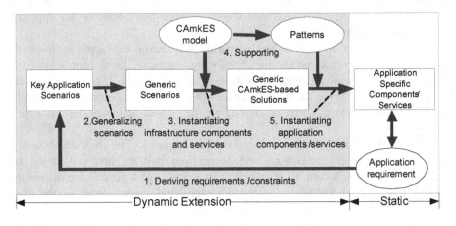

Fig. 1. Scenario-driven component-based development approach

4   Case Study: Developing a PCI Bus Driver

In order to illustrate how our approach is used in the development of a real system we discuss a simple (but relevant) case study: the development of a PCI bus driver. Most systems that incorporate a PCI I/O bus use a driver that scans the bus at start up in order to determine what devices are attached. There are two ways to build and use such a PCI driver.

The first is a static approach in which the developer knows which devices will be attached to the bus and the PCI driver is simply used to provide initialisation information for the drivers of the attached devices. The second approach is a dynamic approach where the PCI driver scans the bus and the resulting information about which devices are attached is used to find, instantiate, and initialise appropriate drivers.

Implementing the static approach using CAmkES is straightforward and does not require functionality beyond that provided by the core model. The components implementing the bus driver as well as the required device drivers (e.g., an Ethernet driver), their clients (e.g., a network stack component) and connections between them are all specified at design time and are created at system initialisation time. The bus driver component includes functionality to scan the bus and to invoke the connected device driver's configuration interface in order to initialise it correctly. It does not need to create any components at run time since the driver component is already there and connected to it.

Implementing the dynamic approach, on the other hand, is not possible using only the core CAmkES functionality. In particular, at design time the system developer does not know what specific device will be connected to the PCI bus and so cannot include this in the system specification. As such, the device driver component cannot be created at system initialisation time nor is it possible to specify the connections to the device driver component at design time. It is up to the PCI bus driver to determine which device driver components to create and to ensure that the clients are connected to those drivers. In order to do this at runtime we must add appropriate extensions (in the form of extension components) to CAmkES.

In the following we use the approach described in this paper to design and implement generic CAmkES extensions that allow us to build a system taking the dynamic approach to PCI bus driver design.

4.1 Deriving Key Scenarios

To keep the case study feasible we specify further details about the actual scenario that we wish to implement. We assume that the possible devices connected to the bus are limited and known ahead of time so that driver code can be made available in the loaded image (this simply prevents us from having to include discussion of functionality to download the code or search for it on external storage). We also assume that the family of devices (e.g., Ethernet card, audio device, etc.) that we discover on the bus is fixed. This means that the client knows the family of device that it will connect to, and therefore the interfaces that it wants to connect to, and prevents us from having to introduce interface discovery into the example. Another simplifying assumption is that there will be only one device attached to the bus (i.e., only one instance of the device driver component will need to be created). Finally, while the client does need to find the driver to connect to, there will be a predetermined way for the client to find the driver component.

Note that many of these further details comprise constraints on the system. Other constraints are provided by the application environment, and may relate to resource restrictions, temporal requirements, security requirements, etc.

These constraints together with the initial application requirements allow us to perform the first step and distil key application scenarios, which results in the following:

- Bus driver determines component required for a specific device.
- Bus driver finds loaded device driver component code.
- Bus driver creates device driver component instance.
- Bus driver connects to device driver component's configuration, interrupt, and IO interfaces.
- Bus driver initialises device driver component.
- Bus driver registers device driver component instance in a registry with a predetermined keyword.
- Client searches registry for desired device driver component by keyword.
- Client connects to device driver component interfaces.

The second step is to generalise these scenarios so that they are no longer application specific. We start by noting that we have at least two different types of components involved:

- The bus driver and client components are included in the system specification at design time and are created at system initialisation time.
- The device driver component, on the other hand, is created at runtime.

Likewise there are different types of connections involved, either created at system initialisation time or at runtime. There are more distinctions possible, and Table 1 provides an overview of the various aspects to consider when distinguishing between the types of components and connections.

Based on the different combinations of these aspects we can identify all the different types of components and connections. For further clarity we have given names to some of the more common combinations.

We call components that have property A1 and B1 *static components*. Components with A2 and B1 are called *dynamic components*, while those with A2 and B2 are called *dynamically loaded components*. We call connections with property C1 and D1 *static connections*, those with C2 and D2 are *dynamic connections* and those with C2 and D1 are *partially dynamic connections*.

Note that some combinations are not feasible, including: A1 and B2, C1 and D2, and A2 and C1 as they violate the logic of the component model.

4.2 Generalising Scenarios

In this case study the bus driver and client components are static components, while the device driver is a dynamic component. While the connections between the static components and the dynamic component can be dynamic connections, for simplicity sake we will assume that they are all partially dynamic connections.

Table 1. Component and Connection Category

A. How component instances are created
1. Statically created components are components that are created at system initialisation time.
2. Dynamically created components are components that are created at runtime (after all static components have been created and the system has been started).
B. How component code is loaded into the system
1. Statically loaded components are loaded into the system memory at system boot time (from the boot image).
2. Dynamically loaded components are loaded into the system memory at runtime, typically from secondary storage (e.g., disk, RAM disk, flash disk, etc.) or network.
C. When the connections are created
1. Statically created connections are created at system initialisation time.
2. Dynamically created connections are connections that are created at runtime (after all static components and connections have been created and the system has been started).
D. When the connection type is defined
1. Statically defined connections have the connector types defined at design time in the ADL specification. Practically this means that communication stubs are compiled directly into the component.
2. Dynamically defined connections have the connector types defined at bind time. Practically this means that the stubs are not compiled into the component code but must be dynamically linked in some way (e.g., using dispatch tables).

Generalising from the application-specific scenarios we arrive at the following. The components involved can be generalised based on their role:

- **Creator** (*static component*): requests that a new component be created. In the application-specific scenario this is the bus driver component.
- **Created** (*dynamic component*): a component created at runtime. In the application-specific scenario this is the device driver component.
- **Connecter** (*static component*): requests a connection to be created between the interfaces of two components. Both the bus driver and the client components play this role in the application-specific scenario.
- **Client** (*static component*): a component that is connected to the created component. In the application-scenario both the bus driver and the client components take on the client role.

Based on this, the generic scenarios we arrive at are:

- Find loaded code for a given component type.
- Create a component instance given a component type.
- Connect the corresponding interfaces of two component instances; this requires being able to identify component instances and interfaces.
- Register component instance at a registry with keywords.
- Search the registry with keywords.

4.3 Extending CAmkES

Next we design CAmkES extensions that allow us to implement these generic scenarios. Our main goal is to design and implement extensions in such a way that they are generic and reusable. It is also important to consider how the extensions can utilise the existing tools associated with the component architecture (e.g., the compiler and loader of CAmkES) in order to reduce the engineering effort and cost of development. Our solution to address these requirements is that the extension components will all be static components, and all connections to the extension components will be static as well. We end up with three extension components as shown in Table 2. These components will implement the interfaces shown in Table 3.

Table 2. Extension Components

Factory	does the actual work to create a new component instance
Registry	Maps a keyword string to an opaque piece of binary data
Binder	does the actual work to connect two component instances at given interfaces

Table 3. Extension Interfaces

```
// IFactory interface:
component_instance_id create (component_id)
// IRegistry interface:
register (component_instance_id, keyword[])
{component_id, keyword[]} lookup (component_instance_id)
component_instance_id[] find_keyword(keyword[])
// IBinder interface:
bind(component_instance_id, interface_id, component_instance_id, interface_id)
```

These extensions are used to implement the general scenarios as follows.

- The factory component is responsible for locating loaded component code given a component identifier. The result of such a lookup is platform specific and will be used internally by the factory component in the following scenario.
- The creator component invokes the factory component's create method. The factory component locates the appropriate loaded component code and creates a new instance (the details of this are platform dependent). It returns a component instance identifier, which is an opaque platform-specific data type.
- The connecter invokes the bind method on the binder component providing component instance identifiers of the two target components and their corresponding interfaces.

- A component invokes the register function of the registry component, providing the identifier of the component it wishes to register along with relevant keywords.
- A component invokes the find_keyword method of the registry component, passing a keyword and receiving the identifiers of matching component instances.

We apply knowledge of design patterns in this step to come up with extensions that can be used as parts of appropriate patterns when possible. For example, the factory design pattern is applied to create new instances of components while the registry component adopts the service locator design pattern.

4.4 Developing Application Components

Finally, given the extensions and their use in the generic scenarios we can implement the desired application by defining the appropriate application components and having them use the extensions as required.

For the PCI scenario, the three application components are: the bus driver component (PCI bus driver), the client component (TCP/IP network stack), and the device driver component such as an Ethernet driver, which is to be created by the factory. The first two are static while the device driver component is dynamic. The design-time component architecture of the application is shown in Fig. 2. It contains the two static application components and the three extension components with appropriate connections between them. The interfaces of the application components are shown for completeness, however, we do not discuss them further.

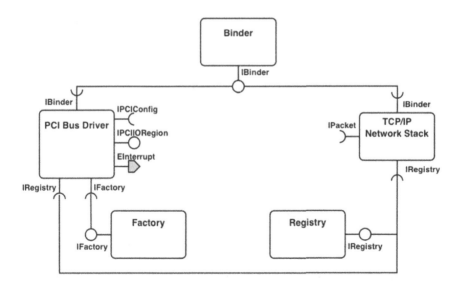

Fig. 2. Design-time component architecture

At runtime the following steps are taken:

1. The bus driver scans the bus and maps the found device to an appropriate component identifier using internal (and driver-specific) data, such as PCI vendor ID and device ID fields in the PCI device configuration header.
2. The bus driver creates a device driver component by calling the factory with the appropriate component identifier.
3. The bus driver connects to the device driver component by invoking the binder component's bind method.
4. The bus driver registers the device driver component with the registry component by invoking the register function and using a preset keyword (e.g., "ethernet").
5. The client queries the registry component for the preset keyword until a positive result is returned (an alternative approach would involve the client registering with the registry to be notified when a match for the keyword is available).
6. Given the results from the registry the client connects to the device driver by invoking the binder component's bind method.

The component architecture after these steps is shown in Fig. 3. Note that we now have one new component and several new connections.

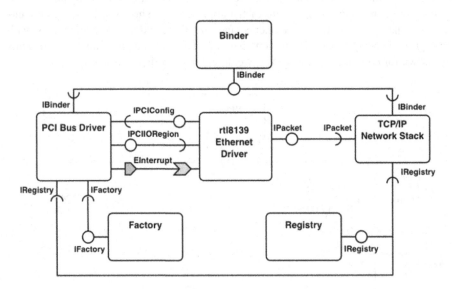

Fig. 3. Run-time component architecture

To further develop the extensions, we can remove each of the scenario assumptions made earlier, thus broadening the scenario and changing the requirements. Doing so may affect some of the decisions made so far (in terms of what extensions to provide and the details of the interfaces) but will make the extensions more broadly applicable and therefore more general. In this way the design process can feed back into itself, allowing iterative feedback-based development of applications and generic CAmkES extensions.

4.5 Evaluation

We have followed this approach and implemented prototypes of the extension components as presented above. In our prototype, the extended dynamic functionality was fully contained in the static extension components. Future work will include the relaxation of several assumptions regarding the application scenario, and will lead to the development of further extensions such as those required for dynamically loading code and more flexible dynamic binding.

In terms of the overhead introduced by this implementation, it is mainly incurred by the static core CAmkES components. This is because the extension components for the dynamic features in this case are implemented as static components.

5 Applying the Approach to Non-functional Requirements of Embedded Systems

The previous case study illustrated the use of our scenario-based approach based on the analysis and generalisation of application-specific functional requirements. The approach is also suitable when the application-specific requirements are non-functional. For embedded systems important classes of non-functional requirements include temporal requirements relating to timeliness of execution and worst-case execution times, power management, reliability, etc. Following the approach as outlined earlier, we would start with application-specific scenarios that illustrate the non-functional requirements and remove the application-specific aspects to arrive at generalised scenarios relating to the requirements. We would then use these scenarios to design extensions to the component model that enable the implementation of such scenarios. The specific extension mechanism used may differ for these requirements than for functional ones, that is, we may need to make more changes than simply adding extension components. The details of extending the CAmkES model for non-functional requirements are future work.

6 Related Work

The basic characteristics of embedded systems, their requirements and constraints, and the implications to component models are summarised and presented in [9]. The challenging issues of devising an appropriate component model for embedded systems are recognised when component-based software engineering is adopted in developing embedded systems through experience. That is existing technologies for enterprise systems such as CCM, J2EE and .Net/COM+ cannot be used, or at least used directly for embedded systems [9]. The constraints of embedded systems are further articulated in [5]. This essence is also acknowledged in this paper. The approach we proposed in this paper is based on our existing CAmkES component model, which takes into account the constraints and requirements for embedded systems. We focus on the reusable extension of this core CAmkES component model. Our contribution is to demonstrate that this approach is feasible for developing the extension by reusing existing component models and making them general for different applications.

Andrews et al summarised the impact of embedded system evolution on real-time operating system use and design [3], in which how to map components onto application specific requirements remains a challenging problem. We consider dynamic updates as typical extension requirements for embedded system evolution. Research and engineering effort has been devoted to the field of dynamic updates. For a good overview, we refer to [12]. This paper focuses on a method to extend the capability of component-based design and implementation for embedded systems. We used dynamic updates as an example to illustrate our scenario-based approach to extending capabilities of CAmkES component model for embedded systems. The approach integrates application specific requirements to the development of generic and reusable extensions.

Another potential use of our approach is realising non-functional requirements through extensions to existing component models. Most component models do not address or at least have limitation in providing support for non-functional properties, such as timeliness, security, safety, reliability and fault tolerance. Ibrahim et al presented the ongoing research at Philips Semiconductors on improving productivity and reliability. It provides a literature survey of some techniques that address the issues of productivity and reliability [1]. In [7][16] solutions to address the timeliness and safety of embedded systems are proposed within their component model. In this paper we only briefly suggest that non-functional requirements can be implemented following our approach. It remains our future work on how to extend the component model to support non-functional requirements on quality attributes.

Scenario-based approaches are widely applied in software architecture evaluation. Methods and mechanisms are well established. For a good overview, we refer to [2][4]. In this paper we adopt a scenario-based approach to drive the design and implementation of extensions. The general scenarios constructed in this paper are consistent with the concept of a general scenario used in [13], which describes what achieving a quality attribute goal means. In [13], general scenarios describe how the architecture should respond to a certain stimulus. In this paper, a general scenario is abstracted and derived from key scenarios for quality attributes of interest. It is described to be generic and less application specific than the key scenarios. It remains our future work to apply this approach to more case studies and further validate its practical use.

7 Conclusion

Given the resource restrictions of embedded systems, component models specifically targeted for such systems are typically minimal, providing only limited functionality with which to build systems. In order to be widely useable and to fulfil demands imposed by modern embedded systems and their applications it is often necessary to extend the capabilities of such component models. In CAmkES, our component model for embedded systems, extending functionality is achieved by including extension components in a system's design. The need for extensions typically comes up when designing specific applications, however, the functionality provided by such extensions should be generalised such that the extensions can be reused to provide similar functionality for other applications.

We introduce a scenario-based approach to developing such generalised component model extensions. In this approach we start with an application's requirements and iterate through the steps of distilling key scenarios and then generalising these scenarios to make them independent of any specific application. The general scenarios provide requirements and context, which we use to guide development of the extensions. Finally, with the help of architectural patterns we use the extensions during the development of applications.

This approach has been applied during the development of CAmkES extensions that provide dynamic capabilities (e.g., creating and binding components at runtime). We describe a part of this experience in our case study section. Future work involves investigating the application of this approach to create extensions that address non-functional application requirements, as well as other constraints imposed by an embedded system's environment.

Acknowledgement

National ICT Australia is funded by the Australian Government's Department of Communications, Information Technology, and the Arts and the Australian Research Council through Backing Australia's Ability and the ICT Research Centre of Excellence programs

References

[1] Ibrahim, A.E., Zhao, L., Kinghorn, J.: Embedded Systems Development: Quest for Productivity and Reliability. In: Fifth International Conference on Commercial-off-the-Shelf (COTS)-Based Software Systems (ICCBSS 2006), pp. 23–32 (2006)

[2] Ali Babar, M., Gorton, I.: Comparison of Scenario-Based Software Architecture Evaluation Methods. In: 11th Asia-Pacific Software Engineering Conference, pp. 600–607 (2004)

[3] Andrews, D., Bate, I., Nolte, T., Otero Perez, C.M., Petters, S.M.: Impact of Embedded Systems Evolution on RTOS Use and Design. In: 1st International Workshop Operating System Platforms for Embedded Real-Time Applications (OSPERT 2005) (2005)

[4] Dobrica, L., Niemela, E.: A Survey on Software Architecture Analysis Methods. IEEE Transactions on Software Engineering 28(7) (2002)

[5] Hammer, D.K., Chaudron, M.R.V.: Component-based software engineering for resource-constraint systems: what are the needs? In: 6th International Workshop on Object-Oriented Real-Time Dependable Systems (WORDS 2001), Rome, Italy, pp. 91–94 (2001)

[6] Heiser, G.: Secure embedded systems need microkernels. USENIX;login 30(6), 9–13 (2005)

[7] Hansson, H., Akerholm, M., Crnkovic, I., Torngren, M.: SaveCCM – a component model for safety-critical real-time systems. In: 30th EUROMICRO Conference (EUROMI- CRO 2004) Rennes, France (2004)

[8] Kuz, I., Liu, Y., Gorton, I., Heiser, G.: CAmkES: A component model for secure microkernel-based embedded systems. Journal of Systems and Software Special Edition on Component-Based Software Engineering of Trustworthy Embedded Systems 80(5), 687–699 (2007)

[9] Crnkovic, I.: Component-based approach for Embedded Systems. In: Ninth International Workshop on Component-Oriented Programming (2004)

[10] Liedtke, J.: On μ-kernel construction. In: 15th SOSP, Copper Mountain, CO, USA, pp. 237–250 (1995)

[11] Bass, L., Klein, M., Moreno, G.: Applicability of General Scenarios to the Architecture Tradeoff Analysis Method, Technical Report, CMU/SEI-2001-TR-014 (October 2001)

[12] Hicks, M.: Dynamic Software Updating. PhD thesis, Department of Computer and Information Science, University of Pennsylvania (June 2001)

[13] Kazman, R., Abowd, G., Bass, L., Clements, P.: Scenario-Based Analysis of Software Architecture. IEEE Software 47–55 (November 1996)

[14] Gheorghita, S.V., Basten, T., Corporaal, H.: An Overview of Application Scenario Usage in Streaming-Oriented Embedded System Design. Eindhoven University of Technology, Report number: esr-2006-03 (May 20, 2006) ISSN 1574-9517

[15] Vandewoude, Y., Berbers, Y.: Run-time Evolution for Embedded Component-Oriented Systems. In: 18th IEEE International Conference on Software Maintenance (ICSM 2002) (2002)

[16] van Ommering, R., van der Linden, F., Kramer, J., Magee, J.: The Koala component model for consumer electronics software. Computer 33(3), 78–85 (2000)

Architectural Knowledge: Getting to the Core

Remco C. de Boer[1], Rik Farenhorst[1], Patricia Lago[1], Hans van Vliet[1], and Viktor Clerc[1], and Anton Jansen[2]

[1] VU University Amsterdam, the Netherlands
{remco, rik, patricia, hans, viktor}@cs.vu.nl
[2] University of Groningen, the Netherlands
anton@cs.rug.nl

Abstract. Different organizations or organizational units are likely to store and maintain different types of information about their software architectures. This inhibits effective management of architectural knowledge. We experimented with a model of architectural knowledge to characterize the use of architectural knowledge in four different organizations. Based on this experimentation we identified four perspectives on architectural knowledge management, and additionally adjusted the model to better align theory with practice. The refined model defines a minimal set of concepts with supposedly complete coverage of the architectural knowledge domain. Because of the minimalistic aspect of the model, we refer to it as a 'core model' of architectural knowledge. Supporting evidence for the validity of our model, i.e. the supposed complete coverage, has been obtained by an attempt to falsify this claim through a comparison with selected literature. Application of the core model to characterize the use of architectural knowledge indicates possible areas of improvement for architectural knowledge management in the four organizations.

1 Introduction

The notion of software architecture is one of the key technical advances in the field of software engineering over the last decades. The advantages of using an explicit software architecture include early interaction with stakeholders, its basis for a work breakdown structure, and the early assessment of quality attributes [1]. Although considerable progress has been made in this area, we still lack techniques for capturing, representing and maintaining knowledge about software architectures.

Various authors (e.g. [2,3,4]) address the notion of 'architectural knowledge' and provide a model of what this notion entails. Key elements in all models are design decisions and their rationale. However, different authors use different words for what might be the same. For example, some models consider design decisions, others architectural decisions, but it is hard to determine whether these actually denote the same concept.

Having different notions of what architectural knowledge entails can hamper effective management of that knowledge. If, for instance, different organizations – or even departments within a single organization – use different concepts to communicate architectural knowledge, terminological misunderstandings may arise. Sharing architectural knowledge between these parties then becomes very hard, if not impossible. We need a

S. Overhage et al. (Eds.): QoSA 2007, LNCS 4880, pp. 197–214, 2007.

model of architectural knowledge that acts as a common frame of reference and enables architectural knowledge sharing.

The question we address in this paper is what this model should entail. As an answer, we propose a model of architectural knowledge that has maximal expressivity in the architectural knowledge domain and functions as a reference model for sharing architectural knowledge. Real-life models of what architectural knowledge entails can be expressed in the form of extensions to this model. These extensions are domain-specific, organization-specific, or both.

2   Related Work

In an overview of the maturation of the software architecture field [5], Shaw and Clements conclude with an outlook on future work in software architecture research. Promising topics mentioned include a focus on architectural design decisions and their link to quality attributes, and the organization of architectural knowledge to create reference materials. Our work serves both these goals.

The research field already shows increasing focus on the management of architectural knowledge (i.e. knowledge pertaining to a particular software architecture), such as architectural design decisions and their rationale [3,6,7,8]. A growing number of researchers acknowledges that a software architecture can – or should – be viewed as the collection of architectural design decisions [9], or as the design decisions plus the resulting design [4]. Others target tracing architectural decisions to concerns [10], or link business goals to the software architecture [1].

Hofmeister et al. define architecting as an iterative process in which the architecture 'grows' over time as architects perform architectural activities, such as analysis, synthesis, and evaluation [11]. In our research we build further on this view, by considering the iterative nature of architecting as a 'decision loop'. We focus not only on the design decisions themselves, but also on the result of this iterative process – the architectural design – which is reflected in various design artifacts such as architectural descriptions.

In recent years, several other models or frameworks have been proposed to capture architectural knowledge. Akerman and Tyree propose an ontology that focuses on architectural assets, architectural decisions, stakeholder concerns and an architecture implementation road map [12]. A framework for capturing and using architecture design knowledge is proposed by Ali Babar et al. in [2].

All methods and frameworks described above share a common understanding of what 'architectural knowledge' is, or should entail. Then again, each of the methods and frameworks has a different focal point and may use terminology differently from others. In an attempt to aggregate the common understanding, while allowing for different specializations of the central concepts, we have constructed a reference model of architectural knowledge that is described in Section 5.

3   Research Methodology and Structure of This Paper

The structure of this paper, schematically depicted in Fig. 1, is tightly coupled to the research approach we followed. In the remainder of this section we outline the research

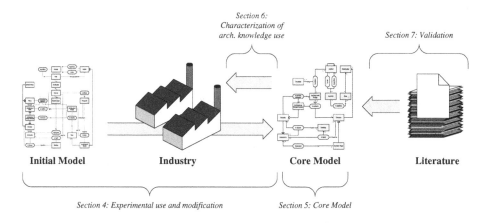

Fig. 1. Structure of this Paper

methodology we employed, the steps we followed, and in which sections the respective results are elaborated upon.

The research methodology that we followed can best be described as an instantiation of action research. Action research is an iterative research approach in which the researcher actively participates in the studies he performs. The researcher wants 'to try out a theory with practitioners in real situations, gain feedback from this experience, modify the theory as a result of this feedback, and try again' [13].

Our research commenced with a 'theory' of architectural knowledge that stemmed from our earlier work [14]. This initial model of architectural knowledge was an abstract conceptualization of the architectural knowledge domain. We experimented with the model, and tried to characterize the use of architectural knowledge by (and together with) four industrial partners. Experience from those characterization attempts taught us that there were a number of mismatches between our theory and industrial practice. Reflection on the apparent mismatches led us to conclude that our model should exhibit a number of properties in order to overcome those mismatches. This reflection process is elaborated further in Section 4. In order to accommodate for the desired properties identified, we refined the initial model and arrived at a new 'version' of our theory of architectural knowledge: a core model of architectural knowledge presented in Section 5.

With the mismatches between theory and practice removed, we could successfully employ our core model of architectural knowledge to characterize the use of architectural knowledge by the four partners. This characterization, which is the subject of Section 6, led to a number of hypotheses regarding the probable cause of problems with architectural knowledge management in the collaborating organizations. We plan to alleviate the identified problems by removing the probable causes in the near future. This illustrates the iterative nature of action research, where the result of the action research cycle we performed is input for the next cycle.

Since we want our model to be useful as a reference model to align different architectural vocabularies, we believe our model can be regarded as 'valid' when concepts from different architectural approaches can be expressed using terms from the model.

Unfortunately, it is impossible to prove that our model is valid in this sense. However, we can make the validity of our model plausible by trying to falsify our model by comparing the model with (accepted) literature. This falsification attempt, which falls outside the scope of the action research cycle itself, is discussed in Section 7.

4   A Theory of Architectural Knowledge: Experimental Use and Modification

The goal of our research was to characterize the use of architectural knowledge in four different organizations. The four organizations that participated in our research can be described as follows:

- **RFA** is a large software development organization, responsible for development and maintenance of systems for among others the public sector.
- **VCL** is a large, multi-site consumer electronics organization where embedded software is developed in a distributed setting.
- **RDB** performs independent software product audits for third parties.
- **PAV** is a large scientific organization that has to deal with software development projects spanning a long time frame (up to a period of more than ten years).

The theory that we used to characterize the organizations' architectural knowledge use was a model of architectural knowledge that is presented in detail in [14]. This model had been constructed to structure software architectural knowledge in such a way that it is clear what can exist and what can happen during the architecting phase of a software development project. We aimed to use this model as an abstract view of the architectural knowledge domain, to allow for clean reasoning about the use of architectural knowledge in the four organizations.

Experience with the model from [14] in the four industrial organizations taught us that the model did not entirely fit all organizations. The original model highly conformed to the IEEE-1471 standard for architectural description [15]. IEEE-1471 prescribes the use of so-called 'Viewpoints' to describe the architecture from the perspective of different stakeholders. The resulting 'Views' (partial descriptions of the architecture) are aggregated in a single architecture description. Although stakeholders and their concerns play a key role in any software architecting process, the tight coupling of the model to IEEE-1471's Views and Viewpoints turned out to be a mismatch with most organizations' practice. In hindsight this need not come as a big surprise, since organizations can (and do) use other approaches for documenting their architectures, which need not coincide with the IEEE-1471 way.

Although the model from [14] did not entirely fit all organizations, diagnosis of the use of architectural knowledge in those organizations at least showed that each of the organizations has its own perspective on architectural knowledge management, resulting in different issues at each of the organizations. The central issue within RFA was how to *share* architectural knowledge between stakeholders of a project. The main question within VCL was how *compliance* to architectural rules can be enforced in this multi-site environment. RDB was mainly concerned with how auditors can *discover* the architectural knowledge they need to do a proper audit. The main challenge for PAV was how to improve *traceability* of its architectural knowledge. While the mismatches between theory and practice still prevented us from pinpointing the exact areas of improvement, at least we had an idea where to search for those areas in a next research iteration. However, this required that we removed the identified mismatches to further align theory with practice.

From a closer inspection of the mismatching concepts we learned that those concepts could either be expressed in terms of other concepts already present in the model, or as more generic concepts that *are* used by the organizations. This led us to believe that we should strive to construct a model of architectural knowledge that is both minimalistic and complete. We believe the model can be regarded as 'complete' if there are no concepts from other approaches that have no counterpart in the model. If there turns out to be such a missing concept, our model should be extended. With 'minimalistic' we signify the feature that it should not be possible to express some concepts from the model in any other concepts from the model.

Based on these insights we modified the initial model from [14] to obtain such a model that is both complete and minimalistic. Especially because of this latter feature, we refer to our model as a core model of architectural knowledge; elements that can be modeled in terms of core elements do not belong to the core.

5   A Core Model of Architectural Knowledge

Our core model of architectural knowledge is depicted in Figure 2. As a result of the minimalistic aspect of this model introduced in Section 4, the core model leaves room for the use of different architecture description methods, including IEEE-1471. This contrasts with the model from [14] in which the use of IEEE-1471 was assumed and which therefore did not match those organizations that use other architecture description methods.

In our core model of architectural knowledge, the concepts of Stakeholder and Concern coincide with the, widely accepted, definitions of these terms in IEEE-1471: a stakeholder is "an individual, team, or organization (or classes thereof) with interests in, or concerns relative to, a system" [15]. Both IEEE-1471 concepts of *Architectural Model* and *View* are subsumed in our notion of Artifact, i.e. an inanimate information bearer such as a document, source code, or a chapter in a book. Storing or describing the Architectural Design in either of these artifacts can be abstracted to a single action 'to reflect'. The Architectural Design can be reflected using different Languages, including models, figures, programming languages, and plain English.

Constructing an architectural design is essentially a decision making process. In our core model, decision making is viewed as proposing and ranking Alternatives, and selecting the alternative that has the highest rank, i.e. the alternative that, after careful consideration based on multiple criteria (i.e. Concerns), is deemed to be the best option available with respect to the other alternatives proposed. It is especially this process of proposing, ranking, and selecting which is hard to articulate and distinguishes the good architects from the weaker. The chosen alternative becomes the Decision. The alternatives that are proposed must address the Decision Topic, and can be ranked according to how well they satisfy this and other concerns. We view Decision Topic as a special type

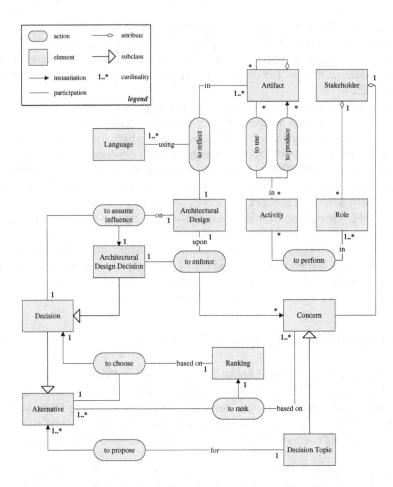

Fig. 2. Core Model of Architectural Knowledge

of Concern, namely a Concern for which a Decision must be taken. Example concerns for which no further decisions need to be taken – and which hence are no decision topics but do need to be taken into account when evaluating (ranking) proposed alternatives – are constraints, such as budget constraints, technological limitations, et cetera.

Architectural Design Decisions are defined as those Decisions that are assumed to influence the Architectural Design and can be enforced upon this Architectural Design, possibly leading to new Concerns that result in a need for taking subsequent decisions. This 'decision loop' captures the relations between subsequent Architectural Design Decisions. This loop also corresponds to the 'divide and conquer' technique of decision making, in which broadly scoped decisions are taken which may result in finer grained concerns related to the broader concern. Furthermore, it enables in theory traceability from concerns through decisions to artifacts, although this very much depends on whether those traces have been captured in the reflection of the architectural design. Note that architectural design decisions need not necessarily be 'invented' by the architect himself; architectural patterns, styles, and tactics are examples of architectural design decisions (or, more precisely, alternatives) that are readily available from other sources. The 'decision loop' described above also captures the rationale of an architectural design; the answer to the question why an architectural design is the way it is. Rationale is in our opinion extremely interwoven with all elements in this loop, and is therefore not represented as a distinct element in our model.

The Architectural Design (often called 'architecture' for short) is the result of all architectural design decisions. Note that reflection of (part of the) Architectural Design is not limited to a single Artifact: a single Architectural Design Decision might for instance be represented in the architecture description as well as impact the source code. Artifacts themselves can again be composed of various (sub)Artifacts, e.g. chapters in a document, or methods in a class. The concepts Role and Activity are borrowed from SPEM, which defines the software development process as "a collaboration between abstract active entities called process roles that perform operations called activities on concrete, tangible entities called work products" [16]. The 'work product' from SPEM resembles our notion of Artifact. The latter is in our opinion a better known and widely accepted concept in Software Engineering.

6   Core Model Application: Characterization of Architectural Knowledge Use in Four Industrial Settings

We initially started our research with the goal to characterize the use of architectural knowledge in four industrial organizations. Although we were able to discover four different perspectives on architectural knowledge within those organizations (see Section 4), the mismatches of our initial model of architectural knowledge with the observed practice in those organizations hampered a further diagnosis of the problems those organizations encounter. Since those mismatches have been removed in our core model of architectural knowledge, it is interesting to see how the organization-specific 'models' of architectural knowledge of all four organizations can be expressed in terms of the core model. From a superficial look, each of the organizations appears to use architectural knowledge very differently. Alignment of the organization-specific models to the core model, however, allows for a more fundamental characterization of how the organizations perceive and use architectural knowledge.

The use of architectural knowledge in RFA and VCL is mainly located in the upper 'description' part of Figure 2, i.e. the reflection of architectural design decisions in artifacts. The use of architectural knowledge within RDB and PAV is positioned more in the lower 'decision' part, i.e. the decision making process reflected in the decision loop. We hypothesize that the problems that the organizations experience in managing architectural knowledge are partially due to their focus on only a part of the theory of architectural knowledge as expressed by our core model.

An overview of the result of the four characterizations is provided in Table 1. In this table we list for each of the organizations their prevalent perspective on the use of architectural knowledge, the main architectural knowledge concepts encountered (both organization-specific and at a core level), the hypothesized cause for the diagnosed

Table 1. Diagnosis of Industrial Problems with Architectural Knowledge Management

	RFA	VCL	RDB	PAV
Perspective	Sharing	Compliance	Discovery	Traceability
Main org. concepts	Design choices, Principles, Starting Points, Prerequisites	Architectural rules	Quality criteria, Quality in use	Knowledge entities
Mainly used core concepts	Arch. design decisions	Arch. design decisions, *to enforce*	Arch. design decision, Concern, Arch. design, *to reflect*	Concern, Decision topic Alternative, Arch. design decision
Problem	Ambiguous terminology	No sense of urgency regarding compliance with architectural rules	Implicit relation between architecture and "quality"	Lack of traceability between knowledge entities
Hypothesized cause	Decision making process not captured	Tacit decision making process	'Quality' and related arch. knowledge not confined to a single artifact	Implicit relations between artifacts
Possible solution	Explicit focus on relations between decisions through iterative "decision loop"	Explicit focus on rationale of decisions through 'decision loop' elements	Uncover architectural design decisions, their cause, and their effect on the software product	Annotate architecture documents with specific knowledge entities

problems, and a possible solution to this problem. In the following subsections, we further elaborate on these aspects for each organization in turn.

6.1   RFA: Development Organization

RFA is a large development organization that develops and maintains software systems for among others the public sector. These systems are typically critical for the public, large in size and complexity, and long lasting. Because of the size of the organization and the projects, this organization focuses on how to effectively share architectural knowledge. To this end, RFA developed its own methodology and tooling to aid the software architects in creating and documenting architectural knowledge by means of architectural descriptions.

Architectural descriptions within RFA basically consist of a number of views based on predefined *viewpoints*, and a set of specific *architectural models* such as an object model, a functional data-model, etc. These models reflect a number of *architectural choices*, which are based on *decisions* that relate to *business objectives*. The choices take into account the *design principles*, *starting points*, and *prerequisites* to which the architect needs to adhere to when designing the software architecture, as well as the *stakeholder concerns*.

An example of a business objective documented in one particular architectural description is: *"The data of the subsystems needs to be easily accessible"*. A stated design principle based on this objective is *"The system needs to be accessible using web services as well as the Enterprise Service Bus"* and the final architectural choice made based on this principle is *"The system information exchange uses InfoMessaging and MS.NET Web Services"*.

We interviewed architects and managers from RFA, who in these interviews acknowledged that they are currently struggling with the different concepts, their relations and their more effective usage. This impairs effective sharing of architectural knowledge, since architects are unsure which concepts to use to describe their architectural design. As a result, readers are unsure where in the architecture description they can find the information they are looking for.

If we express the organization-specific terminology in terms of core concepts, an interesting pattern emerges. The 'different' notions of business objectives, design principles, and architectural choices all are in fact Architectural Design Decisions, which are somehow related to each other. However, the organization's methodology does not define very concrete guidelines to distinguish between those decisions. RFA's struggle with terminology might partially be blamed on the use of different terms for the same architectural knowledge concept without a good definition of the discriminative features for these terms.

The explicit use of architectural knowledge within this organization can be primarily found in the 'description' area of the core model: reflecting architectural decisions in an architectural description. The decision making process – reflected in the decision loop in the model – is left implicit by the organization's methodology.

Our core model captures relations between different architectural design decisions in the decision loop, where a certain architectural design decisions leads to a new concerns that in turn leads to new decisions. A more explicit focus on this loop would help defeat the ambiguity in terminology within RFA. A design principle could then for instance be defined as a decision taken because of new concerns introduced by a business objective. In the example above, the concern introduced by the business objective would be the need for accessibility. Architectural choices are related to design principles analogously.

6.2   VCL: Consumer Electronics

VCL is a large organization within the consumer electronics domain. This organization has arranged software development along subsystems. A release of the software for a consumer electronic product consists of integrating the relevant subsystems. Each subsystem is developed by a small, dedicated development team. The teams are located at multiple, geographically spread development sites.

This arrangement of the software and the software development activities demands guidelines to maintain the subsystem-based software architecture. To this end, a central architecture team issues architectural rules: a set of principles and statements on the software architecture that must be complied with throughout the organization.

Architectural rules originate from various *issues* that influence VCL's software development, such as defects identified in subsystem releases, change requests, or additional requirements. These issues need to be addressed in the software architecture. *Solutions* to these issues – which affect all subsystems – are captured in text-based documents. These documents are sent to all development teams as *architectural rules* that need to be adhered to.

The creation of architectural rules can be expressed in terms of the core model. The issues identified by the various stakeholders correspond to Concerns of Stakeholders. The architectural rules, i.e. the chosen solutions for these issues, are Architectural Design Decisions that are enforced upon the Architectural Design through dissemination of the Artifacts in which they are reflected.

Although VCL is similar to RFA in that the focus of architectural knowledge use is on the 'description' area of the core model, development in teams at distinct locations should put a particular emphasis on *enforcement* of architectural design decisions. However, once the architectural rules have been disseminated to the individual development teams, adherence to the rules on the subsystem architectures is the responsibility of the teams themselves. In practice, some of the rules are disregarded by the teams. Our core model suggests that one of the reasons for this might be the fact that only the architectural design decisions themselves are being communicated, while the decision making process itself remains tacit. This lack of insight into the reason of the architectural design decisions taken make that the development teams do not feel a sense of urgency regarding compliance with these decisions. We believe that more information about the rationale of the architectural rules, including the concerns that led up to the decisions, increases this sense of urgency with the developers.

6.3 RDB: Quality Audits

RDB is a company that performs independent software product audits for third parties. A software product audit consists of comparison of *quality criteria* with the actual software product. Most quality criteria assess the effects of *architectural decisions* as reflected in the *software product artifacts*. A quality criterion might for instance be *"All access to data in a relational database should take place through dedicated data access objects. No direct communication of business objects with the database is allowed"*.

The customer that acquires a software product expects this product to have a certain 'quality in use' [17]. Given the concern 'quality in use', there are various quality characteristics for which quality criteria must be selected. For instance, the criterion that all data access must take place through data access objects favors the maintainability of the software product over its efficiency. Selection of quality criteria therefore depends on the relative importance of each of the quality characteristics indicated by the customer. The example criterion will only be selected if maintainability of the software product is indeed more important to the customer than efficiency.

The problem an auditor faces when performing a software product audit is that architectural design decisions and the resulting architectural design are usually not reflected in a single artifact. Even if there is a document called 'the architecture description', architectural decisions impact other product artifacts (e.g. documentation and source code) as well. There is no guarantee that the information in an architecture description is complete, or even up-to-date.

The reflection of the effects of architectural decisions in different software product artifacts can be readily identified in our core model. The Language used to reflect Architectural Design in Artifacts can be a natural language (e.g. English in software product documentation), but also a programming language (source code) or graphics (e.g. diagrams and figures in a software architecture description). A more interesting and less apparent mapping is the mapping of 'quality' to the core model.

In terms of our core model, *quality in use* is a Concern of the customer, who is a Stakeholder. The quality *characteristics* and *subcharacteristics* are Decision Topics for which *quality criteria* are proposed and selected. The proposed criteria are the Alternatives. Selection of quality criteria is based on their impact on the quality in use – the Concern– in terms of prioritized (sub)characteristics, as indicated above. In this way, trade-off analyses are being made regarding conflicting criteria. The chosen quality criteria describe the architecture in terms of how it ought to be. In other words, quality criteria are a special type of Architectural Design Decisions: decisions that are expected to have influenced (rather than enforced upon) the Architectural Design.

In RDB the relation between architecture and quality is not obvious at first sight. The core model helps us to describe quality in terms of architectural decisions and their effect on the software product, and shows us that quality criteria that apply to the architectural design are themselves architectural decisions. Using the core model, we can express a software product audit as a comparison of two types of architectural knowledge: architectural knowledge that is present in the software product, reflected in the Artifacts that make up the product, and architectural knowledge that is expected by the customer, reflected in quality criteria. This makes it more apparent which architectural knowledge is most important for a software product audit: the architectural design decisions as well as their cause (e.g. stakeholder concerns and trade-offs) and effect (e.g. constraints on subsequent decisions) should be discovered from multiple artifacts for an effective assessment of a software product's quality.

6.4   PAV: Scientific Research

PAV is a scientific organization that is involved in the development of large software-intensive systems, used for scientific research. One of their projects is the development of a highly distributed system that collects scientific data from around 15.000 sources, distributed over 77 different stations, each source generating around 2 Gbps of raw data. The challenge for this system is to communicate and process the resulting 30Tbps data stream in real-time for interested scientists.

In this project, architectural decisions need to be shared and used over a time span of more than 25 years. This is due to the long development time (more than 10 years), and a required operational lifetime of at least 15 years. The organization is judged by external reviewers on the quality of the architecture and the outcome of these reviews influences the funding, and consequently the continuation, of their projects. Therefore, it is of paramount importance to keep the system architecture at a high quality. In order to achieve this purpose, PAV needs to evaluate at all times the design maturity, the completeness, the correctness and the consistency of the architecture.

The evaluation of the architecture is to be performed at the level of *knowledge entities*, which are units of architectural knowledge shared and communicated among the project *stakeholders*. There are four different types of *knowledge entities*: *problems* that state how specific functional requirements or quality attributes must be satisfied; *concerns* that comprise any interest to the systems development, its operation or any other aspect that is critical or otherwise important to one or more stakeholders; *alternatives* that solve the described problem, potentially in different ways and with different consequences; *decisions* that denote the selection of one among multiple alternatives.

During the architecting process, the architect takes a number of architectural decisions that are gradually being refined into more low-level, technical decisions. The lowest level of an architectural decision is called a *specification*, and the architecting process finishes when all architectural decisions have been refined into specifications.

Knowledge entities can be expressed in *artifacts* that are documents in electronic or printed format. The organization also considers *artifacts* of smaller granularity, called *artifact fragments*, such as individual sections, paragraphs or pictures in a document, in order to be able to trace fine-grained *knowledge entities* within a single document. Finally, it is of high importance for the organization to keep trace of how the *requirements*, described in the *requirements specification* document are satisfied in the *software architecture* document. Some *requirements* have associated *risks*.

We can express PAV's organization-specific terminology in terms of our core model. A *problem* is being solved by the alternatives, which coincides with the core model concept of a Decision Topic. The *knowledge entity* on the other hand is a generalization of four core model concepts, namely Concern, Alternative, Decision Topic and Decision. A *specification* is a special, refined case of a Decision. An *artifact fragment* is an Artifact contained in other Artifacts. *Requirements* and *risks* are special types of Concerns that need to be taken care of in the decision making process.

During our research in PAV we found that – although many of the core concepts are present – most relations between artifacts remain implicit, potentially leading to traceability issues. The mapping between the core model and the concepts specific to this organization brings to the architect's attention that four of the fundamental core model concepts, namely Concerns, Decision Topics, Alternatives and Decisions are in fact special cases of *knowledge entities*. With this in mind architects can annotate architecture documents with higher level of detail by taking into account the different types of knowledge entities. A more explicit focus on the core model's 'decision loop', and in particular the individual elements that make up this loop, is likely to result in better traceability.

7 Core Model Validation: Attempted Falsification through Literature

The industrial experiences described in Section 6 showed a practical application of our core model of architectural knowledge. In this section we determine the core model's theoretical significance by comparing its concepts to architectural knowledge concepts used in accepted software architecture literature.

As defined in Section 4 our core model is *minimal* in the sense that it is not possible to express some concepts in any other concepts, and *complete* in the sense that there are no concepts from other approaches that have no counterpart in the model. Unfortunately, it is impossible to 'prove' that our model exhibits the desired features of being complete and minimal. The best we can do is to search for counterexamples that prove our model does *not* exhibit those features, thereby demonstrating that our model is *not* valid. If we don't succeed in this falsification attempt, we accept that as supporting evidence for the validity of our model.

To properly apply the falsification approach on our core model, we have mapped on our model the complete set of concepts from three different terminological frameworks for architectural knowledge well-known from literature. Each of these frameworks has a slightly different perspective on architectural knowledge: IEEE-1471 [15] targets architectural descriptions, Kruchten's ontology [18] focuses on architectural design decisions per se, while Tyree and Akerman [6] provide a template to capture architectural

Table 2. Falsification Attempts on Core Model using Software Architecture Literature

Core concept	IEEE-1471 [15]	Kruchten's ontology [18]	Tyree's Decision Template [6]
Stakeholder	*Stakeholder*		
Concern	*Concern, Environment, Mission*	*Requirement, Defect, Risk, Plan*	*Assumption, Constraint, Requirement*
Decision Topic		*scope*	*Issue, Group*
Alternative		*Idea, Tentative*	*Position*
Ranking			*Argument*
Arch. Design Dec.		*Decision*	*Assumption, Decision, Principle*
"decision loop"	*Rationale*	*relationships*	*Related decisions / requirements / principles*
Arch. Design	*Architecture*		
Language	*(Library) viewpoint*		
to reflect	*(Library) viewpoint*	*trace from/to*	*related artifacts*
Artifact	*System, View, Model, Arch. description*	*Technical artifact*	*Artifact*

design decisions – thereby relating architectural decisions to architectural descriptions. Together, these perspectives cover all 'corners' of our core model.

Our falsification attempts are summarized in Table 2, which shows the mapping between core model concepts and the concepts of the three terminological frameworks for architectural knowledge. We failed to find any concepts that do not fit our core model; we accept this result as support to the claim of validity of our core model. In the following subsections the relationships between core model concepts and concepts of each of the literature frameworks are elaborated upon.

7.1   Architectural Descriptions: IEEE-1471

IEEE-1471 prescribes the use of so-called *view*s to describe an architecture. Views are reflections of part of the architectural design according to a particular perspective, or *viewpoint*. A viewpoint defines "the language, modeling techniques, or analytical methods to be used in constructing a view based upon the viewpoint" [15]. In other words, a viewpoint defines the Languages to use as well as how to *reflect* the architectural design in a view. The IEEE-1471 terms *model* and *view* are both subsumed in the core model concept Artifact.

A *library viewpoint* is a *viewpoint* that is defined elsewhere, i.e. a specialized instance of a normal viewpoint. The core model captures the *rationale* of an architectural design decision in the trajectory from Concern and Decision Topic through ranking of Alternatives to the eventual choice of the Decision.

In IEEE-1471 terms, a *system* has an *architecture*, reflected in the core model as an Architectural Design that is reflected in a set of Artifacts, which together correspond to the IEEE *system*. The *architectural description* is a particular Artifact that conforms to the IEEE prescription of how the Architectural Design should be reflected, i.e. using a *viewpoint* as Language. The *environment* in which a system operates determines the setting and circumstances of developmental, operational, political, and other influences upon that system. These influences are represented by Concerns in the core, as described in Section 5.

Finally, a *mission* is defined as 'a use or operation for which a system is intended by one or more stakeholders to meet some set of objectives'. This is a special case of a Concern, i.e. 'an interest which pertains to the system's development, its operation or any other aspects that are critical or otherwise important to one or more stakeholders'.

7.2 Ontology of Architectural Design Decisions

In [18], Kruchten defines an ontology of architectural design decisions. Kruchten argues that 'design decisions deserve to be first class entities in the process of developing complex software-intensive systems' and proposes a model to do so. Due to space restrictions, this section only highlights some of the concepts from the ontology to capture the spirit of this model and its relation to the core model. For a more elaborate discussion, please refer to [19].

Kruchten defines a number of attributes of architectural design decisions, all of which can be mapped to concepts in our core model. The *scope* of a decision, for example, can be mapped on the Decision Topic concept. In our core model, Concerns consist of one or more Decision Topics for which a Decision must be taken. These Decision Topics are concrete subjects for which a solution is proposed. A single Decision Topic limits the scope of a Decision to the concrete subject it represents.

The evolution of design decisions is captured in the *state* attribute. In the early decision making phase, for instance, *Ideas* and *Tentative* decisions (i.e. decisions with a state 'idea' or 'tentative') correspond to the core concept of an Alternative. Both are not yet decisions, and might never become one. Tentative decisions can be used in running 'what if' scenarios, i.e. a ranking of different ideas.

The ontology further defines a number of relations between decisions. All these relationships are manifested in the 'decision loop' in the core model, described in Section 5. For example, the relation 'decision A *constrains* decision B' implies that B is tied to A and must be in the same state as A. For instance, 'Must use J2EE' constrains 'use JBoss as Application Server'. In terms of the core model, the Decision 'Must use J2EE' introduces a new Decision Topic 'which application server to use?'. The Alternative 'JBoss' could not have been chosen without the decision to use J2EE.

Besides relations between decisions, Kruchten names several relations with 'external artifacts'. Design decisions *trace from* technical artifacts upstream: requirements and defects (i.e. Concerns in the core model), and *trace to* technical artifacts downstream: design and implementation artifacts (i.e. Artifacts in the core model). They are also traceable to management artifacts, such as risks and plans (again Concerns). Finally, Kruchten notes that it may be useful to track which portions of the system are *not compliant with* some design decisions. In the core model, this non-compliance corresponds to a reflection in Artifacts of an Architectural Design upon which some Architectural Design Decisions have not yet been enforced.

7.3 Documenting Design Decisions

In [6], Tyree and Akerman consider important decisions as the major forces that drive architecture. They present a template that can be used to document design decisions. According to this template, *assumptions* and *constraints* limit the alternatives that can be selected. Assumptions are Decisions that are assumed to have been taken and to influence the Architectural Design, often resulting in new Concerns for Stakeholders. Constraints are posed by decisions already taken, reflected in new Concerns. These new Concerns are to be taken into account when ranking Alternatives for a Decision Topic.

During the architecting process, an architect comes up with *positions* for a certain *issue*. Ultimately, one of the *positions* is chosen based on some *argument*. This position becomes the *decision*. This sequence of steps is also visible in our core model, as the proposal of a set of Alternatives, out of which one Alternative is chosen as Decision.

A *group* can be used to organize a set of decisions based on their topic (e.g. integration, presentation, etc.). In our core model, Decision Topics (i.e. concrete subjects for which a solution is proposed) correspond to the *group* concept from [6]. The example template in [6] lists the positions (i.e. Alternatives) 'Rearchitect existing batch logic in System A', 'Extend System B to handle a new product type', and 'Develop a replacement for System A' for the issue 'Current IT infrastructure doesn't support interactive approval functionality for most financial products', with a grouping labeled 'System structuring'. The example template clearly shows the proposed *positions* all target the group (i.e. Decision Topic) 'System structuring'.

According to [6], a *decision* states the architecture's direction. This corresponds to our notion of an Architectural Design Decision that is enforced upon the Architectural Design. The template has room for the documentation of *related decisions*, *related requirements*, *related artifacts*, and *related principles*. The way in which Decisions (that include principles), Artifacts, and Concerns (i.e. requirements) can be related has been extensively described in Section 7.2.

8   A Vision on Architectural Knowledge Sharing

We can look at the core model from two perspectives, namely data integration and service integration. For data integration the core model becomes a reference model for sharing architectural knowledge. For service integration, it provides the means to integrate the services that a grid infrastructure may provide.

Having a core model of architectural knowledge has a number of advantages. First of all, from a data integration perspective, the core model defines a vocabulary for architectural knowledge: the minimal set of common notions that is needed when architectural knowledge has to be made explicit. Terminology, processes, and concerns particular to a specific organization or domain can be expressed in terms of core model concepts. Metaphorically speaking, the organization-specific terminology lies like a shell around the core model. One can even envision multiple layers of shells, for instance when an organization defines its own methodology (the outer shell) as an extension to the IEEE-1471 standard (the inner shell). Thanks to this separation between core model and shells, we gain in terminological stability (the core model acts as a reference model used by all companies), extensibility (the architectural knowledge of new companies or domains can always be added as a new shell without any increase in complexity), and reuse (by adding new shells, the architectural knowledge vocabulary is incrementally enriched).

Moreover, with a shared core model it becomes easier to agree on a common terminology. This common terminology sticks to the essence and neglects the specific

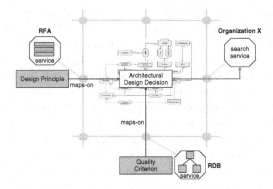

Fig. 3. Sharing Architectural Knowledge in a grid-setting

concepts delegated to the shells. These benefits are reaped whenever multiple departments in the same organization, or even different partner organizations, have to collab-
orate in the same software project: terminological misunderstandings are avoided.

Furthermore, from a service integration perspective the core model can be the means
to integrate the services that a grid infrastructure may provide. These services may
'speak the same language' by exchanging data expressed in concepts from the core
model. A direct benefit of this language uniformity is that the core model, being shared
among multiple sites, realizes a more generic architectural style aimed at integration
via an enterprise data model [20]: the enterprise data model (i.e. our core model) is the
target format for all messages between the grid members, which transform their specific
formats to the target format. Such transformations are defined as shells.

We envision architectural knowledge sharing in a grid-setting, an instantiation of the
knowledge grid discussed in [21]. The basic idea is sketched in Figure 3. The model
depicted in the center is the core model of what concerns architectural knowledge.
Organization-specific models provide a specialization hereof. In the figure, *design principles* (a kind of Architectural Design Decision) are made available by RFA, while
quality criteria (another kind of Architectural Design Decision) are made available by
RDB (see also Section 6). Both organizations may offer visualization services (e.g. tab-
ular versus graph-based) to visualize Architectural Design Decisions. Suppose a third
organization, X, is looking for Architectural Design Decisions that are shared on the
grid. Because of the specializations of the notion of an Architectural Design Decision
at RFA and RDB, this query translates into a search for *design principles* at RFA, and
quality criteria at RDB. Both results will be returned, even using the local visualization
services of RFA and RDB.

We have started to use our core model to realize our envisioned grid-like setting to
share architectural knowledge. We have built some simple services to process specific
architectural knowledge: a word processor plug-in to annotate the rationale in architectural documents, and a service to visualize architectural design decisions using cluster-
based browsing [4]. Future work includes construction of the grid service infrastructure
based on the core model and specific shells, as well as new services to be shared among
organizations participating in the grid.

9   Conclusions

In this paper we have presented a core model of architectural knowledge. This core model is the result of the execution of an action research cycle. Experimentation with an earlier version of the model identified mismatches between the model and industrial practice. Those mismatches have been overcome by ensuring the new version of our model of architectural knowledge is both complete and minimalistic. It is this latter feature that led us to adopt the term 'core model'. The validity of the claim of completeness of our core model is made plausible by an attempt to falsify this validity using various sources from literature.

During experimentation with the earlier version of the model, we identified four perspectives on architectural knowledge management in four different industrial organizations: sharing, compliance, discovery, and traceability. Subsequent application of the core model allowed us to identify probable causes and remedies for problems with architectural knowledge management encountered in those organizations: implicit relations between architectural decisions is the likely cause for the problems with sharing architectural knowledge a particular software development organization encounters; the compliance issues in a multi-site development organization are probably due to a decision making process that remains invisible to the affected parties; an organization that performs software product audits has to deal with the fact that, since the result of architectural decisions is not confined to a single product artifact, the relation between 'quality' and 'architecture' is often not obvious at first sight; long-term development projects in a scientific organization benefit from improved traceability if a better distinction is made between different concepts that play a role in the decision making process. We aim to alleviate those problems in a next iteration of our research with tools, methods, and techniques that address the probable causes of these problems with architectural knowledge management.

Acknowledgment

The authors would like to thank Rich Hilliard for constructive feedback on an earlier version of this paper. This research has been partially sponsored by the Dutch Joint Academic and Commercial Quality Research & Development (Jacquard) program on Software Engineering Research via contract 638.001.406 GRIFFIN: a GRId For inFormatIoN about architectural knowledge.

References

1. Bass, L., Clements, P., Kazman, R.: Software Architecture in Practice, 2nd edn. SEI Series in Software Engineering. Addison-Wesley Pearson Education, Boston (2003)
2. Ali Babar, M., Gorton, I., Jeffery, R.: Capturing and Using Software Architecture Knowledge for Architecture-Based Software Development. In: 5th International Conference on Quality Software (QSIC), Melbourne, Australia, pp. 169–176 (2005)
3. Bosch, J.: Software Architecture: The Next Step. In: Oquendo, F., Warboys, B., Morrison, R. (eds.) EWSA 2004. LNCS, vol. 3047, pp. 194–199. Springer, Heidelberg (2004)

4. Kruchten, P., Lago, P., van Vliet, H.: Building up and Reasoning about Architectural Knowledge. In: Hofmeister, C., Crnkovic, I., Reussner, R. (eds.) QoSA 2006. LNCS, vol. 4214, pp. 39–47. Springer, Heidelberg (2006)
5. Shaw, M., Clements, P.: The Golden Age of Software Architecture. IEEE Software 23(2), 31–39 (2006)
6. Tyree, J., Akerman, A.: Architecture Decisions: Demystifying Architecture. IEEE Software 22(2), 19–27 (2005)
7. van der Ven, J.S., Jansen, A., Nijhuis, J., Bosch, J.: Design decisions: The Bridge between Rationale and Architecture. In: Dutoit, A. (ed.) Rationale Management in Software Engineering, pp. 329–346. Springer, Heidelberg (2006)
8. Tang, A., Ali Babar, M., Gorton, I., Han, J.: A Survey of the Use and Documentation of Architecture Design Rationale. In: 5th Working IEEE/IFIP Conference on Software Architecture (WICSA), Pittsburgh, USA, pp. 89–98 (2005)
9. Jansen, A., Bosch, J.: Software Architecture as a Set of Architectural Design Decisions. In: 5th Working IEEE/IFIP Conference on Software Architecture (WICSA), Pittsburgh, USA, pp. 109–120 (2005)
10. Wang, Z., Sherdil, K., Madhavji, N.H.: ACCA: An Architecture-centric Concern Analysis Method. In: 5th Working IEEE/IFIP Conference on Software Architecture (WICSA), Pittsburgh, USA, pp. 99–108 (2005)
11. Hofmeister, C., Kruchten, P., Nord, R.L., Obbink, H., Ran, A., America, P.: Generalizing a Model of Software Architecture Design from Five Industrial Approaches. In: 5th Working IEEE/IFIP Conference on Software Architecture (WICSA), Pittsburgh, USA, pp. 77–86 (2005)
12. Akerman, A., Tyree, J.: Position on Ontology-Based Architecture. In: 5th Working IEEE/IFIP Conference on Software Architecture (WICSA), Pittsburgh, USA, pp. 289–290 (2005)
13. Avison, D., Lau, F., Myers, M., Nielsen, P.A.: Action Research. Communications of the ACM 42(1), 94–97 (1999)
14. de Boer, R.C., Farenhorst, R., van der Ven, J.S., Clerc, V., Deckers, R., Lago, P., van Vliet, H.: Structuring Software Architecture Project Memories. In: 8th International Workshop on Learning Software Organizations (LSO), Rio de Janeiro, Brazil, pp. 39–47 (2006)
15. IEEE: IEEE Recommended Practice for Architectural Description of Software-Intensive Systems. Standard 1471-2000, IEEE (2000)
16. Object Management Group: Software Process Engineering Metamodel Specification. Technical Report formal/05-01-06, Object Management Group (2005)
17. ISO/IEC: Software engineering - Product quality - Part 1: Quality model. Technical Report ISO/IEC 9126-1, ISO/IEC (2001)
18. Kruchten, P.: An Ontology of Architectural Design Decisions in Software-Intensive Systems. In: 2nd Groningen Workshop on Software Variability Management, Groningen, The Netherlands (2004)
19. Farenhorst, R., de Boer, R.C.: Core Concepts of an Ontology of Architectural Design Decisions. Technical Report IR-IMSE-002, Vrije Universiteit Amsterdam (2006)
20. Gorton, I.: Essential Software Architecture. Springer, Heidelberg (2006)
21. Zhuge, H.: The Knowledge Grid. World Scientific Publishing Co., Singapore (2004)

The Influence of CMMI on Establishing an Architecting Process

Eltjo R. Poort[1], Herman Postema[1], Andrew Key[2], and Peter H.N. de With[3]

[1] LogicaCMG, P.O. Box 159, 1180 AD Amstelveen, The Netherlands
{eltjo.poort,herman.postema}@logicacmg.com
[2] LogicaCMG, Stephenson House, 75 Hampstead Road, London NW1 2PL, United Kingdom
andrew.key@logicacmg.com
[3] Eindhoven Univ. of Technol., P.O. Box 513, 5600 MB Eindhoven, The Netherlands
P.H.N.de.With@tue.nl

Abstract. A large IT company is creating a generic architecting process. Since the company has set an objective to achieve Maturity Level 3 of the Capability Maturity Model Integration (CMMI), the process needs to comply with the relevant requirements set by the CMMI. This paper presents the elicitation of such requirements, and the resulting set of requirements. It analyzes their potential impact on generic architecting processes found in literature. It turns out that many key architectural concepts are at best loosely defined in the CMMI. CMMI is strong in support of the development-related architecting activities, but gives only indirect support for other architecting activities, particularly in a product development context.

1 Introduction

The setting of this paper is a large IT company, in which it was established that an institutionalized architecting process would help control technical risks in projects and products. At about the same time, a company-wide objective had been set to achieve CMMI Maturity Level 3. This made it necessary to obtain insight into the requirements that architecting processes need to fulfill in order to comply with CMMI Maturity Level 3 [1]. This paper documents the process of establishing these requirements. Apart from this paper, we will elaborate on the establishment of this architecting process in a separate paper that is still under development.

As references we have chosen two generic processes found in literature: Architecture Based Development [1], because its scope is close to our purpose and because it represents one of the better known approaches to architecting in both industry and academia, and Hofmeister *et al.* [2], because their model represents the commonalities between five industrial approaches.

First, in Sect. 2 we will present the organizational context and scope of a generic architecting process. In Sect. 3, the CMMI Process Areas that are relevant to such an architecting process will be identified, and their requirements on architecting processes extracted. In Sect. 4 follows a discussion on the impact of the CMMI requirements on

---

[1] *CMMI Maturity Level 3* is abbreviated to *CMMI Level 3* in the rest of this paper.

S. Overhage et al. (Eds.): QoSA 2007, LNCS 4880, pp. 215–230, 2007.

generic architecting processes found in literature, and on the coverage of architecting processes by CMMI. We will finish up with some conclusions and further work to be done.

2 Architecting Process Context and Scope

2.1 Organizational Context

The analysis described in this paper was done by and for an IT Corporation of 40,000 people across 41 countries. The company has a diverse business portfolio, consisting of services centered on business consulting, systems development and integration and IT and business process outsourcing.

One of the company's Technical Directorate's activities is controlling technical risks in the various IT projects and products. It was felt that technical risk control could be enhanced by developing and institutionalizing a process that would provide guidance for making technical decisions: in short, an architecting process. Two of the authors of this paper work within the company's technical directorate at group and subsidiary levels, and have terms of reference that include management of technical risks.

The decision to institute an architecting process coincided with the setting of a maturity objective by the company's executive management. Encouraged by benefits experienced through local CMMI driven process improvement, management set an objective to achieve CMMI Maturity Level 3 for relevant organizational units throughout the whole company. This meant that the architecting process to be developed would be subject to the requirements set by the CMMI.

2.2 Scoping an Architecting Process

The terms Architecture and Architecting are used in a great variety of meanings in the IT world. Rather than risking a non-converging discussion on the meaning of the terms, it was decided to scope the architecting process in terms of a set of business goals and usage scenarios. The details of this work and the resulting process description will be the subject of a separate paper. For the purposes of this paper, a high-level summary is provided:

Business Goals. The business goals for the architecting process were established as *Consistency in Delivery, Risk Management, Customer Satisfaction* and *Knowledge Incorporation*.

Usage Scenarios. The process will be used for architecting activities in the following scenarios: *Responding to a Request for Proposal (RFP), Software Development Project, System Integration Project* and *Product Development*.

The business goals and usage scenarios were analyzed to determine the scope of the architecting process. Apart from literature and the existing experience of the authors, additional input for the analysis came from other stakeholders, specifically the company's sales community, quality assurance community and technical community, obtained in a workshop.

The most significant elements in the outcome of this analysis are listed below.

– Analysis of the business goals and experience indicates that *architectural decisions* are critical to the success of projects in terms of cost and timing of delivery. The process should therefore give guidance on how to identify and make architectural decisions. This matches requirements from CMMI about decision analysis and resolution, and with recent publications about the status of architectural decisions [3,4,5].
– Many architectural decisions are made during the *sales* phase of projects; the architecting process has to facilitate that process.
– A certain level of *reviewing and control* has to be facilitated by the process. This is the convergence of the architecture assessment practices from literature [6,7], and the responsibilities of the authors to control technical risks. Not only are reviewing and control necessary parts of the process, it also has to be facilitated by a certain level of standardization in *documentation* of architectures.
– The involvement of architects in the *implementation* phase of solutions is essential in order to assure that the selected solution will be adequately implemented *conforming* to the architecture. The architecting process has to facilitate this.
– To contribute to the business goal of knowledge incorporation, the process should support a structure for organizational *learning from experiences*. Learning points may be both process-related (like best practices) and product-related (like best architectural constructs).
– The objective is to implement a process that gives guidance on aspects of architecting that are *not specific* to particular types of applications, e.g. not just software development, but also system integration, ERP implementations, and embedded system development. This means its concept of "architecture" covers both *software* and *system architecture*. For such a generic process to be useable, it must be accompanied by a set of guidelines for *tailoring* the process to the specific needs and characteristics of the usage environment. This is also required by CMMI Generic Practice 3.1 "Establish a Defined Process".

The result of all this is an architecting process description under development that focuses on requirements analysis, architectural decision making, shaping, selection and evaluation of the best-fit solutions, documenting and implementing architectures and controls like architectural governance and reviewing.

At the time of writing this paper, it is being considered to extend the scope of this process to better support the product development scenario, by adding e.g. reusable asset harvesting and product roadmapping.

The scope of what is meant by an "architecting process" in this paper is documented as a list of requirements[2] in Table 1. In Sect. 4.1, we will identify a number of generic architecting processes in literature that are similar in scope.

The scope of the architecting process has been determined by the analysis of the business goals and usage scenarios, with limited consideration of CMMI. We will now focus on the influence of CMMI in more detail.

---

[2] A note on the tagging of requirements in this paper: the reader will notice the use of mnemonic, hierarchical tagging [8]. The use of dots indicates a hierarchical grouping, with an implicit traceability to higher level requirements.

Table 1. Scope of architecting process: high-level requirements

rq.arch A process giving guidance on architecting technical solutions.
rq.arch.decision Guidance on how to make architectural decisions.
rq.arch.sales Facilitating the sales process.
rq.arch.documentation Standardization of architectural documentation.
rq.arch.controls Guidance on architectural controls.
rq.arch.conform Assuring conformance with architecture during the implementation process.
rq.scalable Scalable over business unit sizes (20 - 2000) and project/programme sizes (80 K - 500 M), and over a broad range of size and complexity of solutions.
rq.generic Flexible / generic to work in diverse applications.
rq.generic.tailoring Be accompanied by a set of tailoring guidelines.
rq.accessible Simple, accessible to all.
rq.accessible.terminology Terminology familiar to company staff.
rq.cmmi CMMI Maturity Level 3 compliant.
rq.learning.product Bottle product experiences and make available to architects in controlled manner.
rq.learning.process Support a structure for organizational process learning.

3 Architecting and CMMI

The Capability Maturity Model Integration (CMMI) is a process-improvement model developed by the Software Engineering Institute (SEI) of the Carnegie Mellon University. It is scoped towards the development, acquisition and maintenance of systems or services.

The "staged representation" of the CMMI consists of five maturity levels. With increasing maturity level, the process capabilities increase, resulting in a higher probability that development or maintenance targets will be realized. Each maturity level consists of a number of Process Areas (PAs). Each PA consists of a small set of "goals" followed by a collection of practices that must be performed in order to realize the goals. A process complies to a certain maturity level if the goals and practices of all PAs of that level are satisfied. The PAs are customarily referred to by a set of fixed tags; all level 2 and 3 PAs and their tags are listed in Table 2.

Goals and practices of a PA are divided into specific ones and generic ones. Specific goals and practices directly refer to the PA itself, whereas generic goals and practices represent mechanisms to institutionalize the specific goals and practices. These practices are called generic because they apply to multiple PAs.

CMMI Maturity Level 3 requires that for all PAs belonging to Level 2 and Level 3 a "defined process" is established. A defined process is tailored from the organization's "standard process" according to a set of tailoring guidelines. In addition, a defined process has a maintained process description, which implies that all (generic and specific) practices are described. For more information, the reader is referred to [9] or [10].

This section starts with an exploration of what a *CMMI Compliant Architecting Process* actually means. This is followed by a discussion on the use of architectural concepts in the CMMI. We then proceed to identify the Process Areas that have a significant contribution to architecting according to the scope set out in Sect. 2.2. We call this set the *Architecting Significant Process Areas (ASPAs)*.

3.1 CMMI-Compliant Architecting Process

The boundaries (scope) of the architecting process are determined in Sect. 2.2. Because of the structure of the CMMI, the practices related to this process may be distributed over a number of Process Areas.

The CMMI Level 3 coverage of the architecting process can be obtained by analyzing every Level 2 and Level 3 specific practice to determine whether or not the practice is inside the scope of the architecting process. The generic practices of Level 2 and Level 3 will always be in scope because they apply to all PAs. This analysis will be performed further on in this paper.

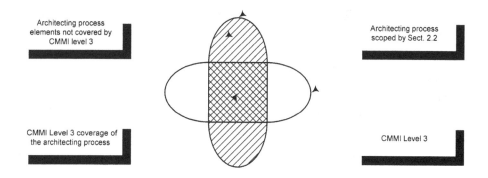

Fig. 1. CMMI coverage of the architecting process

Figure 1 illustrates the CMMI coverage of the architecting process. As can be derived from the figure, the architecting process may include elements that are not covered by CMMI Level 3. These may for example be elements that are beyond the scope of system development (like architectural roadmapping) or elements that are considered critical for a successful architecting process but cannot be found in the CMMI.

Summarizing the above information, it can be stated that a CMMI Level 3 compliant architecting process:

- has a maintained description of all specific and generic practices that are in scope of the architecting process (the square box in the figure)
- has a maintained description of guidelines to tailor the process to the specific needs and characteristics of the usage environment
- is consistently deployed inside the company in the context of the user scenarios referred to in Sect. 2.2.

The scope of this paper is the determination of the practices that should be part of the maintained description mentioned in the first two items. These practices will be presented as a list of requirements imposed on an architecting process description. In Sect. 3.3 we will present the elicitation of these requirements, but first we will have a more general look at the use of architecture concepts in the CMMI.

3.2 Architecture Concepts in the CMMI

The word "architecture" is used extensively in the CMMI. It appears in 7 out of 25 Process Area descriptions [9]. The CMMI is a collection of industry best practices and not a formal theoretical model. Effort was put in making the model consistent and unambiguous, but many parts are still subject to different interpretations.

Architecture itself is not defined in the CMMI glossary. The word is mostly used informally to denote a number of concepts, some of which are related to our architecting process, and others are not.

Architecting the company processes: the CMMI describes how to set up and maintain a company's processes in order to best achieve its business goals. The design and overview of these processes and their alignment with the company's IT resources require architecting skills. This type of architecting is relevant in the OPD and OPF processes. It is outside the scope of this paper as defined in Sect. 2.2.

Architecting the product: the bulk of the CMMI PAs describe how to improve systems and software engineering processes. Architecting is an essential part of those processes, especially RD, TS, PI, PP, REQM, DAR and RSKM.

Furthermore, several architecture-related terms are defined in the CMMI glossary:

Functional Architecture is defined as "The hierarchical arrangement of functions, their internal and external (external to the aggregation itself) functional interfaces and external physical interfaces, their respective functional and performance requirements, and their design constraints."

Process Architecture is defined as "the ordering, interfaces, interdependencies, and other relationships among the process elements in a standard process". This concept is on a different level than the "architecture" in the architecting process as described in this document.

Shared Vision is defined as "a common understanding of guiding principles including mission, objectives, expected behavior, values, and final outcomes, which are developed and used by a group, such as an organization, project, or team."

A significant finding is the fact that "product architecture", though used extensively, is not defined in the CMMI glossary.

These considerations show that the concepts and terms relevant to architecting are generically defined (e.g. Shared Vision) or not defined at all (e.g. Product Architecture) in the CMMI. Hence the terms provide little guidance in themselves. The word architecture is used in many different ways, making it inadequate as a basis to establish direction for an architecting process. We have therefore selected a different approachto establishing the CMMI requirements on an architecting process, which will be the subject of the following section.

3.3 Process Areas Relevant to Architecting

Our approach to establish which requirements CMMI imposes on architecting processes is to first identify which PAs are relevant for the process, and then to extract requirements on the process from the practices in their descriptions. An analysis of the CMMI Level 3 PAs against the architecting process scoped in Sect. 2.2 results in a set of PAs that have a direct and significant contribution to the objectives of this process. As discussed before, these PAs are called *Architecting Significant Process Areas* (ASPAs).

The PAs of the CMMI are grouped into four categories:

Process Management. These PAs contain the activities related to defining, planning, implementing, monitoring, evaluating and improving all other processes. The architecting process is subject to these process management PAs in order to assure the required level of capability.

Project Management. These PAs cover the project management activities related to planning, monitoring and controlling the development or maintenance project. The architecting process is generally performed in the context of a project.

Engineering. These PAs cover the development and maintenance activities that are shared across engineering disciplines (e.g. systems engineering and software engineering). The architecting process falls mainly within these PAs.

Support. These PAs cover the activities that support all other PAs like establishing measurement programs, verification of compliance, and effective decision making. The architecting process is also subject to these PAs.

Table 2 identifies the categorized set of Level 3 PAs and indicates which PAs have been qualified as an ASPA. It should be noted that *all* PAs of the CMMI contribute to the objectives of the architecting process. Their contribution may be direct because the PA is actually part of the architecting process, or indirect because the PA is establishing the context and preconditions for a successful architecting process.

As stated before an ASPA has a direct contribution and this contribution should also be significant. This is the case for all Engineering PAs, one Project PA (Risk Management, RSKM) and one Support PA (Decision Analysis and Resolution, DAR). Both RSKM and DAR are actually part of the architecting process and contribute significantly to its objectives. The architecting relevance of the set of ASPAs is shortly explained below. Where relevant, underpinning references to the CMMI text have been added in [braces].

REQM *Requirements Management.* The role of architecting in Requirements Management focuses around the impact of requirements and their traceability to the architecture. [Specific Practice 1.1 *Obtain an Understanding of Requirements* describes the process of the acceptance of requirements according to objective criteria. "Does not break the architecture" is an important criterion to assess requirements, implied in the example criterion "Appropriate to implement". It is also implicit in the impact

Table 2. Categorized Process Areas and their Architecting Significance

Tag		Process	Project	Eng	Supp	ASPA
OPF	Organizational Process Focus	X				N
OPD	Organizational Process Definition	X				N
OT	Organizational Training	X				N
PP	Project Planning		X			N
PMC	Project Monitoring and Control		X			N
SAM	Supplier Agreement Management		X			N
IPM	Integrated Project Management		X			N
RSKM	Risk Management		X			Y
IT	Integrated Teaming		X			N
ISM	Integrated Supplier Management		X			N
REQM	Requirements Management			X		Y
RD	Requirements Development			X		Y
TS	Technical Solution			X		Y
PI	Product Integration			X		Y
VER	Verification			X		Y
VAL	Validation			X		Y
CM	Configuration Management				X	N
PPQA	Process and Product Quality Assurance				X	N
MA	Measurement and Analysis				X	N
DAR	Decision Analysis and Resolution				X	Y
OEI	Organizational Environment for Integration				X	N

analysis mentioned in SP1.3 *Manage Requirements Changes*. SP1.4 *Maintain Bidirectional Traceability of Requirements*: traceability to architectural components is implied, as is traceability to architectural decisions.]

RD *Requirements Development.* This process area is where a system's functional architecture is defined, and where the requirements are analyzed and developed. Architecting is important here both as a source of new requirements and as a means to structure requirements. ["Analyses occur recursively at successively more detailed layers of a product's architecture". Specific Goal 2 *Develop Product Requirements* identifies the selected product architecture as a source of derived requirements. SP2.1 *Establish Product and Product-Component Requirements* prescribes that "architecture requirements addressing critical product qualities and performance necessary for product architecture design" be developed, and that "requirements that result from design decisions" be derived. SP2.3 *Identify Interface Requirements* prescribes the definition of interfaces as an integral part of the architecture definition.]

TS *Technical Solution.* This process area covers the core of architecting: developing a solution that fulfills the requirements. [TS specific goals are SG1 *Select Product Component Solutions*, SG2 *Develop the Design* and SG3 *Implement the Product Design*. SP1.1 *Develop Detailed Alternative Solutions and Selection Criteria* prepares architectural decision making by identifying alternatives and selection criteria. SP1.2 *Evolve Operational Concepts and Scenarios* prescribes the use of scenarios to help assess alternative solutions for usability.

SP1.3 *Select Product Component Solutions* and SP2.4 *Perform Make, Buy or Reuse Analyses* are about making design decisions and documenting them, including rationale. SP2.1 *Design the Product or Product Component* establishes the product architecture. It describes architecture definition, driven by the architectural requirements developed in RD SP 2.1. It identifies elements of architectures, such as coordination mechanisms, structural elements, standards and design rules. It also mandates architecture evaluations to be conducted periodically throughout product design. SP2.2 *Establish a technical data package* and SP3.2 *Develop Product Support Documentation* are about documenting, giving guidance on where the architecture definition and the rationale for key decisions are documented. SP2.3 *Design Interfaces Using Criteria* supplies requirements to the interface design process.]

VER *Verification.* Verification is an essential part of the architecting process because its purpose is to ensure that the work products of this process meet the specified requirements. Typical work products of the architecting process are the architecture and design documents and the architecture and design itself. Means for verification may be peer reviews (for documents) and architectural assessments. Verification activities should be prepared, performed, the results analyzed and corrective actions identified.

VAL *Validation.* Validation is in fact a variant on verification but its objective is to demonstrate that a (work) product fulfills its intended use (i.e. that it meets user needs). Regarding the architecting process, the work products and means for validation are similar to verification.

DAR *Decision Analysis and Resolution.* Key to architecting is decision making [3,4]. The DAR process area prescribes a formal evaluation process for decisions of this kind: evaluation criteria should be established, alternatives should be identified, evaluation methods selected, alternatives evaluated and a solution selected. There should also be guidelines establishing which decisions should be subject to this formal evaluation process.

RSKM *Risk Management.* Better risk management is one of the business goals of the architecting process. The inherent risk in a requirement is an important factor in determining whether or it is an architectural requirement. [A requirement that, when not fulfilled, heavily "impacts the ability of the project to meet its objectives" (SP1.1 Determine Risk Sources and Categories), has a good chance to be considered architectural. The RSKM process area prescribes how to deal with such risks: risk parameters should be defined (SP1.2), a risk management strategy should be established (SP1.3), the process should give guidance on how risks are identified and analyzed (SG2), and mitigated (SG3). Insofar as architectural requirements involve risks, they should be treated the same way.]

An analysis of the texts of these ASPAs yields the requirements imposed on the architecting process by the CMMI. These requirements are listed in Table 3. In agreement with the nature of the CMMI, this table is effectively a list of 67 best practices that support companies in creating and implementing an architecting process. The tags allow traceability to the PAs that the requirements originated from, and give the list a clear structure. The largest contributor is TS with 31 requirements, confirming our earlier observation that TS covers the core of architecting. The next largest contributor is RD with 16 requirements, indicating that an architecting process within our scope includes

Table 3. Requirements imposed on Architecting Process by CMMI

rq.cmmi.reqm.arch	Use architectural fit as criterion when assessing requirements and changes.
rq.cmmi.reqm.trace	Maintain traceability between requirements and architectural components and decisions.
rq.cmmi.rd.fun-arch	Develop a functional architecture.
rq.cmmi.rd.recursive	Recursive analysis of requirements.
rq.cmmi.rd.arch-req	Develop architectural requirements.
rq.cmmi.rd.alloc-comp	Allocation of requirements to product components.
rq.cmmi.rd.alloc-fun	Allocation of requirements to functions.
rq.cmmi.rd.elicit	Elicit needs from stakeholders by proactively identifying additional requirements.
rq.cmmi.rd.derive	Derive requirements that result from design decisions.
rq.cmmi.rd.if	Identify interface requirements.
rq.cmmi.rd.trace	Document relationships between requirements.
rq.cmmi.rd.analyze	Analyze requirements.
rq.cmmi.rd.scenario	Develop operational concepts and scenarios.
rq.cmmi.rd.balance	Use proven models, simulations, and prototyping to analyze the balance of stakeholder needs and constraints.
rq.cmmi.rd.risk	Perform a risk assessment on the requirements and functional architecture.
rq.cmmi.rd.lifecycle	Examine product life-cycle concepts for impacts of requirements on risks.
rq.cmmi.rd.assess	Assess the design as it matures in the context of the requirements validation environment.
rq.cmmi.rd.measure	Identify technical performance measures.
rq.cmmi.ts.alt	Develop detailed alternative solutions to address architectural requirements.
rq.cmmi.ts.alt.crit	Develop selection/evaluation criteria for alternative solutions.
rq.cmmi.ts.alt.crit.assess	Assess adequacy of selection criteria after use.
rq.cmmi.ts.alt.req-alloc	Obtain a complete requirements allocation for each alternative.
rq.cmmi.ts.alt.scenario	Develop timeline scenarios for product operation and user interaction for each alternative solution.
rq.cmmi.ts.alt.eval	Evaluate alternative solutions against criteria.
rq.cmmi.ts.alt.issues	Identify and resolve issues with the alternative solutions and requirements.
rq.cmmi.ts.alt.select	Select the best set of alternative solutions that satisfy the established selection criteria.
rq.cmmi.ts.alt.alloc	Establish the requirements associated with the selected set of alternatives as the set of allocated requirements to those product components.
rq.cmmi.ts.alt.doc	Establish and maintain the documentation of the solutions, evaluations, and rationale.
rq.cmmi.ts.reuse	Identify the product-component solutions that will be reused or acquired.
rq.cmmi.ts.reuse.analyze	Perform make, buy or reuse analysis.
rq.cmmi.ts.scenario	Evolve operational concepts and scenarios.
rq.cmmi.ts.technology	Identify technologies currently in use and new product technologies.
rq.cmmi.ts.design	Establish the product architectural design.
rq.cmmi.ts.design.struct	Establish product partition into components.
rq.cmmi.ts.design.struct.if	Identify and document major intercomponent interfaces.
rq.cmmi.ts.design.struct.id	Establish product-component and interface identifications.
rq.cmmi.ts.design.state	Establish main system states and modes.
rq.cmmi.ts.design.if	Identify and document major external interfaces.
rq.cmmi.ts.design.crit	Establish and maintain criteria against which the design can be evaluated.
rq.cmmi.ts.design.method	Identify, develop, or acquire the design methods appropriate for the product.
rq.cmmi.ts.design.standard	Ensure that the design adheres to applicable design standards and criteria.
rq.cmmi.ts.design.fulfill	Ensure that the design adheres to allocated requirements.
rq.cmmi.ts.design.doc	Document and maintain the design in a technical data package.
rq.cmmi.ts.design.levels	Determine the number of levels of design and the appropriate level of documentation for each design level.
rq.cmmi.ts.design.impl	Base detailed design descriptions on the allocated product-component requirements, architecture, and higher level designs.
rq.cmmi.ts.rationale	Document the rationale for key decisions made or defined.
rq.cmmi.ts.if	Establish and maintain interface descriptions.
rq.cmmi.ts.if.crit	Design interfaces using criteria.
rq.cmmi.ts.implement	Implement design adhering to design decisions and architecture.
rq.cmmi.pi.seq	Guidance on determining the product integration sequence.
rq.cmmi.pi.if	Ensure interface compatibility of product components, both internal and external.
rq.cmmi.pi.if.review	Review interface descriptions for completeness.
rq.cmmi.pi.if.manage	Manage interface definitions, designs and changes.
rq.cmmi.ver.prepare	Prepare verification activities.
rq.cmmi.ver.review	Perform peer reviews on architecture and design documents.
rq.cmmi.ver.verify	Verify (part of) the architecture or design.
rq.cmmi.ver.analyze	Analyze verification results and identify corrective actions.
rq.cmmi.val.prepare	Prepare validation activities.
rq.cmmi.val.validate	Validate (part of) the architecture or design.
rq.cmmi.val.analyze	Analyze validation results and identify corrective actions.
rq.cmmi.dar.guid	Specify when a technical choice or design decision is architectural and subject to architecting process.
rq.cmmi.dar.rank	Evaluation criteria for alternative solutions should be ranked.
rq.cmmi.dar.evalmethod	Guidance on selecting evaluation methods for alternatives.
rq.cmmi.rskm	Guidance on handling architectural requirements as risks.
rq.cmmi.rskm.id	Identify architectural risks.
rq.cmmi.rskm.analyze	Analyze architectural risks.
rq.cmmi.rskm.mitigate	Mitigate architectural risks.
rq.cmmi.gen	Architecting process should be institutionalized according to CMMI's Generic Practices.

a substantial amount of requirements development practices. All other PAs provide only 4 or less requirements.

4   Discussion

In this section, we will discuss our results in conjunction with two generic architecting process models found in literature, and we will discuss the coverage of architecting processes in CMMI.

4.1   Generic Architecting Process Models in Literature

The CMMI imposes requirements on processes used by organizations. So if an organization were to institutionalize an architecting process based on a model found in literature, what would that organization have to do to make their architecting process CMMI level 3 compliant?

Although this analysis of CMMI's influence on architecting processes was based on an initial scope set out in the context of a particular company setting, the results of the analysis should be relevant for other generic architecting processes. This section explores that relevance. We examine the impact of the CMMI requirements derived in this paper on two generic architecture process models found in literature: one from a technical report and one from a recent conference paper. Please note that the architecting process models treated here differ significantly in scope: one focuses on design and analysis and the other focuses on architecture playing a central role throughout the software development lifecycle process. Also note that the models only roughly overlap the architecting process scope set out in Sect. 2.2. A discussion on how exactly these processes match or mismatch this scope will be presented in a separate paper.

Architecture-Based Development (ABD). This is the generic architecting process as developed by the Architecture group at the SEI. It is described in [1], but aspects of it are present in most of the publications of the SEI Architecture group (e.g. [11]). It is used as a reference here because its scope is close to that determined in Sect. 2.2, and because it represents one of the better known approaches to architecting in both industry and academia.

The ABD process consists of six steps:

1. Elicit the architectural requirements.
2. Design the architecture.
3. Document the architecture.
4. Analyze the architecture.
5. Realize the architecture.
6. Maintain the architecture.

Table 4. ASPAs Mapping onto ABD Steps

	Elicit	Design	Document	Analyze	Realize	Maintain
REQM	X					
RD	X	X				
TS		X	X	X	X	X
PI					X	
VER		X	X	X	X	X
VAL	X	X	X	X	X	
RSKM	X	X	X	X	X	X
DAR	X	X	X	X	X	X

Table 4 shows how the ASPAs map onto these steps. In order to make the ABD process CMMI Level 3 compliant, each of these steps should be implemented in such a way that the practices belonging to the ASPAs related to this step are satisfied. The following explanation applies to this mapping:

- RD is not only mapped onto the Elicit step but also onto the Design step. This is because the establishment of the "functional architectural structure" as part of this step is actually a practice that is part of RD.
- VER activities start from the Design step because, as discussed before, verification refers to the requirements produced during the Elicit step.
- The ABD process defines that each step includes validation (VAL) activities. For the Elicit step this refers to the validation of behavioral and quality scenarios.
- The Maintenance step is not well defined and scoped in the ABD process description. The existing text refers to means to prevent that the architecture drifts from its original precepts due to poor maintenance. This may include activities to extract the architecture of the as-built system, verify its level of compliance with the architecture of the as-designed system and performing the required corrective actions. In this respect, TS and VER should be mapped onto the Maintenance step.
- Because RSKM and DAR generally support all development and maintenance activities, they are related to all steps of the ABD process.

Generalized Software Architecture Design Model. In [2], Hofmeister *et al.* compare five industrial approaches to architectural design, and extract from their commonalities a general software architecture design approach. The approach involves three activities:

1. *Architectural analysis*: define the problems the architecture must solve. This activity examines architectural concerns and context in order to come up with a set of Architecturally Significant Requirements (ASRs).
2. *Architectural synthesis*: the core of architecture design. This activity proposes architecture solutions to a set of ASRs, thus it moves from the problem to the solution space.
3. *Architectural evaluation*: ensures that the architectural design decisions made are adequate. The candidate architectural solutions are measured against the ASRs.

It should be noted that this generalized model is of a higher level of abstraction than the ABD process discussed before, and that its scope is explicitly limited to the Design step of architecting.

Table 5 shows how the selected set of ASPAs map onto these activities. In order to make a process based on this generalized model CMMI Level 3 compliant, each of these activities should be implemented in such a way that the practices belonging to the ASPAs related to this activity are satisfied. The following explanation applies to this mapping:

- Unlike the ABD process, the generalized model has limited its scope to the design step of the architecture. For this reason, PI and VAL cannot be mapped to this model.

Table 5. ASPAs Mapping onto Generalized Architecture Design Model Activities

	Analysis	Synthesis	Evaluation
REQM	X		
RD	X		
TS		X	
PI			
VER			X
VAL			
RSKM	X	X	X
DAR	X	X	X

– The Architectural Evaluation activity ensures that the architectural design decisions made are adequate. The candidate architectural solutions are measured against the ASRs. Although the result is called the *validated* architecture, this activity is *verification* (VER) in CMMI terms because it refers to the requirements (ASRs) produced during the Architectural Analysis activity.
– Since RSKM and DAR generally support all development and maintenance activities, they are related to all activities of the generalized model.

4.2   CMMI Coverage of Architecting Processes

As discussed in Sect. 3, the architecting process scoped in Sect. 2.2 may include elements that are not covered by CMMI Level 3. An analysis of the information in this section against the CMMI results in the following elements that are not or only indirectly covered.

rq.arch.documentation. Standardization of architectural documentation: the activity to document architecture and design information is part of the practices of TS, including roughly what kind of information should be documented. In this way the CMMI guides standardization of documents. Concrete standards, however, are not provided.

rq.arch.conform. Facilitating conformance to architecture during the implementation process: The implementation phase as such is part of the practices of TS, including references to VER in order to verify the implementation once it is finished. However, the CMMI does not provide any explicit support in ensuring that the architecture and design will be adequately implemented during implementation (e.g. by involvement of the architects).

rq.learning.product. Bottle experiences and make available for architects: the CMMI has many PAs that deal with establishing an infrastructure for organizational learning and improvement. Because the CMMI is a process framework, this is strongly focussed on the process dimension (like the architecting process), not on the product dimension (like architectural solutions). Only at Level 5 the PA Organizational Innovation and Deployment (OID) addresses improvements on processes and (process and product related) technologies. Product related technologies may also be interpreted as architectural solutions.

Reuse development. Although not indicated as a requirement in Sect. 2.2, reusable assets like product components, source code libraries and technical documents may
be developed and maintained in the context of the usage scenario Product Development. Although the CMMI addresses the concept of reuse in a number of PAs, the
development and management of a reusable base of core assets is not adequately
covered. The SEI has an area of work called Software Product Lines in the context
of its Product Line Systems Program to cover this. Although this includes some
process related support, no CMMI-like reference model exists.

Roadmapping. Like reuse development, the development and evolution of architecture and technology roadmaps has not been indicated as a requirement in Sect. 2.2
although it is relevant in the context of the usage scenario Product Development.
Roadmapping is not supported by the CMMI because it is mainly a product planning (pre-development) activity.

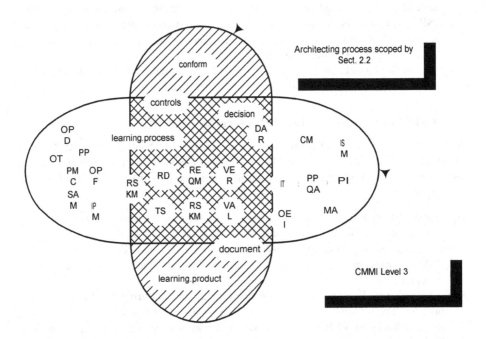

Fig. 2. CMMI, architecting process and cross-section

An informal visualization of the overlap between CMMI and the architecting process
is presented in Fig. 2.

A note on the meaning of the fact that these elements are not covered by CMMI. We
have not made any statement on the relative merits of these elements. One could argue
that this lack of coverage is a shortcoming of CMMI; conversely, one could argue that,
given the success of CMMI, how do we know that the elements in the square aren't
by themselves good enough for an optimal architecting process? The current state of
affairs does not allow us to answer this question in a general sense; the analysis in

Sect. 2.2 merely indicates that in the current organizational setting, the elements would contribute to achieving the business goals set.

5 Conclusions and Further Work

Our starting point in this paper was a large IT company with a need to institutionalize a generic architecting process that is compliant with CMMI Maturity Level 3. To this end, we have studied and discussed the relation between architecting and CMMI, resulting in the identification of PAs significant to architecting, and a list of requirements to make a generic architecting process compliant with CMMI Maturity Level 3. Furthermore, we have compared our findings with two well-known process models from literature.

We have concluded that:

– Architecture is not a well-defined concept in the CMMI; the word is used in many meanings, most of which are not defined in the glossary.
– CMMI implicitly provides considerable support in establishing an architecting process. However, in some areas of architecting, the CMMI only gives indirect support. The weaker areas are documentation, facilitating the implementation of the architecture, and learning from architectural choices.
– In product development contexts, there are two activities generally associated with architecting that are insufficiently supported by the CMMI: architectural roadmapping and the exploitation of reusable assets.

Besides these conclusions, other relevant findings worth mentioning are:

– Although the scope of this paper was limited to CMMI Level 3, an investigation of the level 4 and 5 PAs shows that none of these are Architecting Significant according to our scope. This resonates with remarks made informally by Grady Booch [12].
– Although architecting is generally viewed as an engineering activity, two PAs outside Engineering are crucial to a good architecting process: RSKM and DAR.

Further Work. The work described in this paper was based on CMMI version 1.1. Since August 2006, CMMI version 1.2 exists. This is the "CMMI for Development". There are now three CMMI variants: Development, Service and Acquisition. Since support for CMMI 1.1 will be dropped in time, we will update the work in this paper to CMMI 1.2 for Development in the coming months.

As has been mentioned previously in this paper, the work described here was done in the context of designing a generic architecting process for a large IT company. Since this other work also yielded some interesting insights, we will describe it in more detail in a separate paper, which will also contain a comparison of our developed architecting process to the generic architecting processes discussed in Sect. 4.1.

An architecting process that complies with a maturity model also begs a comparison with Architecture Maturity Models (AMMs), such as the IT Architecture Capability Maturity Model (ACMM) developed by the US Department of Commerce [13]. This comparison could be subject of a future analysis. Conversely, the development of architecting enhancements to the CMMI would be an attractive idea for CMMI-compliant companies that wish to enhance their architecting maturity levels, but would rather not introduce another maturity model on top of CMMI. This could be another interesting avenue to explore.

References

1. Bass, L., Kazman, R.: Architecture based development. Technical Report CMU/SEI-2000-TR-007, SEI (April 1999)
2. Hofmeister, C., Kruchten, P., Nord, R., Obbink, H., Ran, A., America, P.: Generalizing a model of software architecture design from five industrial approaches. In: WICSA 2005. 5th Working IEEE/IFIP Conference on Software Architecture, Pittsburgh, Pennsylvania, pp. 77–86 (2005)
3. Bosch, J.: Software architecture: The next step. In: Oquendo, F., Warboys, B.C., Morrison, R. (eds.) EWSA 2004. LNCS, vol. 3047, pp. 194–199. Springer, Heidelberg (2004)
4. Tyree, J., Akerman, A.: Architecture decisions: Demystifying architecture. IEEE Software 22(2), 19–27 (2005)
5. van der Ven, J.S., Jansen, A., Avgeriou, P., Hammer, D.K.: Using architectural decisions. In: Hofmeister, C., Crnkovic, I., Reussner, R. (eds.) QoSA 2006. LNCS, vol. 4214, Springer, Heidelberg (2006)
6. Abowd, G., Bass, L., Clements, P., Kazman, R., Northrop, L., Zaremski, A.: Recommended best industrial practice for software architecture evaluation. Technical Report CMU/SEI-96-TR-025, SEI (1997)
7. Clements, P., Kazman, R., Klein, M.: Evaluating Software Architectures. Addison-Wesley, Reading (2002)
8. Gilb, T.: Principles of Software Engineering Management. Addison-Wesley, Reading (1988)
9. CMMI Product Team: Capability maturity model integration (cmmi(sm). Technical report, SEI (2002) staged representation, version 1.1, CMU/SEI-2002-TR-012, ESC-TR-2002-012
10. Chrissis, M.B., Konrad, M., Shrum, S.: CMMI: Guidelines for Process Integration and Product Improvement. Addison-Wesley, Reading (2003)
11. Bass, L., Clements, P., Kazman, R.: Software Architecture in Practice, 2nd edn. Addison-Wesley, Reading (2003)
12. Booch, G.: Observations from the road (May 2006),
    http://www-03.ibm.com/developerworks/blogs/page/gradybooch?entry=observation_from_the_road
13. US Department of Commerce: It architecture maturity model
    http://www.osec.doc.gov/cio/arch_cmm.htm

The Architect's Mindset

Viktor Clerc, Patricia Lago, and Hans van Vliet

Department of Computer Science
VU University , Amsterdam, the Netherlands
{viktor,patricia,hans}@cs.vu.nl

Abstract. Software architecture and software architecture practices become increasingly important for information systems since they enable reasoning on the design of the system. The concept of *architectural knowledge*, i.e. architectural design decisions and the resulting design, plays a pivotal role in architecture. In order to get the most out of architectural knowledge, we need insight into the ways in which architectural knowledge is used. Currently, we lack this insight. We performed survey-based research in the Netherlands to collect feedback on the importance of architectural knowledge for the daily work of practitioners in architecture. We present our findings using two perspectives: the architectural roles practitioners fulfill and the architecture level practitioners are engaged in. We use these perspectives to construct and reflect on the architect's mindset on architectural knowledge. This mindset of architects reveals an approach which is focused on 'to create and communicate' rather than 'to review and maintain' an architecture.

Keywords: software architecture, architectural knowledge.

1 Introduction

A software architecture is a transferable abstraction of a system and allows for communication of that system to different stakeholders [1]. Software architecture and software architecture practices are gaining importance since they enable reasoning on the design of the system and verifying quality attributes of a system at an early stage in the development cycle.

Rather than viewing the software architecture as a set of components and connectors, recent literature regards the software architecture as the set of architectural design decisions [1,2]. The collection of architectural design decisions and the resulting design together constitute *architectural knowledge* [3]. Besides providing insight into the current software architecture, architectural knowledge also caters for the 'why' of the software architecture, its rationale.

To get the most out of the architectural knowledge of information systems in general, we need to determine in what way different stakeholders use architectural knowledge. We term these typical uses *use cases for architectural knowledge*. Some of these use cases may depend on the roles that stakeholders fulfill or the architecture level stakeholders are engaged in. E.g. architects may favour other use cases than designers or technical specialists, and enterprise architecture practitioners may give priority to other use cases than software architecture

S. Overhage et al. (Eds.): QoSA 2007, LNCS 4880, pp. 231–249, 2007.

practitioners. Currently, we determine what information is particularly important for certain stakeholders, by using approaches and standards such as [4,5]. But we do lack insight into what intention these stakeholders have with architectural knowledge.

We have conducted a survey-based study to address the lack of insight into the importance of architectural knowledge. We designed a survey which includes use cases for architectural knowledge. These use cases are based on earlier work [3,6], experiences in industry, and our own experience.

This paper reports on the results of our study. We provide insight in the way practitioners in the Netherlands view and use architectural knowledge. In doing this, we reveal the mindset of practitioners with respect to the use of architectural knowledge by listing what uses are important for what roles and on what architecture levels.

Based on the survey results, we make the following observations. Architects regard the architecting process as a forward engineering discipline and do not see clear benefits of reflection, assessment, and change of the architecture. Yet, literature argues that these are precisely the intended benefits of architecture (e.g. [1]). Apparently, these intended benefits of architecture have not yet been firmly established in the mindset of architects nor transferred to practice. Furthermore, a forward decision-making process is reflected by the mindset of architects, but the value of managing the set of decisions ('architectural knowledge management') is not yet clear. Finally, the importance of stakeholder communication of the architecture is generally recognized.

The results of this research call for further knowledge transfer on the more innovative concept of viewing architecture as architectural decisions. Furthermore, it is important to quantify the benefits of this concept. At the same time, further research is needed into the foundation for the mindset to identify the activities needed to further establish the concept of architectural knowledge in the architect's mindset.

The remainder of this paper is organized as follows. Section 2 discusses related work in the field of architectural knowledge, design rationale, and architectural roles. Next, Sect. 3 describes the design of the research. Sections 4 and 5 present the findings and a discussion of their limitations. Section 6 reflects on the results and provides conclusions. Finally, Sect. 7 provides directions for future work.

2   Related Work

In recent work [7], the use and documentation of architecture design rationale has been analyzed. The survey reveals the view of the participants on several generic uses of design rationale. The study shows that although participants regard design rationale as important, they do not capture the rationale. The main reason for this is a lack of appropriate tools to support the architects. Furthermore, the survey shows that architects tend to focus on the positive aspects of architectural decisions and design rationale instead of looking for problems in a specific architecture. We view design rationale as a specific subset of architectural knowledge [3]. We revert to the use cases for architectural knowledge, initially described in [3] and elaborated on in [6], and provide a detailed view on possible uses of architectural knowledge.

A template for architectural decisions is provided by [8]. This template describes a decision, its underlying assumptions, related requirements, and implications. The template is useful for organizing architectural knowledge but does not provide insight into the use of architectural knowledge. Multiple templates or tailoring of existing templates may be necessary to fully support architects in their use of architectural knowledge. Our work can provide input for this. Zimmermann et al. [9] report on a framework that can be useful in identifying, making, and enforcing architectural decisions *during* the architecting process.

The meaning of architecture in practice has been extensively described in [10]. Smolander describes four metaphors for architecture: 'architecture as blueprint', 'architecture as literature', 'architecture as language', and 'architecture as decision'. The metaphors explain the meaning of architecture in practice. This meaning may differ depending on the role practitioners fulfill or the architectural levels they are engaged in. We provide insight into the importance of use cases for architectural knowledge and relate this insight to the metaphors from [10]. Thus, we show what metaphors are accepted and in use by practitioners.

A good description of possible roles and activities of an architect is given in [11]. Examples include a visionary, technical consultant, decision maker, and coach. These different activities could be supported by appropriate use cases for architectural knowledge. Use cases for architectural knowledge that are deemed important for aforementioned roles enable the architect to effectively capture and reason about architectural knowledge. The other way around, the relevance of use cases for architectural knowledge for the practitioners could indicate to what extent the possible roles and activities from [11] in fact are established.

Clements et al. [12] performed a study on publicly available resources to identify the duties, skills, and knowledge of software architects. They show that the role of an architect implies more than only making technical decisions. Rather than focusing on the competences of architects, our study focuses on the use of architectural knowledge to support the architect in satisfying the competences.

3   Research Design

We aim to find out how practitioners engaged in architecture in the Netherlands view architectural knowledge. This helps us to construct the mindset of architects with respect to architectural knowledge. In order to reveal this mindset, we use a survey instrument. Survey instruments are widely used in software engineering research [13]. In survey-based research, a number of factors should be taken into account: the design of the survey, the selection of participants, and how to control the response rate of the survey. The remainder of this section describes how we have addressed these factors.

3.1   Survey Design

The ultimate objective of the survey is to identify the way practitioners view and use architectural knowledge. We took the typical uses distilled from experienced practitioners within the GRIFFIN research project [3,6] as a starting point. We validated and augmented the list of use cases with the industrial partners in our research project and with our own experience. Next, we reformulated each use case into a clear, self-explaining statement on architectural knowledge. We allowed the survey participants to indicate the importance of each use case using a 5-point Likert scale [14] ranging from 'not important' to 'very important'.

We hypothesized that the importance of certain use cases may depend on the roles practitioners fulfill and on the level of architecture that practitioners are engaged in. We posed some demographic questions and specifically asked the participants to *a)* indicate the architectural roles they typically fulfill and *b)* indicate the relative amount of time they spend on certain architecture levels. Using the information on the roles and architecture levels, we constructed two different perspectives to analyze the way respondents perceive architectural knowledge.

As a first step, we conducted a pilot with the survey on a focused group consisting of selected employees of one of our industrial partners. We then developed a web-based survey for administration of the complete population.

3.2   Selection of Participants of the Survey

We needed to construct a representative subset of Dutch practitioners that play a key role in architecture. To come to this subset, we identified three dimensions by which we selected participating organizations: domain (e.g. banking, telecommunications, insurance, governmental), type (IT service providers, software development organizations), and market (commercial, non-commercial). Next, we selected organizations or platforms (such as *communities* of enterprise architects and embedded architects) in each of these dimensions and identified practitioners that play a key role in architecture at these organizations. This gives us confidence that we have selected a representative subset of Dutch practitioners to give us feedback on the use of architectural knowledge.

3.3   Control of the Survey

In order to keep control on the response rate, we directly contacted key practitioners at the organizations involved. We enquired their willingness to act as on-site representative for that organization. We sent these representatives the hyperlink to the on-line survey. The on-site representatives forwarded the hyperlink to knowledgeable colleagues and notified us of the total number of colleagues involved (*snowball sampling* [13]).

4   Findings

This section describes our findings. We first provide demographic information in Sect. 4.1, after which we discuss the two different perspectives for presenting the results as described in Sect. 3.1. Next, Sect. 4.4 describes how we clustered the use cases for architectural knowledge. After that, we present our main results: the way practitioners view and use architectural knowledge.

4.1   Demographic Information

We sent out the survey to 36 persons acting as on-site representatives. They forwarded the survey to 348 practitioners. In total, 384 practitioners were reached. We collected 143 responses, of which 107 were complete. This corresponds to a response rate of 27.86 %. We took these as a basis for our survey.

Of the total population, 213 practitioners are employed at one of the large IT service providers included in our survey. We discuss the overrepresentation of practitioners employed at IT service providers in Sect. 5. We received 75 responses from these practitioners, corresponding to a response rate of 35.21 %. The remaining 171 practitioners are employed at smaller IT consultancy firms or e.g. IT departments of banks, insurance organizations or governmental organizations. We received 32 responses, corresponding to a response rate of 18.71 %.

4.2   Architecture Levels

A list of definitions of architecture [15] shows that different views on architecture exist. Examples include a systems-oriented view and a view focusing on the information flow in or surrounding a software system. In our survey we used concise definitions from [16] for the so-called *architecture levels*:

software architecture the structure and relations of a software system.
systems architecture the architecture of a single system, taking into account both software and hardware.
information architecture the information needs and flows of business functions as they are identified.
enterprise architecture architecture at the level of an organizational unit or an organization as a whole.
process architecture a description of the processes running in or surrounding a software system.

Each practitioner indicated the amount of time spent on a certain level of architecture. To be able to compare the data collected, we normalized the total amount of time spent by each practitioner to 100 %. The relative amount of time spent on each level of architecture for all respondents is depicted in Fig. 1. We observed that a concrete architecture of a single system (i.e. 'software architecture' and 'systems architecture') receives more attention than company-wide architectures (i.e. 'information architecture', 'enterprise architecture', and

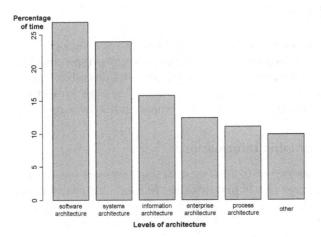

Fig. 1. The percentage of time spent by all respondents on architecture levels

'process architecture'). Other architecture levels that are less often practitioned, are grouped into the *Other* category in Fig. 1.

Since the population is relatively large, we grouped the respondents into clusters and based our analysis on the clusters instead of on the individual responses. Of course, architects may work on different architecture levels simultaneously. We wanted to see if these architecture levels are related based on the responses of the practitioners. E.g. if architects often work on two architecture levels simultaneously, we group these two levels. Moreover, this enables us to group architecture levels that have different names, but in fact appear to be closely related. In order to group similar or closely related architecture levels, we calculated the correlation between each of the architecture levels. This resulted in an n-dimensional space, n being the number of architecture levels. In order to plot the relative distances between the architecture levels, we reduced the number of dimensions to two using *classic multi-dimensional scaling* [17]. In order to assess the accuracy of the distance, we applied *k-means clustering* [18] to cluster architecture levels with a small distance. We observed that the optimal distribution of architecture levels in clusters occured when we used five clusters. We compared the clusters that appeared with *k-means clustering* with the distance plot provided by *classic multi-dimensional scaling*. The comparison revealed that we selected the right number of clusters and that we found the correct distribution of elements over the clusters. Consequently, the clusters contain elements that are different in nature and have overlap reduced to a minimum. We observed the elements in these clusters of architectural levels and labeled the clusters. The results are shown in Table 1.

Table 1 shows that distinct clusters provide for the relation of a software system and the hardware it runs on (*Systems Architecture*), the structure of a software system (*Software Architecture*), the structure of the organization or department using the software system (*Enterprise Architecture*), and the process and

Table 1. Clusters of architecture levels

Cluster label	Levels of architecture
Systems Architecture	systems architecture
Software Architecture	software architecture, management of architecture
Enterprise Architecture	enterprise architecture
Information and Process Architecture	information architecture, process architecture
Other	development coach, integration architecture, infrastructure architecture, service architecture, maintenance of architecture, solution architecture

information flow in or surrounding a software system (*Information and Process Architecture*).

Of the most significant architecture levels, only 'information architecture' and 'process architecture' are very often worked on by a single respondent simultaneously. Consequently, they fall into the same cluster. The remainder of the most significant architecture levels each fall into a distinct cluster.

Practitioners can potentially work on different levels of architecture simultaneously. In spite of that, apparently practitioners do not do this. They are specialized in working at one specific level of architecture only. Possible reasons for this are the different technical and interpersonal skill-sets required at each architecture level. For example, practitioners who mainly work on the level of *Systems Architecture* are concerned with CPU performance, interrupt levels, and other technical topics, whereas practitioners who mainly work on the level of *Process Architecture* are concerned with implications of decisions on working processes, which places less requirements on technical skills. Required interpersonal skills can vary at different architecture levels as well. As the topics that require to be communicated get less technical, the potential audience could grow. Consequently, the set of stakeholders with which to communicate grows from technology-oriented stakeholders to include more business-oriented stakeholders.

4.3   Architectural Roles

The participants indicated the architectural roles they typically fulfill. The survey contained a list of roles, including 'architect', 'reviewer of architecture', 'project manager', and 'developer'.

We repeated the same analysis as described in Sect. 4.2 to identify clusters of roles typically fulfilled by a single respondent. The optimal distribution of architectural roles in clusters occurred when we used five clusters. Again, we labeled the clusters. The results are listed in Table 2.

The clusters labeled *High-level* and *Low-level* show that, apparently, architectural roles are related based on level of abstraction with respect to a software system and practitioners work at one specific level of abstraction. Our results

Table 2. Clusters of architectural roles

Cluster label	Architectural roles
Communicator	architectural educator, project leader
Low-level	designer, developer, reviewer of source code
Specialist	consultant, technical specialist
High-level	architect, reviewer of architecture
Other	end user, lead architect, security consultant, other

also show that practitioners generally do not switch between the different levels. This contradicts with the view on the role of a software architect as an implementor [11]; according to our survey, architect do not design or implement that often. Furthermore, the roles 'architectural educator' and 'project leader' share a communication responsibility towards a variety of stakeholders. Consequently, we label this cluster *Communicator*.

4.4   Clustering the Use Cases

We listed the use cases for architectural knowledge from [6] and asked the practitioners to indicate the importance of each use case for their daily work. We used the answers of participants of the use cases to reveal underlying structure in the use cases. The structure would excavate similarities between use cases based on the answers and allow us to cluster the use cases accordingly.

First, we used principal components analysis [19] to identify the underlying structure in the use cases for architectural knowledge based on the respondents' answers. It turned out that no underlying structure could be found; the variance in the scores of the use cases was explained by one main principal component.

Since the principal components analysis did not lead to a clustering of the use cases, we next tried to cluster the use cases based on the purpose of the individual use cases. Most use cases for architectural knowledge could be clustered relatively easily. E.g. some use cases clearly dealt with stakeholders only. Consequently, we grouped these use cases into a single cluster. For some use cases, clustering was more difficult. These use cases could be grouped into multiple clusters (e.g. 'add an architectural decision' could point at a forward architecting approach, but at the same time assumes that a set of architectural decisions exists to which the new decision is added as well – see Table 3). We identified the most appropriate cluster for these use cases by analyzing the questionnaire results of the participants for these use cases. We compared the answers on a use case with the average of the answers for each candidate cluster. We assigned the use case to the cluster with the highest similarity in answers (see Sect. 4.5). The interpretation of the survey results also led to the cluster labels. Table 3 lists the resulting clusters of use cases for architectural knowledge.

The use case cluster *Architectural decision set* presupposes that a set of knowledge entities (i.e. architectural decisions) and relations between these knowledge

Table 3. Use cases for architectural knowledge

Use case cluster	Use cases
Architectural decision set	11. View the change of the architectural decisions over time 15. Recover architectural decisions 20. Identify incompleteness 22. Detect patterns of architectural decision dependencies 23. Check for superfluous architectural decisions 24. Cleanup the architecture
Assessment – reqs.→arch.→impl.	1. Check implementation against architectural decisions 5. Check correctness (i.e. architecture versus requirements) 18. Evaluate the impact of an architectural decision 19. Evaluate consistency 27. Get consequences of an architectural decision
Assessment – risk, trade-off analysis	4. Perform a review for a specific concern 16. Perform an incremental architectural review 17. Assess design maturity 21. Conduct a risk analysis 25. Conduct a trade-off analysis
Stakeholder-centric	2. Identify the subversive stakeholder 3. Identify key arch. decisions for a specific stakeholder 6. Identify affected stakeholders on change 7. Identify unresolved concerns for a specific stakeholder 8. Keep up-to-date 9. Inform affected stakeholders 26. Identify important architectural drivers
Forward Architecting	10. Retrieve an architectural decision 12. Add an architectural decision 13. Remove consequences of a cancelled decision 14. Reuse architectural decisions

entities exist (see [3] for a list of possible relations). The use cases in this cluster are aimed at managing that set. Several other use cases have to do with assessing or reviewing an architecture. Within this *Assessment* cluster, we distinguish between use cases that imply a forward-engineering approach to architecture (i.e. from requirements, to architecture, to implementation), and use cases that target at performing different kinds of analyses and reviews. The first set aims at verification of the architecting activities ("are we still on the right track?") whereas the second set aims at validation. Seven use cases form the cluster *Stakeholder-centric*. These use cases concern identification of stakeholders and communication of the architecture to specific stakeholders. The cluster *Forward Architecting*, finally, consists of use cases that create, request, reuse or remove architectural decisions.

4.5   Participants' Views on the Use Cases

Instead of elaborating on each of the 107 responses individually, we took the clusters of architecture levels and architectural roles as described in Sects. 4.2 and 4.3 as two perspectives for analyzing the survey results.

We built a structure to be used to identify the importance of a specific use case for architectural knowledge to a specfic cluster (of architectural roles or architecture levels) as follows. For each respondent i in a cluster with n respondents, we used the Likert scores ($score_i$). Using the relative contribution of the respondent to that cluster ($\%_i$), we calculated the weighted average as shown in (1):

$$score = \frac{\sum_{i=1}^{n} score_i \cdot \%_i}{\sum_{i=1}^{n} \%_i} \tag{1}$$

Next, we identified outliers and intermediate results by defining an upper and lower limit of importance: within the possible range of scores from $1 - 5^1$ we regard a use case with a score of ≥ 3.5 as 'important' and a use case with a score of ≤ 2.5 as 'not important'. The results are listed in Table 4. Each row in Table 4 relates a cluster of use cases for architectural knowledge to both the clusters of architectural roles and the clusters of architecture levels. The importance of each use case cluster for each cluster of architectural roles and each cluster of architecture levels is provided. Important clusters are marked '(+)', not important clusters are marked '(−)'. Impartial results are not listed in the table. The findings are discussed below. An extensive discussion of their implications is given in Sect. 6.

The use cases for architectural knowledge within the cluster *Architectural decision set* assume that a set of architectural decisions is at the practitioner's disposal. In terms of the use cases, architecting thus boils down to managing and manipulating that set of architectural decisions. Table 4 shows that viewing architectural knowledge as a set of decisions has not been established at the *Software Architecture* and *Systems Architecture* levels. Furthermore, viewing the architecture as a set of decisions is regarded as not important for *Communicator* and *Specialist* roles. *High-level* and *Low-level* roles (i.e. 'architects' and 'designers'/'developers') deem these use cases neutral. Apparently, the view on architecture as a set of architectural decisions [2] and managing that set has not yet transferred to practice, nor is it of particular value to the practitioners.

The cluster labeled *Assessment − reqs.→arch.→impl.* covers traceability of architectural decisions to the actual implementation, the relation between decisions themselves, and from architectural decisions back to the requirements that have been set for the information system. Especially respondents who strongly contribute to the clusters *High-level*, *Low-level* and *Specialist* (see Table 2)

---

[1] 1 being not important, 5 being very important.

Table 4. Importance of use case clusters per cluster of architectural roles and cluster of architecture levels. (+) denotes importance, (−) denotes unimportance.

Use case cluster	Cluster of architectural roles	Cluster of architecture levels
Architectural decision set	(−) *Communicator* (−) *Specialist*	(−) *Software Architecture* (−) *Systems Architecture*
Assessment – reqs.→arch.→impl.	(+) *High-level* (+) *Low-level* (+) *Specialist*	(+) *All levels*
Assessment – risk, trade-off analysis	(−) *Specialist* (−) *Communicator* (−) *Low-level*	(−) *Software Architecture*
Stakeholder-centric	(+) *High-level* (−) *Communicator*	(+) *Enterprise Architecture* (+) *Process and Information Architecture*
Forward Architecting	(+) *High-level* (−) *Low-level*	(+) *All levels*

regard these use cases as important. These roles are the 'construction' roles with respect to architecture. This confirms our idea that practitioners involved in the construction of architectures have a need for traceability of architecture. The use cases in the cluster *Assessment – risk, trade-off analysis* are not regarded as important by the *High-level* cluster of architectural roles. Furthermore, especially practitioners engaged in *Software Architecture* regard the use cases in this cluster as not important.

A difference that exists between the two subclusters within *Assessment* could lie in the architect's mindset. The results of the cluster *Assessment – reqs.→arch. →impl.* reveal a mindset with a linear (i.e. non-iterative) approach to designing an architecture that satisfies the posed requirements and subsequently have the implementation satisfy the architecture. Use cases that offer traceability in this approach are regarded as important. The use cases in the cluster *Assessment – risk, trade-off analysis*, on the other hand, all are aimed at having an intermediate period of reflection to verify what risks apply, or what quality attributes could be affected by certain architectural decisions. These use cases are not directly related to either requirements or implementation.

In summary, in contrast to the literature stating that architecture offers a good means to assess the correctness and suitability of the desired solution (e.g. [1,11]), our results reveal architects regard the use cases for architectural knowledge in the *Assessment – risk, trade-off analysis* cluster as not particularly important. Literature points out that an architecture enables us to assess the design maturity, perform incremental, iterative design reviews, and periodically identify the largest risks pertaining to the architecture. Apparently, these benefits of architecture are not valued by our respondents, which is surprising.

Moreover, the use cases in the cluster *Assessment – risk, trade-off analysis* aim at finding possible problems in a certain architecture. Since practitioners do not regard these use cases as important, we might infer that practitioners do not favour a period of reflection in which the current state of the architecture is explicitly tested. Yet, this is one of the main reasons stated in the literature for developing an architecture [1]. Apparently, these intended benefits of architecture have not yet been firmly established in the mindset of architects. The lack of value contributed to the intended benefits reveals a mindset of positiveness ("architects always take the right decisions"), which supports the findings of [7]. Respondents do not like to use architectural knowledge to identify potential weaknesses of their design.

A number of use cases for architectural knowledge are *Stakeholder-centric*. These use cases involve identifying stakeholders and communicating the architecture towards these stakeholders. Five out of the seven use cases in this cluster are regarded as important by the respondents. Especially the *High-level* role deems these use cases important. The remaining use cases 'identify affected stakeholders on change' and 'identify key architectural decisions for a specific stakeholder' are deemed neutral. Furthermore, stakeholder-centric use cases are regarded as more important at the architecture levels *Enterprise Architecture* and *Process and Information Architecture* than on the other levels. This confirms the general idea that the architecture levels *Enterprise Architecture* and *Process and Information Architecture* are suitable for communicating architecture to non-IT stakeholders. The other way around, practitioners engaged in *Software Architecture* and *Systems Architecture* do not regard communication of the architecture to stakeholders as important. Apparently, at these more technically oriented levels of architecture, practitioners mainly capture architectural decisions for themselves and not for communication to other stakeholders. This in itself is not bad, but reveals that different communication needs exist for different architecture levels.

Four use cases for architectural knowledge fall into the cluster *Forward Architecting*. When we regard the use cases in this cluster we see that 'adding an architectural decision' is deemed important at all architecture levels and by most architectural roles (only the *Specialist* role does not regard this use case as important). The use case 'remove consequences of a cancelled decision' is not deemed very important. We can identify two reasons for this. Firstly, this use case requires that a practitioner is able to cancel an architectural decision. Consequently, the practitioner should determine the decision that needs to be cancelled. This requires the practitioner to make a review iteration. Secondly, this use case does not directly contribute to the forward-engineering paradigm we identified when we analysed the *Assessment* use cases. Other use cases in this cluster, such as 'reuse architectural decisions' and 'retrieve an architectural decision' are deemed important by all architectural roles and at all architecture levels. These results show that the practitioners regard architectural decisions as an important asset to be reused in developing a specific architecture.

In addition to the results listed in Table 4, we make another observation. A difference exist with respect to the perceived importance of use cases between the clusters *Communicator*, *Low-level*, and *Specialist* on the one side, and *High-Level* on the other side. The cluster *High-level* regards more clusters of use cases important than the other clusters. A possible reason lies in the fact that practitioners in the *High-level* cluster have a wider perspective on architecture and stakeholders involved, whereas practitioners in the other clusters have a more narrowed focus on architecture. This corresponds with the variety of roles and activities of a software architect listed in [11].

5   Threats to Validity

Our case study faced a number of threats. We list them similar to [13,20]. Our survey was targeted at practitioners in the Netherlands. By carefully selecting the participants for the survey, we have attempted to minimize a selection bias. Nevertheless, IT service providers are somewhat overrepresented in our population. Still, a comparison of the responses of practitioners employed at IT service providers and respondents employed at other organizations did not show significant differences.

We kept control on the population of practitioners we invited to participate in the survey. However, we do not have insight into the reasons why the non-respondents did not participate. We conjecture that these practitioners did not have enough time to administer the survey or could not relate the topic of the survey to their daily work. Although our survey satisfies the guidelines for the number of questions and maximum administration time as posed in [13], our results may suffer from a maturation effect, which means that the attitude of the participants towards the use cases in the survey changes during filling in the survey. On the one hand, use cases in the first half of the survey receive a more important rating than use cases in the second half. On the other hand, the second half does contain several use cases rated 'important'. Therefore, we have confidence that the maturation effect did not influence our results substantially.

It was not possible to obtain a structure in the use cases for architectural knowledge based on the practitioners' answers alone. Apparently, the survey answers varied too much to be used for structuring the use cases. A reason for this could be that our study is based on more recent definitions of architecture as made of a set of architectural decisions [2,3,21]. Some participants may regard architecture as a set of components and connectors and are not yet used to viewing architecture as a set of architectural decisions and rationale. Our approach, which uses a list of use cases for architectural knowledge, may have biased the results since the actual mindset of architects may require additional use cases or other approaches to be fully captured. We provide an architectural knowledge-oriented view towards the mindset.

To be able to reflect on the answers given, we identified a clustering based on the use cases for architectural knowledge alone and related the answers to these clusters. The resulting reflection in Sect. 6 is not only based on the clusters of use cases, but puts the survey results in a broader perspective.

6   Discussion and Conclusions

We conducted survey-based research on how the practitioners in software architecture in the Netherlands view and use architectural knowledge. Our results reveal the importance of certain use cases for architectural knowledge for the daily work of the practitioners. The individual results have been discussed in Sect. 4.5. This section reflects on these results and draws overall conclusions on the architect's mindset and the role of architectural knowledge in that mindset.

Figure 2 provides an overview of the results and depicts the major elements of the reflection. We approach architecture from two different perspectives. One perspective is focused on developing a solution, i.e. the architecture. The other perspective is focused on the underlying reason for that solution, i.e. architectural decisions and rationale. The clusters of use cases for architectural knowledge are depicted as package symbols. The +-mark or − -mark indicate the respondents' view on these clusters. We put the clusters in perspective by depicting the evolution between the different results that we identify in practice. By and large, widespread acceptance of architecture verification activities preceded architecture validation activities, such as performing risk or trade-off analyses. Similarly, viewing architecting as a forward decision-making process preceded managing the set of architectural decisions, i.e. 'architectural knowledge management'. Putting stakeholders central in architecture has been an important characteristic across time and perspectives. The remainder of this section describes our views as expressed in Fig. 2.

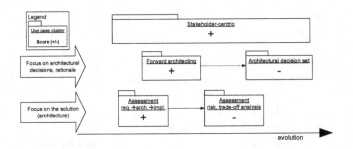

Fig. 2. Overview of the architect's mindset

Forward architecting – Architects regard taking architectural decisions and making these decisions explicit as important. Yet, architects tend to focus on only taking architectural decisions to end up with a correct software architecture for a specific problem. In taking these decisions, architects are supported by e.g. architectural patterns [22], which provide proven architectural solution fragments for certain problems, and by rationale tools such as gIBIS [23] and QOC [24]. We signal an ongoing tension between making architectural decisions and capturing the underlying rationale and other context of these decisions; the time spent on capturing the context is not spent on making new architectural decisions. Consequently, adequate, lightweight tooling is necessary to lower the threshold for capturing the context. Despite the continual tension, progress has been made [25,26].

Architectural decision set – On a more generic level, architects do not regard the architecture as a set of architectural decisions. Although the concept of architectural decisions in itself has gained importance, the architect's mindset lacks focus on reflections on those decisions as building blocks for software architectures. These reflections allow for a step back to actually learn from architecture experiences. Furthermore, architects do not (yet) manage or manipulate that set of architectural decisions (i.e. use cases in the cluster *Architectural decision set*). A reason for this could be that more recent definitions of software architecture in terms of architectural decisions [2,3,21] are not yet completely transferred to practice. In addition, adequate tool support is necessary to fully exploit architectural knowledge as a set of architectural design decisions across architectures and domains.

Assessment – reqs.→arch.→impl. – Software development largely occurs via projects. Depending on the development approach chosen, the architecting phase can run in parallel during the lifetime of the project or the architecting phase is a distinct phase which leads to a deliverable – the architecture. Based on the results of this study, we conjecture that the latter is the case: the practitioners show an approach in which the architecture is delivered based on the requirements. After that, the implementation is checked against the architecture. Our experience shows that this verification phase often is not performed by architects. Architects, often experienced and relatively expensive resources, perhaps run off to other projects to run the architecting phase at that project. Consequently, they may not be offered the time to support the design and implementation phase.

Assessment – risk, trade-off analysis – Our study shows that methods and techniques to validate the architecture (such as the Architecture Tradeoff Analysis Method as described by [27], or their predecessors) are not embedded within the mindset of architects. A recent presentation on the topic of this paper given during the Dutch architecture conference revealed that when practitioners do deem performing a risk analysis important, they do not have clear what the role of architectural knowledge is in a risk analysis. Architectural knowledge may support to evaluate the impact of architectural decisions on the resulting architecture; it allows to (re-)consider alternative decisions as well. Apparently, this rather new view on architecture is not yet generally accepted. Education on viewing architecture as architectural decisions [10] as part of architectural knowledge could help overcome this.

Stakeholder-centric – Another benefit of architecture is that it enables communication among stakeholders [1]. Architecture thus can be regarded as a language to transfer the architect's opinions and views to those stakeholders. Most use cases in the cluster *Stakeholder-centric* rate high, which means that the view of 'architecture as language' [10] is generally accepted. Communication of architecture to stakeholders is clearly established in the mindset of architects.

Our study shows that the mindset of architects is focused on delivering a solution and capturing the related architectural decisions. Consequently, we conjecture that a so-called *micro* view on software architecture largely is in place: architects are focused developing an architecture for a specific solution and (more and more) on capturing the architectural decisions and rationale for that solution. What lacks in the mindset of architects is a view that exceeds specific architectures but puts architectures in context by validating them, and the architectural decisions that led to them. When architects have a set of architectural decisions at their disposal, this offers the opportunity to interrelate architectural decisions taken in the past to identify learning opportunities for future architecting activities. We conjecture that this *macro* view may be achieved by applying initiatives that proved valuable in other disciplines, such as ontology engineering [28] onto the domain of (software) architecture.

In summary, the mindset of architects in the Netherlands reveals an approach which is focused on 'to create and communicate' rather than 'to review and maintain'. This reflects a general pattern as e.g. highlighted in [7]. Furthermore, architectural knowledge and the view of architecture as a set of architectural decisions has not yet transferred to industry. We see two possible approaches to embed the importance of architectural knowledge and design decisions in industry. Firstly, more knowledge transfer is needed on the concepts and intended benefits of this view. Secondly, it is necessary to collect more empirical data on these benefits in terms of throughput and cost to fully sustain the importance of architectural knowledge and architectural decisions.

7   Future Work

Our work describes the mindset of architects in the Netherlands. We provided several reasons for this mindset but acknowledge that additional research is needed on the foundation for this mindset. This additional research could focus on the activities needed to effectively establish the concept of architectural knowledge in the architect's mindset. The possible increase in understanding of architectural knowledge by architects may be monitored by using our survey instrument periodically. Moreover, we can compare the mindset of architects in the Netherlands with the mindset of architects at other countries or continents by reusing this survey.

We envision the use cases for architectural knowledge to define operations on a grid for architectural knowledge. We view this grid to support satisfying the need for architectural knowledge from different perspectives. De Boer et al. [29] define a model that lies at the basis for this knowledge grid and supports capturing architectural knowledge.

Within our research project, we are developing, notations, tools and associated methods to extract, represent and use architectural knowledge. This paper sheds light onto the most important use cases for architectural knowledge from a practitioners' perspective. Although specialized tool support for the architects is still generally lacking, we use these results to develop tools for the most important use cases for architectural knowledge. In addition, we continue the work in our project to further embed the view of architectural knowledge and architectural decisions in practice.

Acknowledgement. We thank Joost Schalken for his support in the statistical analysis of the survey results and Rik Farenhorst and Remco C. de Boer for our discussions to clarify the survey results. This research has been partially sponsored by the Dutch Joint Academic and Commercial Quality Research & Development (Jacquard) program on Software Engineering Research via contract 638.001.406 GRIFFIN: a GRId For inFormatIoN about architectural knowledge.

References

1. Bass, L., Clements, P., Kazman, R.: Software Architecture in Practice, 2nd edn. SEI Series in Software Engineering. Addison-Wesley Pearson Education, Boston (2003)
2. Jansen, A., Bosch, J.: Software Architecture as a Set of Architectural Design Decisions. In: WICSA 2005. 5th Working IEEE/IFIP Conference on Software Architecture, Pittsburgh, Pennsylvania, pp. 109–120 (2005)
3. Kruchten, P., Lago, P., Van Vliet, H.: Building up and Reasoning about Architectural Knowledge. In: Hofmeister, C., Crnkovic, I., Reussner, R. (eds.) QoSA 2006. LNCS, vol. 4214, pp. 43–58. Springer, Heidelberg (2006)
4. Clements, P., Bachmann, F., Bass, L., Garlan, D., Ivers, J., Little, R., Nord, R., Stafford, J.: Documenting Software Architectures: Views and Beyond. SEI Series in Software Engineering. Addison-Wesley Professional, Reading (2003)
5. IEEE: IEEE Recommended Practice for Architectural Description of Software-Intensive Systems. Standard 1471-2000, IEEE (2000)
6. Van der Ven, J.S., Jansen, A., Avgeriou, P., Hammer, D.K.: Using Architectural Decisions. In: Hofmeister, C., Crnkovic, I., Reussner, R. (eds.) QoSA 2006. LNCS, vol. 4214, Springer, Heidelberg (2006)
7. Tang, A., Babar, M.A., Gorton, I., Han, J.: A Survey of the Use and Documentation of Architecture Design Rationale. In: WICSA 2005. 5th Working IEEE/IFIP Conference on Software Architecture, Pittsburgh, Pennsylvania, pp. 89–98 (2005)
8. Tyree, J., Akerman, A.: Architecture Decisions: Demystifying Architecture. IEEE Software 22(2), 19–27 (2005)
9. Zimmermann, O., Gschwind, T., Küster, J., Leymann, F., Schuster, N.: Reusable Architectural Decision Models for Enterprise Application Development. In: QoSA 2007. Third International Conference on the Quality of Software Architectures. LNCS, Springer, Heidelberg (2007)
10. Smolander, K.: Four Metaphors of Architecture in Software Organizations: Finding Out the Meaning of Architecture in Practice. In: ISESE 2002. 2002 International Symposium on Empirical Software Engineering, pp. 211–221 (2002)
11. Hofmeister, C., Nord, R., Soni, D.: Applied Software Architecture. Addison-Wesley Longman Publishing Co. Inc., Boston, MA, USA (2000)

12. Clements, P., Kazman, R., Klein, M., Devesh, D., Reddy, S., Verma, P.: The Duties, Skills, and Knowledge of Software Architects. In: WICSA 2007. 6th Working IEEE/IFIP Conference on Software Architecture, Mumbai, India, IEEE Computer Society Press, Los Alamitos (2007)
13. Kitchenham, B.A., Pfleeger, S.L.: Principles of Survey Research, Parts 1 to 6. SIGSOFT Software Engineering Notes (2001–2002)
14. Likert, R.: A Technique for the Measurement of Attitudes. Archives of Psychology 140 (1932)
15. SEI: Published Software Architecture Definitions (November 10th, 2006) http://www.sei.cmu.edu/architecture/published_definitions.html
16. Florijn, G., Clerc, V., Van Ekris, J., Koning, H., Leih, G., Maat, M., Niessink, F.: Softwarearchitectuur - Overzicht en Compendium (Dutch). Ten Hagen & Stam (2003)
17. Borg, I., Groenen, P.J.F.: Modern Multidimensional Scaling, 2nd edn. Statistics. Springer, New York (2005)
18. MacQueen, J.: Some Methods for Classification and Analysis of Multivariate Observations. In: Cam, L.M.L., Neyman, J. (eds.) The Fifth Berkeley Symposium on Mathematical Statistics and Probability. Statistics, vol. 1, pp. 281–297. University of California Press, Berkely, California (1967)
19. Anton, H.: Elementary Linear Algebra, 9th edn. John Wiley & Sons, Inc., Chichester (2005)
20. Kitchenham, B.A., Pfleeger, S.L., Pickard, L.M., Jones, P.W., Hoaglin, D.C., Emam, K.E., Rosenberg, J.: Preliminary Guidelines for Empirical Research in Software Engineering. IEEE Transactions on Software Engineering 28(8), 721–734 (2002)
21. Rozanski, N., Woods, E.: Software Systems Architecture: Working With Stakeholders Using Viewpoints and Perspectives. Addison Wesley Professional, Reading (2005)
22. Buschmann, F., Meunier, R., Rohnert, H., Sommerlad, P., Stal, M.: Pattern-Oriented Software Architecture, Volume 1: A System of Patterns. John Wiley & Sons, Inc., Chichester (1996)
23. Conklin, J., Begeman, M.L.: gIBIS: A Hypertext Tool for Exploratory Policy Discussion. ACM Transactions on Office Information Systems 6(4), 303–331 (1988)
24. MacLean, A., Young, R.M., Bellotti, V.M.E., Moran, T.P.: Questions, Options, and Criteria: Elements of Design Space Analysis. In: Moran, T.P., Carroll, J.M. (eds.) Design Rationale. Concepts, Techniques, and Use, pp. 53–105. Lawrence Erlbaum and Associates, Mahwah, NJ (1996)
25. Fischer, G., Lemke, A.C., McCall, R., Morch, A.I.: Making Argumentation Serve Design. In: Moran, T.P., Carroll, J.M. (eds.) Design Rationale. Concepts, Techniques, and Use, pp. 267–293. Lawrence Erlbaum and Associates, Mahwah, NJ (1996)
26. Conklin, J., Selvin, A., Buckingham-Shum, S.J., Sierhuis, M.: Facilitated Hypertext for Collective Sensemaking: 15 Years on from gIBIS. In: 12th ACM Conference on Hypertext and Hypermedia, Århus, Denmark, pp. 123–124. ACM Press, New York (2001)
27. Clements, P., Kazman, R., Klein, M.: Evaluating Software Architectures: Methods and Case Studies. SEI Series in Software Engineering. Addison-Wesley Professional, Boston (2001)

28. Gruber, T.R.: Towards Principles for the Design of Ontologies Used for Knowledge Sharing. In: Guarino, N., Poli, R. (eds.) Formal Ontology in Conceptual Analysis and Knowledge Representation, Kluwer Academic Publishers, Deventer, The Netherlands (1993)
29. De Boer, R.C., Farenhorst, R., Clerc, V., Van der Ven, J.S., Deckers, R., Lago, P., Van Vliet, H.: Structuring Software Architecture Project Memories. In: LSO 2006. The 8th International Workshop on Learning Software Organizations, Rio de Janeiro, Brazil, pp. 39–47 (2006)

Author Index

Lecture Notes in Computer Science

Sublibrary 2: Programming and Software Engineering

For information about Vols. 1– 4260
please contact your bookseller or Springer

Vol. 4574: J. Derrick, J. Vain (Eds.), Formal Techniques for Networked and Distributed Systems – FORTE 2007. XI, 375 pages. 2007.

Vol. 4556: C. Stephanidis (Ed.), Universal Access in Human-Computer Interaction, Part III. XXII, 1020 pages. 2007.

Vol. 4555: C. Stephanidis (Ed.), Universal Access in Human-Computer Interaction, Part II. XXII, 1066 pages. 2007.

Vol. 4554: C. Stephanidis (Ed.), Universal Acess in Human Computer Interaction, Part I. XXII, 1054 pages. 2007.

Vol. 4553: J.A. Jacko (Ed.), Human-Computer Interaction, Part IV. XXIV, 1225 pages. 2007.

Vol. 4552: J.A. Jacko (Ed.), Human-Computer Interaction, Part III. XXI, 1038 pages. 2007.

Vol. 4551: J.A. Jacko (Ed.), Human-Computer Interaction, Part II. XXIII, 1253 pages. 2007.

Vol. 4550: J.A. Jacko (Ed.), Human-Computer Interaction, Part I. XXIII, 1240 pages. 2007.

Vol. 4542: P. Sawyer, B. Paech, P. Heymans (Eds.), Requirements Engineering: Foundation for Software Quality. IX, 384 pages. 2007.

Vol. 4536: G. Concas, E. Damiani, M. Scotto, G. Succi (Eds.), Agile Processes in Software Engineering and Extreme Programming. XV, 276 pages. 2007.

Vol. 4530: D.H. Akehurst, R. Vogel, R.F. Paige (Eds.), Model Driven Architecture - Foundations and Applications. X, 219 pages. 2007.

Vol. 4523: Y.-H. Lee, H.-N. Kim, J. Kim, Y.W. Park, L.T. Yang, S.W. Kim (Eds.), Embedded Software and Systems. XIX, 829 pages. 2007.

Vol. 4498: N. Abdennahder, F. Kordon (Eds.), Reliable Software Technologies - Ada-Europe 2007. XII, 247 pages. 2007.

Vol. 4486: M. Bernardo, J. Hillston (Eds.), Formal Methods for Performance Evaluation. VII, 469 pages. 2007.

Vol. 4470: Q. Wang, D. Pfahl, D.M. Raffo (Eds.), Software Process Dynamics and Agility. XI, 346 pages. 2007.

Vol. 4468: M.M. Bonsangue, E.B. Johnsen (Eds.), Formal Methods for Open Object-Based Distributed Systems. X, 317 pages. 2007.

Vol. 4467: A.L. Murphy, J. Vitek (Eds.), Coordination Models and Languages. X, 325 pages. 2007.

Vol. 4454: Y. Gurevich, B. Meyer (Eds.), Tests and Proofs. IX, 217 pages. 2007.

Vol. 4444: T. Reps, M. Sagiv, J. Bauer (Eds.), Program Analysis and Compilation, Theory and Practice. X, 361 pages. 2007.

Vol. 4440: B. Liblit, Cooperative Bug Isolation. XV, 101 pages. 2007.

Vol. 4408: R. Choren, A. Garcia, H. Giese, H.-f. Leung, C. Lucena, A. Romanovsky (Eds.), Software Engineering for Multi-Agent Systems V. XII, 233 pages. 2007.

Vol. 4406: W. De Meuter (Ed.), Advances in Smalltalk. VII, 157 pages. 2007.

Vol. 4405: L. Padgham, F. Zambonelli (Eds.), Agent-Oriented Software Engineering VII. XII, 225 pages. 2007.

Vol. 4401: N. Guelfi, D. Buchs (Eds.), Rapid Integration of Software Engineering Techniques. IX, 177 pages. 2007.

Vol. 4385: K. Coninx, K. Luyten, K.A. Schneider (Eds.), Task Models and Diagrams for Users Interface Design. XI, 355 pages. 2007.

Vol. 4383: E. Bin, A. Ziv, S. Ur (Eds.), Hardware and Software, Verification and Testing. XII, 235 pages. 2007.

Vol. 4379: M. Südholt, C. Consel (Eds.), Object-Oriented Technology. VIII, 157 pages. 2007.

Vol. 4364: T. Kühne (Ed.), Models in Software Engineering. XI, 332 pages. 2007.

Vol. 4355: J. Julliand, O. Kouchnarenko (Eds.), B 2007: Formal Specification and Development in B. XIII, 293 pages. 2006.

Vol. 4354: M. Hanus (Ed.), Practical Aspects of Declarative Languages. X, 335 pages. 2006.

Vol. 4350: M. Clavel, F. Durán, S. Eker, P. Lincoln, N. Martí-Oliet, J. Meseguer, C. Talcott, All About Maude - A High-Performance Logical Framework. XXII, 797 pages. 2007.

Vol. 4348: S. Tucker Taft, R.A. Duff, R.L. Brukardt, E. Plödereder, P. Leroy, Ada 2005 Reference Manual. XXII, 765 pages. 2006.

Vol. 4346: L. Brim, B.R. Haverkort, M. Leucker, J. van de Pol (Eds.), Formal Methods: Applications and Technology. X, 363 pages. 2007.

Vol. 4344: V. Gruhn, F. Oquendo (Eds.), Software Architecture. X, 245 pages. 2006.

Vol. 4340: R. Prodan, T. Fahringer, Grid Computing. XXIII, 317 pages. 2007.

Vol. 4336: V.R. Basili, H.D. Rombach, K. Schneider, B. Kitchenham, D. Pfahl, R.W. Selby (Eds.), Empirical Software Engineering Issues. XVII, 193 pages. 2007.

Vol. 4326: S. Göbel, R. Malkewitz, I. Iurgel (Eds.), Technologies for Interactive Digital Storytelling and Entertainment. X, 384 pages. 2006.

Vol. 4323: G. Doherty, A. Blandford (Eds.), Interactive Systems. XI, 269 pages. 2007.

Vol. 4322: F. Kordon, J. Sztipanovits (Eds.), Reliable Systems on Unreliable Networked Platforms. XIV, 317 pages. 2006.

Vol. 4309: P. Inverardi, M. Jazayeri (Eds.), Software Engineering Education in the Modern Age. VIII, 207 pages. 2006.

Vol. 4294: A. Dan, W. Lamersdorf (Eds.), Service-Oriented Computing – ICSOC 2006. XIX, 653 pages. 2006.

Vol. 4290: M. van Steen, M. Henning (Eds.), Middleware 2006. XIII, 425 pages. 2006.

Vol. 4279: N. Kobayashi (Ed.), Programming Languages and Systems. XI, 423 pages. 2006.

Vol. 4262: K. Havelund, M. Núñez, G. Roşu, B. Wolff (Eds.), Formal Approaches to Software Testing and Runtime Verification. VIII, 255 pages. 2006.